# THE CORE OF THE CITY

*Publications of the Institute for*
*Urban Land Use and Housing Studies*
*Columbia University*

# THE CORE OF THE CITY

*A Pilot Study of Changing Land Uses*

*in Central Business Districts*

*by* JOHN RANNELLS

COLUMBIA UNIVERSITY PRESS, NEW YORK 1956

# PREFACE

THE STUDY of Urban resources is approached, in this book, through examination of land-based activities and their changing patterns—the accommodations provided for them, their locations with respect to each other, and active relationships among them. Activities make the city what it is; the physical structures are enlarged or modified or neglected in response to current levels of activity in different parts of the city and the demand for space and location that results from these activities. It follows that the value of the city's physical assets is not inherent in the actual structures so much as in the use that is made of them. Unrented space in a commercial building or too much unused capacity in a public utility installation becomes an economic liability, however sound the physical structures may be.

In order to comprehend the phenomena of urban land utilization we must go behind the customary measures (such as ground coverage or floor area ratio) or blanket use designations (such as "commercial" or "industrial" or "residential"); we must consider the underlying systems of activity and their effects, as they develop, on the urban resources that are embodied in land and buildings and services. The first five chapters of this study deal with relationships among these activity systems as they occur in any city center. The conceptual approach and tools for analysis developed here are then used for measuring and comparing land-based activities and their patterned relationships in the Central Business District of Philadelphia, using data from a survey made for the Philadelphia City Planning Commission in 1949. The Institute for Urban Land Use and Housing Studies at Columbia University participated in the design and execution of this survey and at the same time conducted another study in Philadelphia for the Bureau of Public Roads of the United States Department of Commerce with the purpose (among others) "to measure the movement of persons and the movement of goods associated with

various characteristics of selected land uses and combinations and patterns of land use." During the course of these
two studies a workable unit for classifying and analyzing land
use was devised—the establishment, which is defined as
people using a definite location for carrying on regular activities. Relationships among establishments with regard to
systems of movement have already been developed in a publication by the Institute: Urban Traffic: A Function of Land
Use by Robert B. Mitchell and Chester Rapkin (New York:
Columbia University Press, 1954). The present book carries
further the analysis of relationships among establishments
in the more general framework of activitiy systems in central urban locations.

Establishments serve as bases for the regular activities
of people and as focal points in the interactions between social and governmental and business organizations. The land-
based activities of a city can be pinned down and catalogued
through an inventory of establishments, classified by major
activity. Thus whole chains and clusters of establishments
engaged in, say, banking or retailing or manufacturing can
be picked out, and threads of relationship among them can be
traced.

The methods developed in the middle section of this
book combine graphic and statistical techniques for applying measures which can be verified and can serve for testing hypotheses. It has been one of the author's pious hopes
that creation of methods acceptable to both social scientists
and physical planners may help to clear a middle ground
which will aid better collaboration between these fields.

In the last few chapters, a beginning is made toward
synthesis of material in the foregoing sections by analyzing
patterned relationships among some of the central activities
in Philadelphia as they interact with each other and with
their accommodations, both buildings and environment. This
analysis is conceived as a prototype study of theory and
method wherein are forged some of the tools for locating
and analyzing land-use relationships in any urban center.

At the time of beginning work on this book it was hoped
that a substantial contribution to urban location theory might
result. This remains a distant goal. The product seems to
have evolved as two half-books: a beginning at theory and
a somewhat fuller treatment of methods. The two still re-

main to be synthesized satisfactorily. A program of further studies leading to a general theory of locational arrangement of urban activities is sketched in the last chapter.

Apparent throughout the present book is the author's indebtedness to Professors Mitchell and Rapkin and to Dr. Ernest H. Jurkat, who conducted the field work in Philadelphia for both the traffic and central distric studies. Not only did these men pioneer the trails which the author has followed; they have continued to help in formulating problems encountered in further journeyings. The author's thanks are due also to Edmund N. Bacon, Executive Director of the Philadelphia City Planning Commission, for permission to use materials from the Commission's files. The book has also benefited from critiques of early drafts made by Dr. Leo Grebler and Dr. David Blank of the Institute's staff, and from critical readings of the final draft by Martin Meyerson and Hans Blumenfeld. Throughout all stages of the work, the skilled editorial assistance of Esther Olmstead has deserved the author's thanks and appreciation.

And finally, the author wishes to acknowledge his debt to Dr. Ernest M. Fisher, Director of the Institute, for giving the push that initiated this book and for his sure insight and unfailing advice during its development.

JOHN RANNELLS

Philadelphia, Pennsylvania
November, 1955

# CONTENTS

changing requirements, is tolerably well suited to the
activities of each city and is also unique for each city.

tween the Delaware and Schuylkill rivers. The
city soon outgrew its original boundaries, but
its business center has remained within them,
its main nuclei gradually shifting to locations
near the middle of the original gridiron.

The patterning of central activities is best described in terms of the mass transit stations and
the surface lines. Its buildings provide a visible
history of the entire area's development, with
examples remaining from all periods.

Description, such as the foregoing, can provide only the background for analysis, which requires for its accomplishment the systematic
measurement of activities and relationships
among them.

Only enough descriptive material has been given
in this chapter to demonstrate that the general approach of preceding chapters can be applied to an
actual urban situation. Analyses will require the
devising of methods for locating and measuring
patterns of activities—to be developed in the
chapters to follow.

Data from a survey of the Philadelphia Business
District are used for developing measures for
evaluating central district establishments, their
characteristics and relationships in terms of
location. Detailed in Appendix A.

The delimitation of the study area and method of
mapping data on a grid of approximately equal
blocks.

Categories for classifying business establishments must be continuously reexamined in terms
of their functional operation. The amalgamation
of two similar classes of establishments in the
Philadelphia survey results in an interplay of
five major groups in place of the six groups of
Chapter VIII.

Tabulating coincidence of location among all
five business groups leads to measures of the
strengths of these relationships.

Methods developed in Chapters VII and VIII are
utilized in this chapter for comparing each major business group with others, stating relationships both on the map and numerically.

Study of changing activities is approached by
setting up diagrammatic patterns of relationships among groups of establishments as they
exist at a given time.

The varied establishments making up each major group are to be reexamined in the light of
broad requirements of space and location which
apply to them all in varying degree.

## APPENDIXES

# FIGURES

# TABLES

# I

## CITIES VIEWED AS CONCENTRATIONS
## OF ACTIVITIES

CITIES, of whatever age or size, exist through the piling up of people's activities which take place in them; changes in the physical makeup of the city come about in response to changes in the organization and arrangements of those activities. The structures of the land and the subdivided land itself—streets, public utilities, open places, old areas or new—all are the result and record of the changing physical accommodations made for people's activities past and present. The same is true for all settled areas where men have modified the existing features of the site to provide accommodation for their patterned actions. Whether a present-day city began as a frontier trading post or an agricultural village, its growth and continuing vitality derive from the innumerable interactions between people and groups which occur there—always changing, always requiring accommodation.

Activities, in turn, are conditioned by the physical environment provided by the city in which the people live and work. At first glance the physical environment appears fixed, the activities transitory. The city's buildings are extremely durable, and the streets and other public works on the map of the city are surely as permanent as any works of man; if they are modified in response to changing activities it is a delayed response. It would seem that the life of the city plays itself out on the stage of the city as it exists and must conform to the conditions imposed by the setting of that stage.

To understand and describe this complex interaction which is city life—both activities and physical environment serving each other, adjusting to each other, conditioning each other—it is possible to begin either with activities or with their physical setting, but neither can be understood without the other. And the key role is played by activities, for in these is the source of the vitality of the entire city or selected parts of it. When activities are seriously curtailed the physical environment begins to deteriorate; as

different kinds of activity change in relative importance, the
physical environment adjusts to the new balance.

The relationship is seen clearly in the engineering
structures which make up the municipal plant: highways,
bridges, underground installations of all kinds. These
scarcely can be discussed, even in the most technical terms,
without including in the discussion those requirements of
people which the structures were built to fulfill. A bridge,
for example, is designed to support loads as heavy as may
reasonably be expected and to cope with a foreseeable volume of traffic. Engineers are continually preoccupied with
both these aspects of design, for too big a structure is subject to adverse comment while too small a structure is
generally considered inexcusable. Water supply and sewer-
age systems would be costly indeed if their capacities were
far in excess of actual requirements. The public utilities
(gas, electricity, and the rest) are in close touch with
changes in population and changing levels of business activity. Their operations, especially the addition of new
facilities, are as responsive to variations in demand as
"management" can make them.

Not so apparent nor so simply stated are the relationships between buildings and the activities for which they
provide accommodation. The need for space in buildings
results from the same intricate complex of activities which
is the source of demand for public utilities. But gas and
light and telephone service and the rest are rather homogeneous commodities, much the same to all their users,
while space in buildings must meet different sets of requirements stemming from a host of different kinds of activity, each of which has further needs as to location relative to associated activities. The construction of buildings
entirely suited to specific requirements has become com-
monplace, but these contain only a fraction of the space
available at any time. The bulk of it is in buildings that have
existed for several decades, and these older buildings have
generally experienced a succession of uses. This succession results from continually changing ways of doing business,
with resultant shifts in location as well as new sets of requirements.

There are some advantages in approaching a study of
the changing life of a city in terms of changes in the use of

its "permanent" structures and the provision of new buildings. These changes present a kind of summation of effects
resulting from many complex forces, a simplification by
which an intricate task can be started on familiar terms
within a manageable scope. "Land-use surveys" of many
cities have been made in such terms by plotting the major
categories of use (residential, commercial, industrial, and
so on) on the city map. Repeated periodically, a series of
such maps can show in a general way the extent of different uses, their changes in concentration or "spread," and
their shifts in location.

        This approach, however, does not carry far toward un-
derstanding, or even describing, the continually changing
relationships between activities that express themselves in
the use of space. It soon becomes necessary to go behind
the resultant demand for space of various kinds in various
locations to see what the underlying activities are and how
they function and interact with each other. And behind the
activities are all the individuals who engage in them or have
dealings with them: the population employed by and in turn
supporting the physical plant of the entire city.

        The continual changes in activities which lie behind
changing demands for space or location are not apparent
to everyone, but they are by no means obscure. Rather, they
are intricate, with elements well understood by those who
are particularly concerned, even though the total aggregation
of these elements may appear at first glance beyond comprehension.

        A country person, for example, visiting a big city for
the first time, finds it hopelessly confusing. The resident
or frequent visitor selects out of the whole confusion those
things that concern him and takes the rest for granted. The
person whose livelihood is bound up with the life of the city
sees it as a series of patterns affecting his work. The fire-
man knows his district as a pattern of call boxes and water
mains and hydrants and fire hazards (warehouses, tenements,
vacant structures). The local real estate dealer knows his
neighborhood as a pattern of available properties or floor
space to be matched against a list of clients, actual or prospective. The proprietor of a local movie house is concerned
with his customers' behavior patterns, mostly in terms of
competition: baseball, other theaters, television, or just

weather. The list is endless, but for each habitual partici-
pant there is a diagram, actual or implicit, whether on paper
or in a card file or in the back of the mind, which states his
particular concern with the whole, larger complex made up
of all the activities performed by people in the urban setting.
Of course, a great deal of urban behavior is unstructured,
but out of the whole tangle we can pick many patterns.

The routines of all city dwellers may be viewed as
touching many different activities, closely connected with
few. There are more different kinds of activity in larger
places and more specialists, but, however intricate the
relationships between activities may become, each particular situation is well within the comprehension of the actual
participants.

The present study deals primarily with that fraction of
urban activities called land use which is based on the land
and is concerned with questions of location and the use of
space. The "activities" approach to description and analysis
of urban patterns which is to be pursued here was first used
in 1925 by Haig in his classic study of "trends and tendencies in the economic activities within the region of New
York and its environs."[1] Haig's question, "Where do things
belong in an urban area?" remains unanswered. Little further research, in fact, has been devoted to the study of
functions performed at various locations by business firms
and the relationships among them. The well-known "con-
centric zone" and "sector" approaches to description of
urban form and structure need only be mentioned here.[2]
They are too generalized to be of use in the description of
functional relationships. More satisfactory is the "multiple
nuclei" description in which the various centers of activity
are designated.[3] Even this, however, is no more than a first

[1] Robert Murray Haig, Regional Survey of New York and its Environs, 10
vols. (New York, 1927). Vol. 1, Major Economic Factors in Metropolitan
Growth and Arrangement. The first two chapters of this study were first
printed in The Quarterly Journal of Economics, Vol. 40 (February and May,
1926).
[2] E. W. Burgess, "Urban Areas," in Chicago: An Experiment in Social Science
Research, ed. T. V. Smith and L. D. White (Chicago: University of Chicago
Press, 1929), and Homer Hoyt in The Structure and Growth of Residential
Neighborhoods in American Cities (Washington, D. C.: Federal Housing Administration, 1939).
[3] C. D. Harris and E. L. Ullman, "The Nature of Cities," Annals of the American Academy of Political and Social Science, Vol. 242 (November, 1945).

approximation of a few important locations, without any
spelling out of relationships among activities.

It is the purpose of the present study to describe and
analyze the changing patterns of land use that are found in
urban centers—patterns made up of the interplay of two
elements: (1) activities carried on in the various structures
of the city and in movement among them, and (2) the structures themselves, including the vacant tracts, streets, and
other common spaces. In the process of describing and
analyzing urban patterns, a formulation of the reciprocal
relationships between activities and structures will be
developed, also new methods for measuring and comparing
groups of activities.

The general orientation to be formulated in the first
part of this study (through Chapter V) will be based primarily on various systems of action as they relate to patterns of land use. Physical structures and their locations
will play a minor role in this development of schematic
relationships.

In Chapters VI through IX, dealing with a mass of empirical data from the central business district of Philadelphia, prime attention will be given to patterns of location
and techniques for expressing them statistically.

In the remainder of the book, patterned relationships
actually found in Philadelphia will be further examined in
the light of the conceptual approach developed in the first
few chapters to see what adjustments are taking place and
what kinds of activities belong together. A concluding chapter will consider the possibilities for designed adjustment of
land-use patterns for the better functioning of cities.

A major difficulty of our "activities" approach to problems of land use consists in drawing the line between what
applies to location and what does not, for location is only
one factor in the operation of any given activity. Systems
of action have their own relationships, in fact, which can be
considered quite apart from location and usually are. In
order to deal with that fraction of activities which does affect location, it is necessary to develop a fairly complete
picture of activity systems as they operate in the urban
scene. It is necessary to take in somewhat more than relates directly to land use, since changes in demand for space
or location may come about as secondary results of business

decisions or consumer preferences which, in themselves,
have no concern with questions of land use. This discussion
may therefore appear at times to circle around the central
concern of the study, but the boundaries of our field are
necessarily indefinite, and it will be better to set a wide
stage than a narrow one.

# II

## SYSTEMS AND PATTERNS
## OF URBAN ACTIVITY

Patterns of interaction between people, both as individuals and in groups, are limitless in complexity, but those which relate to locations within the city can be dealt with effectively in terms of the various systems of action which operate in the urban setting.

Three stages of elaboration are distinguished:

1. In the course of everyday living, each person follows a number of fairly repetitive ROUTINES through which he engages in successive activities, some regularly patterned, some casual or infrequent. For example, the weekday journey to work and occasional social activities, or regular food marketing and irregular shopping for apparel or furnishings.

2. The routines of many people come together in common activities and these repeated, patterned actions take more or less permanent form in INSTITUTIONALIZED PROCESSES. These processes of events between people concentrate at locations where the appropriate activities can be accommodated. The "institutions" (repeated activities at locations) cover a great variety of activities, ranging, for example, from selling newspapers to organized baseball. The accommodations provided for them make up the full catalogue of the city's physical structures, all the way from schools or theaters to office buildings or dwellings.

3. Continued interactions between different institutionalized processes result in the ORGANIZATION OF PROCESSES. These patterned cross relationships between different kinds of activity are the connective tissue of urban life, involving entire clusters of the less elaborate systems. They are seen most clearly in the service processes, such as transportation, advertising, or banking. They stand behind mutually interdependent processes such as manufacture and distribution of goods for the retail market. They include such far-reaching systems as government or education or medical care.

Systems of action at the three levels or stages of elab-

oration just noted may be considered as classifications under
which to account for a multitude of continual or repeated
happenings. The number of such systems which may be
abstracted from the total fabric of city life is limited only
by the purposes toward which a given analysis is directed.
The present study will be concerned with those systems
which come to a focus in the city center, keeping in mind
always that the systems are abstractions, however firmly
they may have become established as separate entities. For
the systems themselves change and subsystems take shape
and die out, whatever may be the basis for setting them up.
Human events remain the significant continuing units on
which theoretical analyses of the changing physical city can
be built.

In dealing with systems of action engaged in by many
people, analysis is greatly simplified by substituting the
role in which each person is functioning at a given time for
the complications of separate individual personalities. Everyone is considered alike for the time being. For example, the
working people of a big city make the daily journey to work
as patrons of the mass transit system and are employed by
various business or public institutions as industrial or office
workers, as salesmen, cabdrivers, policemen, schoolteachers, and so forth. Persons going downtown on shopping
trips enact the same role in relation to the transit system
as do the workers, although in smaller numbers and at different times. Local shoppers follow other routines as pedestrians or as automobile drivers; school children and
teachers participate in the public education system. Some
of the same people make perhaps a weekly visit to a motion
picture theater as customers of an entertainment system,
an occasional visit to dentist or oculist or physician or even
a stay in the hospital as participants in a system of medical
care, and so on. In analyzing any particular mass activity it
makes no difference what roles the participants may play in
the other activities which make up their routines. It does
not matter, for example, in the analysis of a transit system,
whether bus passengers are schoolteachers or schoolchil-
dren, businessmen or their employees. At the moment they
are all customers of the bus line.

The foregoing scheme for classifying and describing the
fabric of city life is set up on the abstract plane of systems,

with little attention given to the physical city itself and the actual location patterns, on the map, of its manifold activities. These patterns of structures and the spaces between will be given a great deal of emphasis in the course of this study. They are sources, in fact, of much basic data for understanding relationships between different kinds of activity. They show where activities of different kinds are actually located or where locations have shifted and outmoded centers have been abandoned or new centers formed. In short, their study reveals the evolution of the city.[1]

Each major episode in the growth process of any city is embodied in permanent structures, and many of these remain in use for generations, either continuing in their original use or adapting to new ones as circumstances require. Even in the most extensively rebuilt areas in city centers it is surprising, when one seeks them out, how many buildings remain from earlier periods—old residence structures, warehouses, business blocks, even the shells of churches or banks—all now converted to current uses. Current uses, in turn, prove to be surprisingly mixed whenever a survey is made of all the different activities in a given area, even so limited an area as a single city block. Because of long-term commitments or conservative management, or both in such case as a building owned by the firm which uses it, many activities continue in their present locations long after they might better have moved. Some activities locate in a particular area because of their dealings with others to be found there, and later they may find it expedient to locate elsewhere as other combinations of activities become more important to them. New types and new combinations are continually entering the picture.

A census of structures and activities in any central area, then, is inevitably mixed, with buildings of all ages used almost indiscriminately by long-established and by newly formed activities. To understand the changing locations of activities it is not sufficient to follow the record of the physical patterns; it is necessary to take into account the schemes of action which lie behind them. In the course

[1] "Of this great process," says Patrick Geddes, "the architecture of a city is but the changing expression and its plan but the record, say rather the palimpsest." Cities in Evolution, (New York: Oxford University Press, 1950), p. 82.

of this study of changing patterns, illuminated by a comprehension of the shifting relationships to which they respond, the groundwork can be laid for approaching that
major goal of urban studies: more efficient, economical,
and healthful arrangement of the location patterns of the
city's activities.

## PATTERNS OF URBAN ACTIVITY

City patterns may be studied effectively by surveying
the actual operating units of the different kinds of activities
found at each location. This is the second stage of the foregoing discussion, where both the routines of individuals and
systems of action between different organizations come together.

The classification of activities at locations has been
worked out in great detail by the Bureau of the Budget,[2]
which lists more than 900 varieties, for study of industrial
organization, volume of business, places of employment,
census purposes, etc. There are eight principal divisions,[3]
each subdivided into a dozen or so major groups. The unit
classified in this scheme is the establishment, which is
defined as "a place of business."

For the purposes of the present study, this "kind of
business" classification must be further delimited as to the
kind of activity which actually takes place in each location,
and it must be expanded to include all the places where
routines of people come to a focus—residences, schools, even
public open places where people habitually come together.
Thus, a firm manufacturing heavy machinery and located in
a downtown office building is obviously not a foundry or machine shop or warehouse, but in the study of changes taking
place in ways of doing business it may be important to know
whether this establishment is an executive office or a branch
office dealing with some special phase of the firm's business.

---

[2] Standard Industrial Classification Manual (Washington, D.C.). Vol. I, Manufacturing Industries (1945); Vol. II, Nonmanufacturing Industries (1949).

[3] A. Agriculture, Forestry, and Fishery. B. Mining. C. Construction.
D. Manufacturing. E. Wholesale and Retail Trade. F. Finance, Insurance,
and Real Estate. G. Transportation, Communication, and Other Public
Utilities. H. Personal, Business, Recreational, Public, Semipublic, Professional, and Other Services.

Residential establishments must also be included in the
classification, because they are not only essential units in
systems of action of individuals whose routines are patterned among all those establishments which serve them as
bases of operation; they are important units in many systems of commercial or government activity. The great
emphasis on advertising which is directed toward home
consumption comes to mind immediately, also the fact that
all the elaborate systems of manufacture and distribution of
consumer goods eventually terminate in a host of residential establishments. A surprisingly large proportion of retail sales, however, is accounted for by the people who work
downtown. And perhaps most important in an expanding city
center, residential areas provide the space into which additional business activities can spread out—in fact, they
provide even the structures to accommodate a great many
commercial establishments before specially designed buildings are needed.

## ESTABLISHMENT AND LAND USE DEFINED

For the purpose of this study, then, an establishment is
not only a place of business; it is both a concentration of
people's activities at a definite location and in turn a unit
in the chains of action which link all kinds of activities into
the continually changing networks that make up city life. It
is both a unit of land use and a unit of organization. The
key terms are defined as follows:

ESTABLISHMENT: Individuals or groups using a definite location as a recognizable place of business, residence,
government, or assembly.

LAND USE: Repeated activities of individuals and establishments as they relate to the use of space at fixed locations and among these locations.

Different activities (establishments classified as to
kind of business) tend to concentrate in fairly definite locations: some in a single group, such as those highly specialized businesses (wholesale jewelry, for instance) in which
the entire "trade" is found in a single small area, some in
combinations, with a main concentration plus scattered subsidiary patterns. The latter may be illustrated by the activities of municipal government, with a " City Hall" group

of offices and courts plus scattered police and fire stations
and such features of the city's municipal plant as water supply and sanitary installations and the like. The centers in
which these different types of activity are clustered are
again of different sorts: sometimes fairly homogeneous, as
in a wholesale food market which occupies a few concentrated blocks; sometimes quite heterogeneous, as in an outlying business center which has existed for a long time and
may contain almost as many different kinds of establishment
as the central business district itself.

There is no apparent consistency between the types of
location pattern characteristic of different kinds of business
and the types of center in which these kinds of business are
found. There seems to be no limit to the variety of patterns,
whether we look at the spread on the map of a particular kind
of business, or the patterning of related interacting groups,
or the arrays to be found together at each location. Even in
a small area which appears to be devoted entirely to one
business group, a great many activities unrelated to the
predominant ones are found whenever a listing is made of
all establishments in the area.

These location patterns of establishments on the map
set the stage for the multitudes of separately patterned activities which taken all together make up the life of the city:
a huge multidimensional complex web, its threads the
routines of people and interrelationships between establishments, continually repeating and continually changing. The
activities and interrelationships are so complex that we can
look at any one portion of its continually weaving fabric from
one standpoint after another and get a sequence of quite different pictures, many of them apparently contradictory but
all of them valid.

Every city dweller is familiar with rather extensive
segments of the city scene: the buildings, streets, and traffic within view from the path of his routine movements and
occasional wanderings. And those persons engaged in the
activities of each establishment are familiar with the interrelationships between their own and other establishments of
the same kind or of different kinds, nearby or distant. In the
aggregate, all these myriads of routines and interrelationships add up to the full catalogue of urban activities that are
continually playing out their manifold permutations and com-

binations in every nook and corner of the city. The total aggregation of activity patterns, however, is far too intricate and far too difficult to pin down in space and time to be useful for analysis within the limited scope of the present study. It has been sketched only to show the importance of activities as forces underlying the vitality of the city, causing changes in its physical patterns.

Although establishments are the most nearly fixed entities in the whole flux that we are seeking to comprehend, it is possible and even necessary to study them in the first instance without regard to their locations. All the routines of individuals, acting in their various roles, take place in or between establishments, and the same is true for the activities and dealings of all business organizations. All the relationships in which an establishment is concerned—with people, with other establishments, with larger organizations—can best be understood by setting up system patterns, diagrammatic statements of activities and relationships.

Thus, for example, the routines of individuals can be delineated in terms of the activities of different kinds in which they repeatedly are engaged, in the form of diagrams stating what activities are participated in, for example, what kinds of establishments are visited or dealt with, their relative importance, and their sequence. The same can be done for establishments by delineating their interactions with units in the same or other kinds of business, for example, establishments from which goods are obtained, establishments to which goods are shipped, establishments regularly visited on business, and so forth. Such diagrams show systematic relationships which are valid without regard to location.

## ESTABLISHMENTS AS UNITS OF LAND USE

At first glance a commercial establishment might appear to be the same thing as a "business" or "firm," and sometimes it is; but the activities of a firm may be carried on in one place or in several, depending on its organization, and so may include a number of establishments. In the classification of land uses it makes no difference what position in the organization a particular establishment occupies. It makes no difference, for example, whether a retail store,

selling men's hats, is one of a chain, an independent firm
in the hat business, or an outlet for a hat manufacturer; in
any case it is a specific kind of business at a definite location, an establishment classified by its activity.

The establishment-firm relationship in any given business enterprise may change repeatedly, especially when the
business is growing rapidly. As a typical example, consider
a small manufacturing concern which at first performs all
of its operations under the same roof, say in the space of
a single floor of a loft building—activities such as processing of materials, storage, packaging, shipping, office work,
display, and sales. At this stage the firm and the establishment are one; but as the business expands, some of the
operations will require more space. A series of decisions
will determine the most effective disposition of the various
activities requiring space among available locations. It
might become desirable to relocate the processing of materials, for example, either by setting up a new establishment or by "farming out" the manufacture of the firm's
product to another firm, which might even be located in
another city where manufacturing costs are lower. In any
such case the remaining activities are free to expand in the
original establishment, now somewhat changed in character.
The change will also have effects on patterns of activity outside the firm; for example, the workers relocated along with
the processing of materials are shifted from one portion of
the city's traffic network to another and the total pattern of
goods-handling and its effect on truck traffic is somewhat
changed also. Further decision might place the firm's salesroom in a location more accessible to buyers, resulting in a
new establishment; or it might become expedient to handle
the storage of goods and filling of orders at a warehouse
conveniently located with regard to shipping facilities. It
might even be decided to turn over all marketing functions
to an agent, thus changing the internal organization of the
firm itself.

In time, then, a business firm that started with all its
activities housed under one roof (a single establishment)
may have its operations separated into several establishments occupying different units of space, and some of these
will be taken over by other firms. Thus, a group of activities formerly comprised with a narrow range may become

merged with the organizational processes of an entire industry.

But however intricate an enterprise may become in its internal organization and external relationships, the constituent establishments are definite items that can be pinned down in space and time. And whether they are independent units or branches of larger firms, the existence of groups of establishments of any particular type, their decline in one location and increase in another, their concentration or dispersion, all demonstrate the results of processes or pressures making for change in urban life. Whatever the underlying causes, they continually take the form of changing organizational patterns which are reflected in turn by changes in characteristics of individual establishments and changes in their location patterns; that is, changing patterns of land use.

This is as true of residential establishments as it is of commerce or industry or government. Changes made in the organization of a household as its composition changes are not very different, schematically, from those made by business enterprises. As the family grows, the need for additional space may bring about movement of the household to larger quarters; children away at school are, in a sense, branches of the home establishment; the line of connection with all sorts of institutionalized activities are continually changing. Housework itself has changed greatly, with an increasing proportion of it taken over by industry through packaged foods, mechanical refrigeration, mechanical household appliances, and services such as commercial laundries. The public utilities themselves—water supply, sewage disposal, electrictiy, gas, telephone—which make modern urban life possible, have modified the typical accommodations for family living in cities almost as completely as they have reshaped the accommodations for commercial establishments.

But despite the changes continually taking place and despite the increasingly intricate organization of city life, the elements (such as the activities performed by individual establishments), have continued many simple arrangements from the past. Consider "market place."

The primitive market place where producers brought their goods for exchange became the central open place of

a town. There were also market places in desert country
between settled areas, meeting points for caravans, where
traders exchanged goods. Today the central market of the
ancient town has developed (in the city) into intricate clusterings of establishments engaged in retail trade, scattered
among the resident population and also concentrated heavily
in the city center. The marketing process behind the retail
establishments has become fearfully complex, with whole
interlocking systems of credit ordering, wholesaling, shipping. Somewhere in this complex may be found all the elements that existed in the primitive situation, whether the
market place was part of a town or located between settled
areas. Despite the intricacy of organization of the modern
process, each retail store or each goods counter in the
store carries out the original function of the bit of ground
in the primitive market place where goods were spread out
ready for direct personal exchange. The elements remain
simple, but the process leads inevitably to higher special-
ization of land-use patterns and rearrangement of functions.

Such parallels as those between ancient and modern
market place can be drawn for a number of other organizations of activities. In general it will be seen that institutionalized processes are more subdivided in larger urban
centers and that, as establishments become more specialized, that is, less self-sufficient, the relationships between
them become more intricate. The elements are the same,
however, for any urban center. There are no more complications encountered in following any one thread of analysis in large cities than in small. There are just more
threads in the fabric of a large city.

The scheme of analysis suggested in this chapter is the
same, of course, for all kinds of urban concentrations. Each
city was once a small town and each large city, in the course
of expansion, has absorbed a number of formerly separate
towns. Some, at least, of the infant characteristics of each
of these centers still remain to make the city what it is.

## SUMMARY

It is the basis of this approach to the study of urban
land use that the physical city exists because of the patterned activities of its population as they accumulate and

are accommodated at definite locations, in establishments; that individuals and establishments in action make the city, which in turn shapes their activities; that going patterns of action explain the uses to which available structures are put, with the result that the physical environment is sustained by continuance of activities, while physical changes reflect shifts in the underlying activity systems into which the whole complex of urban life is separated for analysis.

The underlying systems of activity, which result in varying patterns of urban land use, are organized around establishments, classified by kinds of business. These establishments, in turn, are the units for analysis of land use.

# III

## ESTABLISHMENTS AND THEIR LINKAGES

WITHIN the general framework set forth in the previous chapter, analysis of urban land use will be carried on at the <u>establishment</u> level where activities come together at definite locations, both the diffuse activities of people, whether as individuals or in groups, and the organized processes within which the establishments themselves interact.[1] The primary emphasis in this chapter will be placed on the systematic relationships that result from the operations of separate establishments and from the transactions taking place among them. The physical environment and the patterns of location into which establishments arrange themselves will be discussed more fully in the next chapter.

Every establishment, in the course of its regular operations, is engaged in several systems of activity and is connected with other establishments in each of these systems. The entire complex of urban activities may thus be described by tracing these manifold connections or <u>linkages</u> between establishments, both schematically, as relationships between different kinds of activities, and empirically, as transactions between pairs of establishments. These transactions may take the form of visits by salesmen or buyers or clients among establishments or the journey to work by all the members of each establishment. They may take the form of exchange of information (by mail or phone or messenger) or the movement of goods in and out.

LINKAGE, the unit by which relationships are traced in our study of land use and its changes, is defined as follows: a relationship between establishments characterized by recurrent interactions which require movement of persons or of goods or the exchange of information.

Each of the many linkages that converge at a given establishment may be imagined as exerting an attractive force between the linked establishments. The net balance of pulls

[1] See page 7. "Land Use" and "Establishment" are defined on page 11

exerted on each establishment by its linkages with others is
a major factor in the spatial arrangement of land uses, so
that each new establishment tends to locate where the forces
of its expected linkages will be in equilibrium. This sug-
gests a free-to-move arrangement, wherein the organized
activities of each portion of a city (tens or hundreds of establishments interlaced by hundreds or thousands of linkages) are continually adjusting themselves in space as the
relationships between separate activities gain or lose in
strength and as establishments are formed and die out.

This conception—as of a multitude of particles held in
position by multiple networks of changing forces—gives a
reasonably true picture of the changing functional relationships among establishments, but it is rather too fluid for
depicting the locational arrangement of the same establishments. Groups of activities may become fixed or anchored
to their locations, whether these activities have a strong
nucleus (as in a major government building or stock exchange) or whether an entire cluster of establishments
functions as an entity (loosely related as in a group of downtown office buildings or closely knit as in a wholesale market). The physical pattern of land uses in any urban area
is strongly shaped by its prior development; further changes
in the pattern will take place around the more firmly fixed
positions of the dominant activities. Thus, while patterns of
land use do respond to the same changing combinations of
pulls exerted by linkages which bring about changes in organization of activities, changes in land-use patterns are con-
strained by the anchored activities. Changes for any one
period of time, therefore, take shape as minor modifications
to the existing dominant groupings.

The free adjustment of land-use patterns is further
restricted by factors other than linkage, such as: availability
and cost, or rent, of suitable space; inertia of long-term
commitments to present accommodations; difficulty and cost
of moving existing installations; legal (e.g., zoning) restrictions; or simply lack of understanding as to the relative
merits of alternative locations.

A full listing and evaluation of the linkages incident to
the normal operation of a given establishment provides a
basis for judging the relative advantages and disadvantages
of its location. Such a linkage study would show that some

of the establishment's functions are better served than others, and this may lead to a decision to discontinue the establishment and set up a new one at a better location or to divide the functions into two separate establishments with the new branch located to best advantage with regard to its own roster of linkages. Indeed, a linkage study might be set up entirely in speculative terms to compare the potential desirability of a given location for establishments of various kinds.

The scheme for analysis of changing land use to be developed here will be largely concerned with establishments and their linkages. By focusing on the roles of establishments as functioning units within the major classes of activities in which they are engaged and as units in related action systems that cut across these primary categories, the ever changing networks of interaction that make up city life can be traced by way of linkages between establishments.

## CLASSIFICATION OF ESTABLISHMENTS

For a first broad classification of urban establishments as they relate to land use, the following, based roughly on the Standard Industrial Classification Manual,[2] appears to have advantages:

1. Residential (not listed in the manual).
2. Manufacturing (including construction and extraction industries).
3. Wholesale Trade.
4. Retail Trade.
5. Business Services (including finance, insurance, real estate).
6. Personal Services.
7. Transportation, Communication, and Other Public Utilities.

Numbers 1, 4, and 6 on this list are concerned mainly with the resident population; numbers 2, 3, and 5 are concerned mainly with business organizations; number 7 with both. Thus, the classification itself tends to reach both ways from the establishment level, to include both the activities of in-

---

[2] Washington, D.C.: Bureau of the Budget. Vol. I, 1945; Vol. II, 1949.

dividuals and groups of people in relation to establishments
and the interactions of the different business organizations
with each other. Analysis at the level of establishments is
given added reality and depth by these tie-ins to higher and
lower systems of urban activity (see page 7).

The foregoing classification will serve for listing establishments by their major activities so that systems of
action may be traced among them. No activity system, however, can operate within any of these categories without involving establishments in other classes as well. Perhaps the
most pervasive is Transportation, connected as it is with
the activities of all urban establishments and providing the
means for movement among all the separate locations of the
land use pattern. Within this category various systems of
movement may be distinguished, utilizing various means
and serving various objectives. Means include rail (railroad, rapid transit, trolley car) or highway (bus, truck,
taxi, private automobile, even bicycles in European cities)
or water transport, where that is available. Objectives include the movement of persons (workers, shoppers, school
children, recreation seekers, etc.) or the movement of goods
(fuel, food, building materials, newspapers, etc.). Any one
of these may be analyzed separately in relation to a whole
range of establishments, or else the subsystems of movement connected  with a particular establishment or business
group or  location may be singled out in order to study the
effect on the total movement system of the city accounted
for by the subsystems converging at the unit under study.[3]

Consider, for example, a newspaper plant: a rather
complex establishment with several subsystems of persons
movement (employees, staff, advertisers' representatives,
and so on) and of goods handling (bulk newsprint and ink,
supplies and equipment coming in, while going out are papers,
both local and by mail, and waste). The locational requirements of each subsystem, some inevitably in conflict with

---

[3] The study of movement and its functional relationship with land use has
been explored in considerable detail in Robert B. Mitchell and Chester
Rapkin, Urban Traffic: A Function of Land Use (New York: Columbia University Press, 1954). The analysis of land use by way of establishments and
their linkages, as they apply to location and movement, was developed in the
course of this earlier study by the Institute for Urban Land Use and Housing
Studies, Columbia University.

others, can be stated readily enough. For employees and
staff the journey to work is most important; the presence
of a fair range of consumer-service establishments (such
as restaurants) in the neighborhood of the plant is not un-
important. For staff and visitors the most important factor
is convenience of location relative to other establishments
having linkage with the operation of the newspaper. To the
firm the economy of its total operation is paramount. In
delivery of papers there are great differences between
morning and afternoon editions, the former tending to follow a distribution pattern matching the distribution of residential establishments and thus reaching far out into com-
muter territory and the latter "hitting the street" where
pedestrian movement is thickest. This last is frequently
the most important factor of all, dictating a central location and outweighing heavy-bulk manufacturing requirements
of the plant which would be better served by locating in an
area of cheaper rents.

All establishments are connected with several movement systems, in situations not so unlike that sketched for
the newspaper plant. And, of course, systems of movement
comprise only one of the different types of systems relating
to land use. Indeed, the major activity carried on at an establishment may account for virtually no direct exchange
among others in the same business. This is especially true
of rival newspapers, between which there is little inter-
course, although each may use the same wire services and
each may send out reporters to cover the same events.
(Among the reporters themselves, of course, connections
may be very close.)

## ROLES OF ESTABLISHMENTS

Establishments serve as bases of operations, both for
organizations (such as business firms, government agencies) and for individuals (members of establishments) engaged in the activities of these organizations. In dealing with
the various systems of activity as they converge on establishments, it will be useful to simplify systems of action
and their effects by dealing with the roles played by establishments, in much the same way that the roles in which
people act are used to simplify the tangle of activities at the

personal level. Thus, in systems involving the flow of goods
to the consumer market, each establishment acts as consumer or supplier to others above or below in the sequence
and may be either collaborator or competitor with other establishments at the same level. To the population at large,
for example, all retail stores are suppliers of household
needs, whatever their other roles may be. Relative to the
transportation and communications industries, all establishments are consumers while within systems of action
which utilize the facilities of these industries, establishments may be either senders or receivers, principals or
agents.

Establishments are functioning units within organizations and in the systems of activities engaged in by them—
the one is a static frame of relationships, the other an action system cutting across several organizations. As units
in systems of organization, establishments may be represented diagrammatically by the "boxes" in the organization
chart of any large firm which carries on its business at
several locations. As units in systems of action they are
like similar "boxes" in flow charts where activities are
traced through a chain of establishments.

The following example is taken from the New York
Telephone Directory. The A & P Food Stores in Manhattan
have executive offices in a midtown office building, a consolidated car department downtown, a central meat purchas-
ing office in the largest meat wholesaling area of the city, a
fresh fish buying office in the midst of the city's main fish
market, a green coffee department in the neighborhood of
the coffee importers, and warehouses outside of Manhattan,
some of which serve a wider area than the city—all these
in addition to the many retail stores, large and small, whose
locations follow the distribution of the resident population
(Figure 1). Listed at the executive offices are a customer-
relations department and the Eastern Division offices, each
of which is potentially a separate establishment. Other
grocery chains are represented in the New York Telephone
Directory by only a single office-and-warehouse establishment in addition to the retail stores. This was no doubt also
the case with the A & P at an earlier stage before its business developed to the point where separate establishments
were set up for specialized functions.

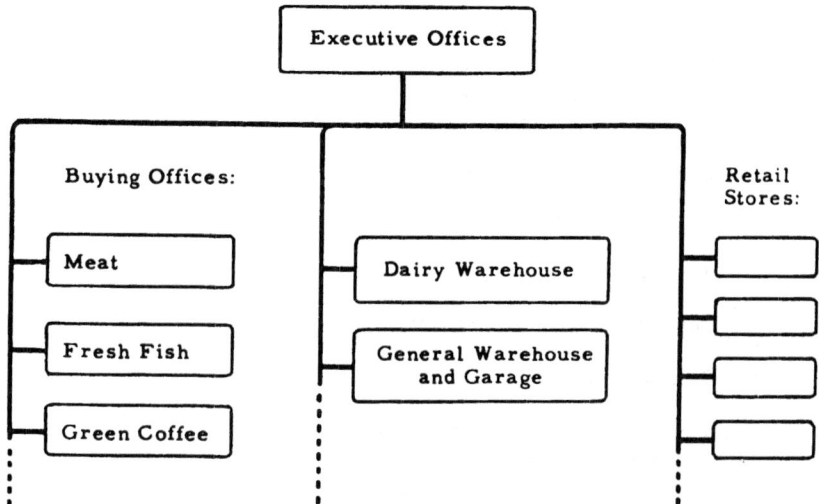

Figure 1.    ORGANIZATION  CHART:  ESTABLISH-
MENTS  IN  A  GROCERY  CHAIN

      Each of these central establishments of the A & P chain
is located in terms of specialized needs, in which linkages
with related activities are of prime importance. The main
office has many linkages with other business organizations
through face-to-face contacts, and its major functions are
best served by its location in a concentration of office buildings near to other central offices and to railroad passenger
terminals. The main warehouse is located on cheap land
accessible to rail and truck transportation and convenient
for the company's own trucks to deliver to the widely dispersed retail stores, each located in a well-populated residential area. The buying offices are all located in their re-
spective markets.
      So much for the relationship of establishments within
the organization. On the activity side, when describing the
flow of goods to the stores, for example, other organizations are necessarily brought into the picture. Milk and
bakery products are delivered by the suppliers direct to
the stores, and to other neighborhood stores at the same
time; packaged goods are delivered in the company's trucks
from its central warehouse where they were shipped by the
suppliers; the central office is only indirectly concerned with

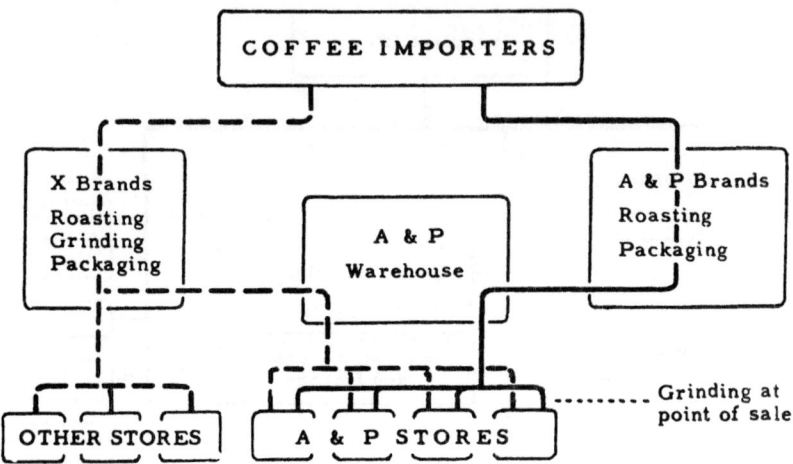

Figure 2.    FLOW  CHART: MARKETING OF COFFEE

this operation. If the supplying of goods were traced
back through packaging and processing to the raw materials, a most formidable network of organizations would
be involved, with many variations in apparently similar
products.

Take coffee as a simple example of a product processed
by the company and sold in competition with other "name"
brands which are carried by the retail stores (Figure 2).
In the one case, the green coffee is purchased direct from
the importers and the processing is all done within the
company organization, the final grinding being done in the
retail stores. In the other case, the product is complete
when it arrives at the company warehouse, like any other of
the huge array of groceries that flows through. When the
packaging materials differ, there is a great difference in
the related industries that are involved—paper vs. tinplate in
the present instance.

Differences might also be followed through the advertising, local and national, by press or radio, of A & P coffee
and, say, Maxwell House. All this might appear to be several removes from the study of land use, but the establishments concerned—executive offices, advertising agencies,
and the rest—will be seen to have strong ties with each
other, and these headquarters establishments will in-

creasingly be found to locate in central business districts, near to each other.

## THE INFLUENCE OF ATTITUDES
## AND EXPECTATIONS

In the scheme for analysis of land use developed in this study—based on establishments and their characteristics and the linkages by which active interrelationships between them are maintained—it is as though all the myriad inter- weaving activities of city life were disregarded except as they are brought to a focus at the establishment level where the analysis is maintained; as though only the patterns ap- pearing at this level were deemed significant. The main focus will continue to be maintained at this level, since it deals with relatively fixed units that can be observed and measured.

But, in the course of analysis of systems of urban ac- tivity based on establishments, it is necessary to refer con- tinually to the activities of individuals and of business or- ganizations to extend and shorten the focus, as it were. It is necessary to view the activities of establishments from these two outside positions: from the standpoint of the popu- lation, specifically of the various individuals who have deal- ings of all sorts with the establishments comprising the pattern under analysis, and from the standpoint of the or- ganizations or groups in whose operations the establish- ments serve as instruments.[4]

Patterns of urban activity, traced through linkages between the establishments taking part in each system, demonstrate what relationships exist and can, to some ex- tent, reveal past history. But, to give meaning to this tracery, the attitudes and expectations and habits of people and of organizations must be kept in mind; these and the

---

[4] It is the role activities of individuals that are significant here, such as their activities as shoppers for specific goods, as employees, as bus passengers or movie-goers—all the multitudes of ways in which people are alike for the time being and for the purpose in hand, however different they may be in any number of other ways. In a similar manner the kind-of-business organiza- tions behind establishments vary over a considerable range—professional groups, manufacturing firms, trade associations, government in any of its manifestations, and so on.

pressure to which they are subjected, as well as opportu-
nities for new arrangements that are continually evolving,
are all part and parcel of the forces making for change in
the systems of urban activities which take shape in the ever
changing patterns of land use.

Urban patterns will be described, then, in terms of
establishments with their characteristics, locations, activities, and linkages, but they will also be considered at
the personal and organizational levels. They will be considered from the point of view of people who prefer one
location to another or one establishment to another, and
from the point of view of a business firm, or any other organization at this level which may be in the process of evaluating the advantages and disadvantages of various locations
for its own purposes, such, for example, as choosing a good
location for setting up a new establishment.

Each person having dealings or expecting to deal with
an establishment judges it and compares it with others, perhaps unconsciously, in terms of its location, convenience,
the services which it renders and their economies in time
or money, even its appearance and that of its surroundings
and the sort of people who deal there. The establishment,
in turn, bears conjugate relationships to the different categories of people with which it has dealings. In other words,
it matters to the establishment how people judge it. Whether
it is the judgment of "the public," "the buyer," "the client,"
or "the trade" that is important will vary with different
kinds of business and in different situations.

For example, a retail store's paramount relationship
is with its customers; its location, appearance, convenience,
and so on are mainly intended to attract and hold customers
who choose it for these selfsame qualities or leave it for
another having qualities which they may have come to prefer. And most important of all these qualities is location—
being where the customers are. None of these items is
especially important in the store's dealings with other establishments. Convenience to employees is also minor,
except as it may help in serving the customer.

A very different situation exists in industries with
groups of related establishments located near one another,
where the activities of each of them is subject to current
conditions "in the trade." This is the case with the needle

trades industries in the large cities, where work on the same product is done by different establishments in turn and the linkages among establishments are subject to frequent change as successive models and styles require different combinations of materials, trimmings, and skills. Nearness of location is of prime importance to these industries, both for flexibility of manufacture, with its frequently changing linkage patterns, and for availability of skilled labor.

The attitudes and expectations of people toward establishments as they are felt to meet requirements, and of organizations judging the same establishments as they may affect business relationships, are compounded of both objective and subjective elements: the stubborn facts of each situation and the evaluation of those facts, which may or may not be realistic and objective. Both the facts and their evaluations change; both are powerful factors in the allocation of activities to different locations.

## CLASSIFICATION OF LINKAGES

Several kinds and degrees of relationship among establishments have been touched upon in the foregoing discussion. These might be approached from several different points of view, but for the present study, concerned as it is with patterns of location, it will suffice to outline a few types of linkage together with different forms of relationship which may occur between the linked establishments The relative importance or independence of one or the other establishment should also be taken into account, for this has a strong effect on location.[5]

Four types of linkages are distinguished:

I. COMPETITIVE LINKAGE: Each establishment strives to hold or increase its own share of the same market, for goods or services, dealing either with a generalized "public," with groups of establishments, or with a single establishment. Competition is so all-pervasive that examples are legion, from newstands to publishers, from peddlers to department stores.

II. COMPLEMENTARY LINKAGE: Both establishments

---

[5] See discussion in Mitchell and Rapkin, Urban Traffic, pp. 110ff.

supply the same market or a single customer-establish-
ment with goods or services which are interrelated. The
products of both establishments may be mutually interdependent; or the product of one establishment may sup-
plement the product of the other. Examples of both kinds
abound among establishments supplying the "bits and pieces"
and subassemblies of manufactured goods of all sorts to the
"prime" manufacturing establishments, from men's cloth-
ing to motor cars.

 III. COMMENSAL LINKAGE: Both establishments use
the same facilities or depend upon the same supplier or the
same market. There may be no direct business relationship between establishments commensally linked.

 IV. ANCILLARY LINKAGE: Services supplied by one
establishment to the members of another. Examples are
especially common in major business centers where cafe-
terias, cigar stores, and various "consumer service" establishments serve the working population.

 Each of the above types may be further classified as to
form or structure of relationship:

 A. Paired linkage: Participation by the two establishments only, without intermediary. Examples are the transactions between supplier and customer, consultant and
client, direct movement from one to the other.

 B. Chain linkage: Participation by two establishments
in joint activity which includes one or more intermediate establishments in the course of its accomplishment. Each
link in the chain is a paired linkage. Examples are supplier-
wholesaler-customer (two links) or supplier's office-sup-
plier's warehouse-shipper-wholesaler-customer (four links).

 C. Systemic linkage: Participation by groups of related
establishments engaged in a common system of activities.

 Types I and II (competitive and complementary linkages)
have much in common. Both may be present in extended
interactions taking place between two establishments, especially when one is in a dominant position. Competition on
some items and collaboration on others is not uncommon.
The greater flexibility of smaller firms often makes it useful for large ones in the same kind of business to "job out"
work to them. Both competitive and complementary linkages
are common among closely related establishments which
comprise a specialized "market." The close proximity of

such groups, often a mixture of manufacturing, wholesaling, and service establishments, stimulates flexibility in business operations, since it provides conveniently a wide range of linkages.

Types III and IV (commensal and ancillary linkages) also have much in common. Both are rather indirect relationships, but they may exert a powerful effect in attracting different kinds of establishments to a given location. The personal service establishment, for example, may have no direct dealings with a firm whose employees it serves (ancillary relationship). The linkage is important to the service establishment, although it may seem inconsequential to the other. The functions performed by service establishments are taken for granted in a downtown center; their importance becomes apparent when offices or factories are set up in outlying locations and services such as "canteens" and recreation facilities have to be incorporated into the new plant itself. In like manner the public utilities supply the sustenance for a host of establishments which may otherwise be unrelated. Indeed, the concept of access to common resources (commensal linkage) might even be extended to include, for example, the advantages of a low-rent area to a firm with scant resources.

The subtypes (paired, chain, and systemic linkages) have to do with more or less direct, more or less simple relationships. A and B are to some extent interchangeable: B is frequently a single strand in the mesh that is C; all may be included in a single transaction between two establishments. For example, an order for goods, originating in face-to-face contact (paired linkage) may be billed through a jobber, requisitioned from a warehouse, and delivered by an outside trucker (chain linkage); when assembly of goods is involved, several chains may converge (systemic linkage). Chain linkages may, of course, become so extended as to lose significance. When the chains are short, however, the difference between paired linkage and chain linkage is one of organization, and the two may be interchanged by a shift in organization. For example, paired establishments might begin dealing through agents, changing from A to B, or the intermediate establishments in a chain linkage may be by-passed, reverting from B to A. In any case, the two establishments do business together and intermediate establish-

ments may, for some purposes of analysis, be ignored. It
matters little to customers of a department store, for example, whether deliveries are made by the store's truck or
by a parcel delivery service, although it may make a great
deal of difference in the office work.

## SUMMARY

Analysis of land use is approached by setting up schematic patterns reflecting the activities and interactions
(i.e., linkages) of establishments, as they relate to the use
of urban land and improvements. These schematic patterns
are expressive of the multiple systems of activity in which
each establishment, classified as to major activity, takes
part. They include systems which follow in sequence through
several establishments of different kinds and also systems
of service, which cut across classes. Examples of major
classes of activity are Manufacturing or Retail Trade, spe-
cified as to kind: cigar-making or men's shoe store, etc.
Systems following through a sequence of establishments, for
example, are manufacture and distribution and sale of ci-
gars or shoes, each system having a similar main sequence
of establishments (factories, wholesalers, retailers) and
touching a number of auxiliary systems (advertising, packaging, transportation, etc.). Such auxiliary systems are
typical of those which cut across major classifications.
Changes in all of these systems and subsystems reflect
changes in organization and bring about changes in establishments. Changing relationships between establishments and
changing locational patterns are thus comprised within the
schematic systems and actual changes can be accounted
for. Formation of new establishments, for example, or regrouping of activities among establishments, do not necessarily modify the basic shemes whereby the effects of different ways of doing business can be assessed. Or if modifications do occur in the basic systems, they do so at a
slower rate than the changes occurring within and between
establishments.
Understanding of systems of land use is greatly enhanced by taking into account viewpoints originating at
levels outside that of establishments, on which the present
analysis is chiefly focused. The reciprocal attitudes and

expectations of people and of organizations toward establishments figure largely in the continuation or atrophy of some
subsystems of land use and the origination of others; they
are at the crux of changing situations. The activities of systems are traced through the interactions taking place, expressed by linkages between establishments. These linkages
can be stated in several different terms: as movement of
persons or goods between the linked establishments, as
number or money value of transactions taking place between
them, as the relative share of a common market captured
by each, and so on.

A schematic method has been set out in this chapter for
studying land use in terms of activities taking place within
and between establishments by tracing the operations of the
manifold systems in which establishments participate
through the linkages between them.

# IV

## THE PHYSICAL SETTING

THE LOCATION patterns of establishments of all kinds among the buildings and streets of a city are visible manifestations of the many systems of activity into which the city's life is organized. Indeed, the operations of past systems have brought about the very accommodations for present activities which are provided by the city's "permanent" structures, both in the buildings themselves and in their spatial arrangements. Changes occur continually in systems of urban activity, some more rapidly than others, and corresponding changes occur in the physical structures, but more slowly. This chapter will be concerned with general questions concerning the locational arrangement of the city's manifold activities in the physical setting of the city's streets and open places, public utilities and buildings.

### ACCOMMODATIONS AND FACILITIES FOR URBAN ACTIVITY

In any analysis of land use the prime elements are the physical setting and the means of operating—that is, the location and accommodation for the designated activity and the facilities for putting that activity into effect. Elaboration of any system of land use may begin with either of these phases—facilities or accommodations—but it will inevitably include the other. For example, we cannot imagine movement of persons or goods in the setting of the city's streets, that is, accommodation for movement, without implying the means for effecting that movement, that is, facilities for transportation in the form of vehicles, rapid transit lines, and the like. Nor do we think of these facilities as other than actively in use. The activities of each establishment are concerned with like elements: accommodations provided by the setting of its building space and location, utilization of the accompanying service facilities, and the establishment's own internal mechanisms for operating.

Space is required for any activity: the dimensions of space and time are inseparable from any system of action, although for purposes of analysis it is possible to describe different aspects of a system without concern for space or time. This was the case in the preceding chapter, where relationships between establishments were treated as they occur in various systems of activity without regard for what kind or amount of space the establishments used, where they were located, when the systems evolved, or what changes may still be taking place in the systems themselves. But, when it comes to analysis of land use, questions of space used by establishments and locations on the map taken or sought by them are of vital concern. Time can be taken for granted in describing current situations. The time dimension relates to the levels of development reached by activities in any given area, for example, the degree of elaboration of linkages among establishments or the extent to which the buildings in the area have become obsolescent.

The main focus of the present analysis is on activities of individual establishments in relation to other establishments and to patterned activities of people as all of these related activities work out in the physical setting, that is, on the map.

## ACTIVITIES OF ESTABLISHMENTS

In analyzing establishments in action, their requirements for space and location are determined by both internal and external activities, that is, by the activities carried on within each establishment and by its relationships and interactions with others. These must be taken up separately, for they deal with other kinds of activity and utilize different operating facilities—have different environments, in fact, which place different constraints upon them. Activities carried on within an establishment determine, in general, the quantities and qualities of space used by itself for work, for display, for processing, for storage, or for circulation (that is, movement within the establishment). These requirements are not unaffected, however, by such external considerations as what goes on in more or less closely related establishments, for business firms have to keep up with their competitors. Choice of location is deter-

mined by a balancing of forces among several external
factors: nearness to transportation or to markets, linkages
to various establishments near by or distant, whether suppliers or competitors or customers, presumed value of
prestige of a good address, and so on.

The different attributes of space and location, the different operations of the inner and outer phases of the activities of establishments, are set forth compactly in the
next few paragraphs to serve as a frame of reference describing the scope and the limitations of our units for analyzing
land use, establishments on the map in action, which in the
aggregate make up the patterns of city life, its slowly changing groundwork and its many-layered interweavings.

The internal activities of establishments bring about
requirements which are practically specifications for building space, equivalent to the sets of attributes possessed by
the properties or listings of real estate brokers. These
requirements are met by the building space used, that is, by
the setting for an establishment's internal activities, and
they are also met by the ways and means of utilizing the
space—that is, by each establishment's use of facilities, its
means of operating.

Descriptive attributes of building space important to
these internal activities, each having certain qualities which
affect usefulness of the space for different kinds of activity,
are as follows:

1. Arrangement: sizes and shapes; headroom; clear
span; ratio of length to width; position and size of windows;
doors; corridors; circulation.

2. Structure: load capacity; type of construction; single
or multistory; partitioning; party walls; finishes; amena-
bility for renovation or major alteration.

3. Attached services and inherent facilities: water,
heat, electricity, telephone, and telegraph; quality of lighting, heating, ventilation, air conditioning; elevator service,
passenger, freight; frontage on one or more streets; show
windows; shipping facilities.

An establishment's use of facilities, including those
provided by the accommodations of the space itself, can be
described in the following terms:

4. Organization of work: scope and sequence of operations; allocation of space among different activities.

5. Mechanisms for operating: equipment for office
work, storage, display; machinery; power, lighting, in excess of "normal" services listed under 3.
This may include alteration of the building space itself for
the establishment's special purposes.

The external activities of establishments, activities relating to other establishments or to markets, bring about
requirements which have to do with locations and with linkages. These requirements are met by the position of the
building in relation to its surroundings, setting for an establishment's external activities, and also by the maintenance of relationships with other establishments and with
customers, through systems of movement and communication, the establishment's means of operating.

Descriptive attributes of location important to the external operations of establishments (the building in relation
to its surroundings), each having qualities affecting suitability for different types of use, include these:

1. Exterior of building: accessibility, entrances, shipping platform, frontage for display; appearance suitable
(symbolic, including height or bulk) for different activities.

2. Site and position: neighboring land uses and natural
features; available services for communication and transportation and services supporting internal activities; location and distance of linked establishments; suitability of
neighborhood (symbolic) for different activities.

An establishment's maintenance of relationships with
others is effected by the following means:

3. Contact with people: shoppers; clients; agents;
representatives of other establishments, etc., effected by
persons-movement and communication. The symbolic attributes of location under #1 and #2 above are frequently
important in this relationship.

4. Communication: face-to-face in closely linked establishments; by telephone, etc.; by exchange of papers by
mail or messenger.

5. Persons movement: pedestrian, mass transit, auto,
rail, etc.

6. Goods handling: by hand truck or by hand for nearby
locations; by direct trucking between linked establishments
or via transportation system through forwarders, freight
terminals, and the like.

The distinction between an establishment's inner and
outer phases of activity is not always clear cut, as is seen
where some items appear on both lists. In the main, however, the differences in their requirements and operations
are such as to account for many of the changes which take
place in the patterns and groupings of urban activities, as
evidenced in the formation and dissolution of establishments
of different kinds in different locations. Whether for the
purpose of a business firm and its profitable operation or
for the purpose of planning a better spatial arrangement of
urban activities in any given area, the items in the outline
are all factors to be taken into account. For it is the goal
of our study of land uses to bring about an ever more efficient allocation of establishments so as to satisfy better
the city's economic and social needs.

It may be well to list again the factors outlined above,
this time in more condensed form, as a device for relating
subsequent discussion of various aspects of land use to the
key subject of our study—the activities of establishments,
including their relationships with people and with other
establishments, as expressed by linkages. (See Figure 3.)

Space requirements brought about by activities carried
on within establishments—requirements for frontage or
shipping facilities, for office or factory or display space,
more or less complicated for each establishment—are ful-
filled by the city's buildings. The requirements of external
activities of the same establishments are met by the physical setting in which these buildings are placed, together
with the services available, and also by the combination of
activities engaged in by near-by establishments. Both these
sets of requirements are satisfied imperfectly at best by
the combination of buildings and locations which constitutes
the total supply of available accommodations in any city or
any designated area within it. For it is inevitable that the
requirements change more rapidly than the great bulk of
the accommodations can be adapted, and it frequently happens
that one set of requirements is better satisfied than the other.
Thus, the patterns on the map taken by different categories
of establishments are largely shaped by their external activities. Hence the apparent anomaly of groups of establishments moving away from accommodations entirely suitable
for their internal activities.

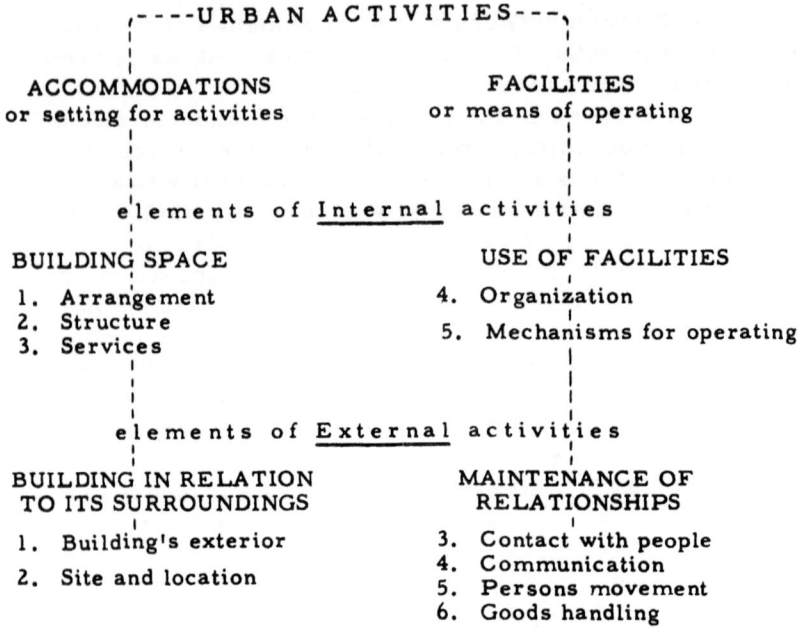

Figure 3.    OUTLINE: ACCOMMODATIONS AND
                    FACILITIES FOR URBAN ACTIVITIES

In every urban setting these accommodations and facilities have been built up over considerable periods of time in response to repeated demands for space in line with requirements current at each period. As requirements change over time the accommodations are modified to suit: new buildings are constructed in the locations and to the specifications currently in demand; old buildings are altered accordingly and the facilities provided by public utilities and public works are adjusted from time to time—each a separate improvement with the purpose of making some part of the city's physical plant a more efficient instrument for carrying on the activities taking place in it. But each improvement is designed, as a rule, on its own merits with small regard for the consequences that may follow in its wake. The builders of a mammoth commercial building, for example, will be little concerned with the vacancies and loss of value which may occur in the properties from which the new tenants are drawn. Or the over-all efficiency of a local area may be upset by dislocation of its service establish-

ments which can ill afford the higher rents brought about
by new construction. The harmful effects of traffic congestion resulting from overbuilding are plain to see—after the
fact—but their prevention demands a much broader basis
for analysis than is provided by the limited concepts of
markets for different kinds of building space which are current in the realm of real estate operations.

## ACCOMMODATIONS: BUILDINGS

The accommodations provided by the city's buildings,
together with their locations relative to streets and other
improvements on the land, the services and facilities
available at each location, and especially the various combinations of activities engaged in by groups of neighboring
establishments—all these constitute the setting for all the
systems of action which together make up the total life of
the city. The part of this setting most in evidence and apparently most permanent is that consisting of the buildings
themselves.

Buildings are constructed, as a rule, in response to
demand for accommodations beyond those available in the
existing structures. The new buildings may be designed to
meet a very generalized demand for office or factory or
shop space, or they may be constructed for a highly specialized establishment such as a bank or church, firehouse or
public school. Between these extremes are buildings designed especially to suit a particular owner-establishment
or group of tenants having specialized requirements somewhat in advance of current standards, such as the home office or factory for a large corporation or a "professional"
building. In any case, new buildings reflect well-established
activities of their prospective users. These are usually
activities such as are current in the older buildings.

Commercial buildings, by far the greatest bulk of central district construction, are most frequently built in the
midst of an existing concentration in order to capitalize on
the advantages of a location proved to be successful. New
and old buildings are thus in competition for tenants, although not entirely for the same ones. New buildings supply
the needs of those best able to lease new (and expensive)

space, while similar older buildings find themselves, in
time, with tenants of "lower" type than the buildings were
designed for. Meanwhile, new assortments of tenants are
always being formed by the continually changing ways of
doing business which are characteristic of commercial
enterprises.

Consider, for example, the central office of an expanding business: records will accumulate, the bookkeeping
burden will increase, more space will be needed. The firm
may seek increased space at the same or a different location, or it may keep its working office in the old location
and set up a new "front office" at a location more accessible
to its customers' representatives. Such differentiation of
needs of separate firms, causing the formation of new establishments, is a vital factor in the markets for different
kinds of space.[1]

Because of this continual rearrangement of the activities
of firms among separate establishments and because of the
normal mobility of tenants, buildings are frequently used
for purposes other than those for which they were designed.
When the business center is shifting away from the building
in question, the process of adaption to different uses is ac-
celerated by the threat of vacancies. The predominant situation is that establishments desiring a given location adjust
to the buildings which exist there, whether they are altogether suited to the internal requirements of each establishment or not.

Establishments use space in different ways, according
to the different functions performed. A given establishment
may contain several functional activities or (rarely) a single
one. When we approach the problem of fitting a particular
establishment (at a particular stage of its development) to
a particular building, the specific functional spaces become
the elements of design or adaptation. Returning to our example of a typical small manufacturing firm (page 14), the
main requirements in its first stage are sufficient space at
reasonable rent, fairly good location with regard to markets
for both goods and workers but with no pretensions as to appearance, except perhaps in the reception and salesrooms.

---

[1] See also Chapter II, page 14, "the establishment-firm relationship" for a
similar case involving a wider range of establishments.

The manufacturing and storage areas must be structurally capable of supporting their loads of machinery and goods, and there must be adequate sanitary and safety conditions (the state and the unions see to that). When the firm has expanded to the extent of maintaining a separate sales establishment, its needs will be conditioned by the "trade" with which it is dealing. Not only is appearance of the building's entrance lobby important but also the fact that competitors are located in the same building. These competitive factors make it worth while to pay for more expensive space for this special function of the firm. The same might be true of the "front office" (resulting sometimes in specialized buildings for a particular business group). Meanwhile, the need for operating economy makes necessary the continued use of cheap manufacturing space.

A multitude of establishments, varying in number and with continually changing requirements, is gradually shifting in location among the available accommodations of a more slowly changing supply of buildings. Establishments with similar combinations of needs tend to cluster together, while there is the greatest imaginable mixture in between these relatively consistent areas. A colossal double-shuffle is taking place all the time—a process in which the space needs of users are somehow matched by the utility of the buildings. The meeting ground between needs and utility is comprised in the measures of the space itself: amount, kind, quality, location. This process is diagrammed in Figure 4.

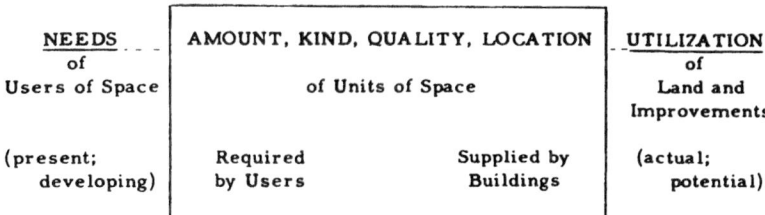

| NEEDS | AMOUNT, KIND, QUALITY, LOCATION | UTILIZATION |
|---|---|---|
| of | | of |
| Users of Space | of Units of Space | Land and Improvements |
| (present; developing) | Required by Users | Supplied by Buildings | (actual; potential) |

Figure 4.    THE MATCHING PROCESS: NEEDS OF
            ESTABLISHMENTS AND UTILIZATION
            OF SPACE

A classification scheme for each side of this diagram is suggested in Figure 5. Items for the middle ground are found in the two lowest levels of each classification. These

| SPACE AS USED | USABLE SPACE |
|---|---|
| by Establishments | in Buildings |

I, II. **Kind of Business**

(of the firm to which
establishment belongs)
such as:
    Manufacturing
    Retail trade
    Consumer Service

I, II. **Kind of Building**

(general purpose for which
building was constructed)
such as:
    Housing
    Commercial
    Industrial

A, B. **Function Performed**

(by each establishment
as a whole) such as:
    Salesroom
    Personnel Office
    Warehouse
    Retail store
Separate lists under each kind
of business, expressive of the
purpose for which each establishment is set up.

A, B. **Type**

(adapted to function)
such as:
    Single-family house
    Multiple dwelling
    Professional offices
    Manufacturing lofts
Separate lists under each
kind of building, with many
specialized building types but
with vast majority of space
listed under only few types.

1, 2. **Functional Differentiation**

(within the establishment)
Space required for:
    Offices
    Manufacturing
    Storage, Shipping
    Selling
A listing of space requirements,
simple for highly specialized
establishments, more complex
for "general" establishments.

1, 2. **Description**

(general form and size)
such as:
    Detached or row houses
    Elevator or walk-up
    Commercial, Office
    or Loft building
Combinations of types will
complicate this level.

a, b. **Measure of Space Required**

(shape, access, services)
Width, Depth, Ceiling height,
Ground or upper floor,
Frontage, Windows, Lighting,
Heating, Construction, Floor
loads, Finishes, Appearance.

a, b. **Measure of Space Available**

Detailed description of
space provided by the building, similar to the list at
the same level for estab-
lishments.

Figure 5.    CLASSIFICATION OUTLINE: SPACE
NEEDS OF USERS AND SPACE PRO-
VIDED BY BUILDINGS

have to do with attributes of floor space, classified both
as to needs of establishments and as to kinds of space
provided by buildings. There will be many duplications at
these levels, for one type of space may suit many needs and
vice versa. The process of cross matching (laborious but
fairly mechanical) will result in a full catalogue of possible combinations.

Analysis of change in the use of building space can now
be attempted, based on the catalogue of all practicable uses
which is suggested by the above diagram of the matching
process (Figure 4) and detailed in the classification scheme
of Figure 5 (p. 44). The range of actual uses and movements among them will be considered in the light of forces
which appear to operate on both sides of this "sorting"
model—those which act on establishments and those which
affect the conditions of utilization of buildings.

At this point the building itself resumes its prime position as an entity in the land-use picture. Throughout the
cataloguing process the characteristics of buildings as such
are practically ignored—such items as appearance, age, or
state of repair, of a particular building and its location
relative to transportation and other land uses. The value
of these items to a user of space is very real, even though
not readily commensurable in terms of the qualities of the
space itself. The direct measure of value (rent per unit of
space) is dependent on a combination of outside circumstances. For example, the economic value of a certain style
of building, located near certain groups of related establishments, is something which may command high rents compared with identical buildings less favorably located. Of
course this circumstance may change as so many of the
patterns of urban life change. Styles of buildings once
deemed necessary for expressing the worth and integrity
of the firms occupying them would now be liabilities to
some of the same firms, which have moved into newer
structures.

The building itself is the unit of change in total space
occupied by establishments, however mixed the functional
uses within buildings. Construction of a new building in the
city entails (almost invariably) the destruction of at least
one existing building and a shifting of the ousted establishments. Thus, a new building, however well suited to the

needs for which it is designed, has side effects along with
the fulfillment of its intended use.

Change in total building space can be stated (for a city:
central business district, "study area," etc.) by tabulating,
for successive time intervals, the additions to the existing
stock of buildings, together with the demolitions and the
remaining total. New buildings and demolished buildings can
be classified as to use on the basis of the public records;
but the great remaining bulk cannot readily be classified
except in the broadest terms, e.g., residential or nonresidential, and the latter into government or commercial-
industrial. When existing buildings are altered structurally,
we again have a chance to look at the record for a statement of intended use. Thus, for new buildings and remodeled buildings (a vital fraction for studying change) the
designed uses can be classified in general terms.

Detailed classification of all uses of space in buildings
can be attempted only for limited areas. However, such
classification, at least in simplified or diagrammatic form,
is a necessary prerequisite for tracing the shifts in city
patterns which result from the various forces and conditions which affect establishments, or for setting up a schematic account of the pros and cons of various available accommodations so that a firm can make realistic decisions
affecting the location of its various activities. Among the
major categories for classifying establishments, listed on
page 21, the first, "Residential," accounts for the distribution of nighttime population and all others except the last
have to do with the flow of goods from raw materials to
final consumption and with specialized services to individuals or to different kinds of business. The last, "Transportation, Communication, and other Public Service Facilities," has a special place in the study of urban land use.

## FACILITIES: TRANSPORTATION, COMMUNICATION, AND OTHER PUBLIC SERVICES

The facilities provided by transportation and communication and all of the other public services, such as
water supply, gas, and electricity, make it possible for
interactions to be maintained between related establishments located at a distance from each other; they are

utilized by all sorts of establishments and activity systems.
Technological developments in these all-pervasive services
have brought about completely new arrangements of activity
patterns and opened up possibilities for planned rearrangement of land uses which can make the city more efficient
for commerce and industry and more agreeable as a place
to live and work.

The far-reaching effects which these services have had
on patterns of land use do not constitute a one-way proposi-
tion by any means. Like all facilities in the urban setting,
these have been developed in response to growing need for
them, while at the same time they have served to develop
new patterns of land use having yet further needs. All relationships are reciprocal in this situation; the effects are
never one-way, except briefly, when the requirements out-
grow the facilities or when new facilities are provided in
excess of present demand and the use of them has not yet
"taken up the slack." The increasing differentiation of urban
activitiy systems and the accompanying developments in
transportation and communication and other public services
are so intermingled that there is no telling which came
first. It would seem that both are cause and both effect.

Before attempting to untangle or even describe these
urban complexities, it may be well to show by a familiar
rustic example how changes in transportation have been
intermingled with changes in several other systems. Rural
education has almost entirely changed its pattern of accommodations; the scattered one-room country schools, to which
pupils walked, have been replaced by consolidated schools
covering large districts, to which pupils are brought by bus.
The organization of teaching has been correspondingly altered, with resulting changes in administration and changes
in relationships between staff and community. The primitive
situation in which each small neighborhood school board
hired one teacher who "boarded 'round" has been replaced
by school boards representing much wider areas, employ-
ing sizable staff with specialized abilities. The entire
change was made possible, of course, by the development of
automobiles and all-weather highways. A related phenomenon is the merging of small farms into larger ones, con-
current with increasing mechanization in agriculture. Of
course, this is a far cry from the city, where situations

are more complex, but the same <u>types</u> of situation do obtain in the city, however many related systems are linked in with a given situation.

The <u>transportation</u> and <u>communications</u> systems provide the means whereby linkages are maintained between establishments, especially between distant locations, while the <u>other public service</u> facilities cater to the internal needs of the same establishments. All are alike, however, in that all serve every establishment in the city. The location of every establishment is, to a large extent, determined by the availability of these services, which take shape as networks on the map, each network an overlay on the topography and soil conditions and drainage of the area. The configuration of these networks—railroads or highways, bus or trolley routes, electric lines of all kinds, water or gas pipes, the street system itself—is determined for each by its own sets of economic and physical requirements. Transportation routes are all strongly affected by the slope of the ground, railroads most of all, so that possible locations for rail lines and yards are severely restricted except in flat country. To a lesser degree the same is true of automotive transport (as it was in the past for horse-drawn vehicles), so that commercial and industrial uses tend to develop in areas with relatively easy slopes. Electric power and communications networks, on the other hand, are practically free of the restrictions of topography, although additions to them are strongly conditioned by their own existing patterns, as is the case with all physical improvements.

Until about a century ago all cities were compact, with closely located groups of associated activities. Workers walked to their places of employment. The only means of communication between establishments, or for that matter within establishments, was by word of mouth or exchange of handwritten notes. Movement of goods within the city was a slow process of horse-drawn drays or hand trucks. Movement of persons and goods between cities was by the slow process of water transport, where that was available, or by a few railroads connecting major centers.

The railroads soon brought cities closer together, but movement within cities remained slow until the development of the trolley car and the automobile. Now the picture is entirely changed, although it has been elaborated on the same groundwork. The expansion of cities has been accompanied by great technological advances in power production and transmission, transportation and communication. Manufacturing operations, for example, once tied closely to water power and water transportation and then to steam and railroads, are now more free to locate where they please, thanks to the development of electric power, highways, and truck transportation. Water and rail transport are still very important, however, for movements in bulk, so that the older patterns of manufacturing location have been not so much displaced as they have been supplemented and given variety by the opening up of new areas between the older centers.

The very existence of urban centers over a long period of time has been accompanied by the development of increasing facilities for transportation and communication and municipal services of all kinds. City growth takes the form of increased concentrations and filling in along the present service networks before the comparatively open sites between existing centers are developed. Provision of all the facilities needed for improving a given area is an engineering problem, compounded of the requirements and limitations peculiar to each branch of engineering concerned. The potential uses of a given site are delimited by the array of services which can be provided as well as by zoning and other regulatory restrictions and by the rent-paying ability of the activities concerned. Efficient solution of the engineering problems can be taken for granted once their scope has been defined by present or anticipated demand. The underlying problem remains—a situation where continually changing needs for services of all kinds are brought about by changing combinations of land use whose "laws" of change are scarcely understood.

## SUMMARY

In this chapter the problems of urban land use are approached on the basis of presently existing patterns of establishments, in terms of the accommodations and facilities provided by the city's buildings and locations and public services. These patterns have come about as a result

of the manifold systems of activity in which all the establishments are involved and are conditioned in turn by the
physical environment, not only as it exists but as it has
been developed over time by a long sequence of changing
activities. Prime clues to the continuing usefulness of the
city's structures are found in the differences which develop
in the internal and external functioning of establishments.
For example, the expanding office work of government tends
to be dispersed in ordinary commercial structures while the
symbolic or ceremonial functions remain in the traditional
setting.

Patterns of buildings and streets and other improvements on the land are relatively permanent in comparison
with the groupings of establishments which they accommodate. These groupings appear and change as requirements
for different kinds of activity are modified and as establishments are formed and dissolved. A great deal of shifting of
activities among existing accommodations goes on continually, while a relatively small proportion of establishments is
set up in newly constructed buildings in any given period.
Additions to the public works or public utilities plant in any
one period are also fractional modifications of existing
facilities. The predominant situation is that of new activities adjusting to the physical accommodations and facilities
as they exist.

# V

## LAND USE
## IN CENTRAL BUSINESS DISTRICTS

T HE main purpose of the present study is to establish
a factual basis for analyzing phenomena of growth and
change in the city center, with the goals of conserving
and enhancing urban resources. The foregoing chapters
have built up a general orientation toward problems of
urban land utilization, an approach formulated in terms of
the entire city's varied activities as they function with
regard to space and location. This general approach may be
applied to the study of almost any kind of urban area, but
it was developed primarily with one type of center in mind:
that major concentration of activities which is loosely referred to as "downtown" or "the business district."

In the central business district of any city is found its
greatest concentration of buildings and of commerce, its
most congested area of pedestrian and vehicular traffic, its
major source of tax revenue. It is, in sum, that chief nucleus of an entire region's activities which makes the city
what it is. It is in this area that the web of linkages has
been longest in process of development and has become
most intricate. It contains more than its share of the oldest
buildings in the city as well as the newest; its business
firms are both the most stable and conservative and the
most enterprising innovators. And here are found the most
apparent advantages of having free choice among closely
located establishments of many different kinds.

Not only does the central district contain the greatest
concentration and mixture of different kinds of establishments: it is most of all characterized by a concentration of
activities not generally found elsewhere, especially those
central offices and banks, retail stores, theaters, and the
like which serve the entire metropolitan area. These central activities could not function, as a group, except in the
central location, but other sorts of activities found in the
center might benefit by removing to outlying locations. Indeed, the process of decentralization is taking place continuously, but so is the process of centralization. The

results of these conjugate processes are seen in the development of outlying centers and the changes which are con-
tinously taking place in the central district. But the key to
understanding both processes lies in the functioning of the
central district itself as it has developed over time.

The chief characteristic of central districts, beyond the
presence of the typically central activities, is the profusion
of establishments of all kinds which are found mixed together in close proximity. Even in limited areas in which
one kind of business appears to predominate, a great
variety of establishments unrelated to the dominant use is
invariably revealed by an actual count. The location and
general extent of this central concentration is seen at once
in the very bulk of its buildings, especially as viewed from
the air. When it comes to drawing a firm boundary for purposes of study, the extent of the central district must be
determined arbitrarily. If limited to the central core
large buildings, which generally includes the hotels and
shopping district as well as the business offices and service establishments, then the predominantly central or near-
central wholesaling and light manufacturing areas may be
excluded. If extended to include a continuous area of manufacturing and wholesaling, the boundary is likely to take in
too much territory, for these industrial areas lose their "central" characteristics as they extend outward and merge with
those industrial concentrations which are not typically central.

In order to trace changes in patterns of land use, the
study area should include the site of former central concentrations from which the present center has shifted, for
in these is found a great variety of changing activities taking
advantage of the reduced rents made available in outmoded
buildings. The area should certainly not be limited to the
main concentration of high-rent, commercial buildings. In
the complete description of central city activities, these
merely provide accommodation for selected groups of establishments whose operations could scarcely be understood without studying their relationships with other kinds
of establishments in the central district. And since further
change is inevitable, it would be well to take in some territory beyond the present main concentration, to include in
the study area some room for future expansion and adjustment of the central activities.

## CENTRAL ACCOMMODATIONS AND FACILITIES

The setting for central district activities, embodied in streets and parks and public works and in buildings and facilities of all kinds, is unique for every city. Each city has its own geographical situation, its own "natural history" through which its present development has been reached. The characteristics of this physical setting have been brought to their present form by a long sequence of events, during which the accommodations and facilities have been modified and developed at intervals or have been allowed to deteriorate in some portions, all in response to changing needs of the major activities of each period.

Increase in accommodations usually tends to build up existing concentrations, whether centrally located or outlying, before the spaces between are developed. Even when new centers are formed they very soon take their place in this scheme and the situation soon becomes the old one of adding to concentrations which already exist. In no case can a well-established city center represent a logical solution of present needs as it might have been planned on the primeval site; in no case have the effects of much earlier arrangements died out entirely. For even though none of the earliest structures remains, and even though the chief focus of activity (the so-called "center of town") has shifted from its original location, the very layout of streets and open places and boundary lines of ownership remains as a mould constraining subsequent patterns. Meanwhile, the networks of public service facilities exert compelling forces for continuance.

The existing stock of buildings is of all ages, with old and new standing side by side, as a rule. Increments to this stock have been constructed at different periods, each in response to the needs of its time and place. Adjustments to the remaining stock of buildings have occurred during the same periods, taking the form of improved services (better elevators, lighting, air conditioning), major alterations (conversion from residential to commercial use, for example, or provision of more street-frontage with show-window space), or even demolition (and use of the ground space as a parking lot "until the time is ripe" for a new building).

New buildings with the most up-to-date services and
advantages of location naturally command the highest rents,
and the very appearance of the more successful of these
buildings becomes a symbol of their desirable qualities.
Well-located older buildings, meanwhile, can maintain fairly
high rents by modernizing their services and altering their
appearance to accord with what is expected of them. In
outmoded locations the same kinds of older buildings continue to serve a less demanding group of establishments at
rentals which their operations can support. In a general
way the quantity and quality and cost of accommodations
provided by the stock of buildings in an established business district all go on adjusting to the requirements of the
entire array of establishments that use them.

The most dramatic happenings in this continuing process of adjustment take place when buildings still useful are
demolished and superseded by new ones. Nearly as dramatic,
and more pervasive, has been the recent wave of costly
front-and-fixture alterations in commerical structures
ranging all the way from small retail shops to large banking establishments. This means of keeping up with developments in commercial efficiency and with their symbols is
most generally applied to "frontage" establishments, thus
highlighting the enormous differences between ground space,
accessible from the street, and upper floor space. These
differences are so marked that there may be little or no
connection between the ground-floor and upper-floor establishments. Centrally located hotels, office buildings, two-
story taxpayers, and even apartment houses all have much
the same assortment of retail shops and small service
establishments at the street level. And old residential
structures are always at hand in the center of any city,
providing a reservoir of space which can be adapted to the
needs of the more volatile elements of central activities.

## SORTING OF ACTIVITIES
## AMONG CENTRAL LOCATIONS

Organizations choose locations for their activities where
they will find suitable accommodations, services, and facilities as well as the associated activities of closely linked
establishments or "the market" which their operations re-

quire, whether this be the labor market or a market for finished goods or a specialized retail market. Small shops, for example, flourish where pedestrian traffic is heaviest— in an "office building" district or in a "department store" district. Service establishments of all kinds are brought into being by the sheer accumulation of activities that exists in the midst of all business districts. Many different groups of activities gather in or near the central core of large office buildings—groups unrelated to each other except by location and what that location has to offer. But wherever they locate, members of every group benefit by nearness to establishments with which they have linkages and by the availability of services of all kinds which they require.

Concentrations of establishments in a central district vary in density, in general conformance with the distribution of floor space in buildings. Each different kind of business, however, has its own pattern of distribution, and related combinations of them tend to congregate in more or less distinct centers, each a somewhat different area, none too definite as to extent and always overlapped by others. The consequent mixture at any one location, say in a single block or a block front, will be characterized as much by the variety of unrelated activities as by the kind-of-business combinations that provide a label for the district. For example, a district of machine tool dealers is usually closely linked with overlapping districts of electric motor dealers, wholesalers of metals, and miscellaneous metal manufacturers. In the same area there may be a group of hotel and restaurant supply houses having little relation to the metals group, or a number of furniture dealers unrelated to any of the other groups, and so on.

Changes in land-use patterns may be observed in two ways: (1) as changes occurring over a wide area, where activities are continually shifting among available locations; and (2) as changes taking place at a given location, where a number of different kinds and combinations of activities follow each other. The first appears as a gradual shift in the location of an entire retail shopping district, for example, or a theater district or a particular kind of manufacturing or wholesaling, over a period of time; or it may take the form of a new center growing up some distance from the old, as in New York's Wall Street and Midtown concentrations of huge commercial buildings; or, most commonly, it appears as a confused scattering and regrouping of miscellaneous establishments. The second is observed as a succession of different kinds of use of a given site (a single block or group of blocks or even a single building). Older buildings, especially, have experienced a sequence of different kinds of tenants as the activities found in their vicinities have shifted. As a result of these continuing changes, there is always a mixture of both related and unrelated activities in each locality.

The array of establishments actually found in a given central location has resulted from both the continuance of previous patterns and the active formation of new business groupings and (from time to time) altogether new kinds of business. The differentiation of the various activities of firms into ever more specialized establishments goes on continually, although the changes are rapid in some kinds of business and slow in others. Size itself is a major conditioning factor in this process of growth by division, and rate of growth is another; establishments are not subdivided until the magnitude or complexity of their operations make it worth while. Locational mobility varies with different business groups, depending on the strength of linkage between related establishments or the relative importance and cost of accommodations and facilities of specific kinds, such as shipping, transit, low-rent space, frontage on a street with heavy pedestrian traffic, and the like. Freedom to relocate may be restricted by long-term leases, by the high cost of moving and installing equipment, or by difficulties in liquidating a real estate investment in the existing location. Or a firm may continue to perform all of its activities in the same locations because of inertia or tradition or sheer unawareness of advantages to be gained by relocating some of the activities at locations which can better meet their needs. But despite a general inertia, a tendency to stay put, the shifting of activities among locations is always going on.

## ANALYSIS OF LAND-USE PATTERNS

Patterns of urban establishments of all kinds as they are accommodated by the central district's buildings and locations make up the groundwork for all the different combinations of central activities; they are also the major nucleus for the life of the entire city and its region. These vital activities may be studied, in so far as they affect changes in land use, by analysis of the functions performed in the various establishments and by tracing linkages between establishments. This analysis may begin with any given kind of business by observing the constituent establishments and their locations, the activities engaged in by them, and the locations of all the other establishments to which the original group is linked. Also of interest in this analysis are the other kind-of-business establishments found in the same locations as the original group, together with their activities and requirements. The latter may be compatible or may interfere with those of the original group.

The differentiation of activities carried on by present-day urban establishments has been brought about largely by technological advances—in production, transportation and communication. Improved production methods affect mainly the internal space requirements of manufacturing establishments—requirements which may bring about removal of some kinds of manufacture from the central district entirely or which may foreshadow further differentiation of the elements going to make up various finished products. Developments in transportation, especially in trucking, figure largely in the changes taking place in the location patterns of activites which are related to each other, while developments in communication—telephone and teletype, for example—have largely released the same activities from the necessity of locating near each other for the exchange of information. Communication within widely separated units of an organization can now be carried on more readily by telephone or telegraph than once it could between next-door neighbors by word of mouth or exchange of messages. Business organizations are now more free to locate each of their separate activities in a place suited to its particular needs. And, in addition to these technological advances, changes taking place in the very organization or the activities themselves are potent factors in the realignment of establishments and linkages among them.

Patterns of activities relating to a single establishment can be diagrammed and studied readily enough. Activities of a single business group are somewhat more intricate but are still easily understood. Both are set against the same background of the entire physical city along with the vast array of the city's other activities, a background that is generally taken for granted or loosely defined at best. But study of the entire roster of activities is another matter. Methods must be developed for evaluating all sorts of establishments on equal terms without losing sight of unfamiliar or scattered groups. The characteristics of a few well-known activities must not be allowed to overshadow the study of those little known. And quite beyond the need for methodical study of the various component activities, their totality is not to be understood without systematic analysis directed toward the entire aggregation. Such analysis is necessarily beset by the hazards of the proverbial situation of being unable to "see the forest for the trees."

### A Parallel from Systematic Forestry

The parallels between city and forest are so apt that a digression may be permitted at this point in order to demonstrate by analogy the need for systematic study of land use, study which can lead to analysis and eventually to conservation and management of urban resources.

In the first place, both city and forest have been with us for ages, and both are taken as given by those who have to do with them. The attitudes of forest dweller and of city dweller are parallel in that each is undismayed by the complexities of his own milieu and utterly confused by the other. When it comes to the question of exploiting the advantages of both environments, the question "for whom?" applies equally.

The city as a place in which to live and work is one thing, and it connotes a continuing, relatively unchanging environment; the forest, at a pioneer level of economy, is much the same. But both become something else entirely when strong measures are brought to bear on their material resources. The primitive woodsman, content to accept what the forest continually gives, has a completely different attitude from that of the primitive lumberman intent on getting out sawlogs in a hurry. Such serenity as the city dweller

may achieve is likely to be disturbed whenever serious
changes in his environment result from real estate operations.

In pursuing this parallel, the total conversion of wood-
lands into farmlands is outside of our picture, and so is the
decay of blighted areas and their total redevelopment after
virtual stagnation. The present discussion is concerned
with the continuing utility of both forest and city. It has
been amply demonstrated that both will deteriorate if the
predatory forces at work on them are allowed to run on un-
controlled.

The systematic study of forestry was developed in this
country at a time when our forests were being plundered
rapidly. The purpose of this study was not to turn the clock
back and restore the primeval forest but to achieve a long-
range utilization of forest resources. The following statement of problems requiring solution in the infant science of
forestry is taken from the presidential address before a
meeting of the American Forestry Association in February,
1878.

Who among us has yet bestowed sufficient attention to the mutual relations of our native and introduced trees to enable him to indicate which of them are obnoxious to one another, and which may be
planted in mixed groups? Yet it is evident that just here we have
much to learn. As to their varied characters in this respect we need
to know respecting each of the species:

1st.  The term or rotation of trees, the time required by them
      to reach their maximum of profit. And this is so various
      that it becomes an important factor in the matter of group-
      ing.
2d.   The height which the trees may attain at maturity is an
      important element in the same problem.
3d.   As also is the rapidity of their growth, for some will in a
      few years so tower above their fellows as to impede their
      advance.
4th.  Some species are found to be really obnoxious or even
      poisonous to others. Such should never be grouped to-
      gether.
5th.  Some trees are so exclusive that they should always be
      planted in masses by themselves, while others seem to
      require the protecting care of nurses or companions.

Upon all these points we are yet almost wholly ignorant, and we
shall need a long series of careful observations to enable us to de-

cide what is best for us.  These are some of the many experiments
which are devolved upon us when we undertake to build up a system
of enlightened American Forestry.

. . . . . . . . . .

Let us indicate a few of the other points upon which our igno-
rance is painfully conspicuous:

Who among us can render a satisfactory statement as to the
proper rotation or period of our own trees, or indicate the proper
succession of different species, which may best follow each other;
or, who can inform us what Preparatory species should be planted
on barren wastes, in order to bring the land into a condition to pro-
duce valuable forests, as is done in many regions of Europe, where
Reboisement or re-foresting the mountain wastes, is successfully
practiced.

. . . . . . . . . .

In the matter of Grouping, who can tell us what species of trees
may be considered Consociates, and which are Disociates? Who can
tell us how, if at all, we can combine Needle-leaved trees with those
that are Broad-leaved? or, which of either grand division will thrive
best when mingled together, or, which species may require to be
planted in masses alone.

. . . . . . . . . .

Then again, who among us is qualified to go into a piece of
woodland and made correct Estimations as to the value of the crop,
and give us the exact contents by Surveys and Measurements, or to
open, with the property in question, a proper system of Accounts?
Who can tell us how to arrange for the Forest management of:
Large Timber growths;
Of Coppice, with its appropriate treatment, thinning and cutting
from time to time; and of the
Mixed Forests, or give us directions as to the proportions of
their several ages, in order to make such most profitable; and
a continuous source of revenue![1]

What we need to know about the healthy functioning of a
city's multiple activities is closely analogous to the situation outlined in the address quoted above. Indeed, one might
substitute different kinds of establishments or types of
buildings for different species of trees and the quotation
would still make sense without any other change. In fact, it
might then serve as a preliminary outline for beginning to
study that interplay between activities and their accommodations which is at the root of changing patterns of urban

[1] John A. Warder, Forestry and Its Needs (Washington, D.C.: American
Forestry Association, 1878). Punctuation is revised in this transcription.

land utilization; for the systematic study of urban activities and their physical accommodations is today in its early stages, not unlike the situation seventy-five years ago with regard to the study of forestry.

## Systematic Research

The material basis for observing and measuring activities and their concentrations in an urban area is provided by a census of establishments, classified as to type of activity. (See, for example, the list on page 21.) Such a listing of all establishments by location and type is the necessary groundwork for describing and analyzing relationships among activities in the central district as a whole. On this groundwork any pertinent data concerning establishments can be used for elaborating the descriptions of separate activities and the relationships among them. Such data will also provide the means for evaluating and comparing establishments and business groups.

Of first importance in the general description and analysis of urban land use is the space actually used by each establishment—its amount, kind, and arrangement; the type of structure in which it is housed; its location relative to public service facilities and to other establishments. Data relating to separate business activities may include (for each establishment) the amount of goods handled or number of persons dealt with; the cost of space; the nature of important linkages; and many more. In the present study, however, the data will be limited almost entirely to a count of establishments of all kinds and an estimate of their floor area, drawn from surveys covering the central business district of Philadelphia in 1934 and 1949. Thus, a broad factual basis will be laid for testing hypotheses having to do with location and distribution of central activities, as they are observed in a representative city.

# VI

## GROWTH AND STRUCTURE OF
## CENTRAL PHILADELPHIA

THE general approach to the study or urban land use that has been developed up to this point will be applied specifically, in the next few chapters, to description and analysis of relationships among land-based activities in downtown Philadelphia. Thus, concepts already presented in general terms will be reexamined in the context of the present physical situation in Philadelphia with its present complex of central activities. Moreover, this study of changing land uses will suggest principles which may be applied to the study of other urban centers, to see what phenomena may be specific to a given city and what may apply generally.

In the course of examining the interplay of activities and locations in the central district, it will be necessary to devise methods of measuring land-use phenomena so that systematic comparisons can be made and hypotheses can be tested. But before commencing to work with the survey data which comprise the chief factual basis of the present study, it would be well to describe central Philadelphia itself in relation to its geographic and historical backgrounds, for this is the stage on which our activities play out their changes. The interplay of activities can be understood only in their own proper setting.

### URBAN ORIGINS

The origin of nearly every city, and Philadelphia is no exception, has been blessed by geographic advantages which persist, even though modern techniques have largely supplanted the original determinants of urban location. Like so many of the older cities in this country, Philadelphia is located on the "fall line" between the coastal plain and the interior upland, where the early needs of manufacture were provided by water power and where water transport was available for commerce—in ships for overseas and coastwise trade and in river boats for inland shipping. The

development of steam power in the early nineteenth century
freed the workshops from their restricted locations at wa-
terfalls while railroads soon replaced much of the water-
borne inland and coastal shipping. But the consequent
changes in urban locations served to build up the more
favorably located existing centers rather than to replace
them with new concentrations. The more recent development of automotive transportation has made all locations
available, with a consequent tendency toward decentralization of activities, yet the major concentrations remain
much as before.

The present situation of Philadelphia's central business
district, its activities and their relative positions, can be
traced continuously from 1682 when William Penn's "greene
countrie towne" was laid out between the Delaware and
Schuylkill Rivers as the chief center for the new Pennsylvania Colony.[1] Philadelphia's site was carefully chosen
under Penn's instructions to locate where "it is most
navigable, high, dry and healthy; where most ships may
ride of deepest draught of water and load and unload without lighterage." The location was most favorable for the
growth of the town and the colony, being at the edge of the
rich, rolling upland which extends sixty miles from the
city to the first ridge of the Allegheny Mountains and from
New England to the South. Midway along this east coast belt,
which was in process of development by the early colonists,
with a fine harbor on the Delaware, with water power on the
Schuylkill and the minor streams, and with the best inland
routes to the northwest frontier, Philadelphia soon became
the country's chief port and first city.

## CENTER AND REGION

Penn's colony had plentiful and diversified resources
and Penn's policy attracted the more substantial European
farmers and skilled craftsmen who rapidly developed a
diversified economy spread out over the entire country-
side east of the mountains. There was timber for smelting
iron as well as for building. Before the local timber became

[1] The area of the original survey is very nearly the same as the present
central business district. See Figure 6A on p. 000.

scarce the apparently inexhaustible coal veins were opened
and the iron industry was so well established in a number
of smaller centers scattered through the region that several
of these survived as manufacturing cities after the exhaus-
tion of the iron ore itself.

As the tide of settlement spread westward, this region
was ready with its tools and goods and wagons to support
the expansion of the colonial seaboard economy across the
mountains and into the Ohio Valley. After the opening of
the Erie Canal in 1825 with its cheaper transportation, the
main stream of westward migration was diverted through
New York to the Great Lakes area, so that Philadelphia lost
its first place to New York in 1830 and was surpassed by
Chicago in 1890, but the resources and manufactures and
transportation facilities of the city and its region have continued to make Philadelphia one of the important centers in
the development of the entire country.

The transportation routes between the urban centers of
the eastern seaboard and the interior—roads, streams,
canals, and finally railroads—became the circulating system that is vital to our present widespread national economy. Philadelphia lies on two main axes of this circulating
system, both now served by several rail lines: (1) the
northeast-southwest axis following the original industrial
development along the "fall line" through the New England
towns, New York, Trenton, Wilmington, Baltimore, Washington, and the South, and (2) the westward axis across the
Alleghenies. In addition to these main axes there are numerous branches and connecting links which together form
a railroad network around Philadelphia.

The highways with their less stringent requirements
as to grades and alignment form a very complete system
throughout the Philadelphia region. The main routes, however, respond to the same pulls as the railroads, with well-
developed connections to all the nearby industrial centers
and through routes corresponding to the same main transportation axes as noted above: U.S. 1 following the "fall
line" and the Pennsylvania Turnpike providing the main
route to the west. The highway system is, of course,
closer-meshed than the railway network, with a greater
number of alternative routes.

The main nuclei of these transportation networks are

the same urban concentrations that have existed since the
early days when the entire built-up portion of Philadelphia
occupied no more than a few dozen blocks near the harbor,
a mere fraction of the present central district. The outlying
towns in Philadelphia County, such as Germantown, Frank-
ford, and Kensington, have been absorbed long since, and
other nearby cities such as Norristown, Bristol, and Chester in Pennsylvania and Camden in New Jersey are now
integral parts of the Philadelphia Metropolitan District.
The spaces between all of the old centers have been largely
subdivided and built up. Indeed, the building-up process
continues everywhere, even at the center itself, with re-
placement of old buildings by new at ever increasing densities.

The relationship of centers to the lower density areas
surrounding them remains much the same as formerly, even
though the open country has been replaced by continuous
suburbs interspersed with parks and industrial uses. The
central city still dominates a wide region. Civil boundaries
"wash out" when we attempt to delimit areas associated with
one or another city activity. For example, the Philadelphia
Retail Trading Zone, as designated by the newspapers' Audit
Bureau of Circulation, includes the four adjacent counties
in Pennsylvania, one county in Delaware, and eight in New
Hersey from Princeton and Trenton south to Cape May,
while the area covered by the United Parcel Service for the
large department stores has amoeba-like boundaries, mostly
within the fourteen counties but reaching out beyond county
lines to other population centers—Reading, Allentown,
Bethlehem.[2] Successive contours delimited by time of
travel (isochronic maps) shape up somewhat differently,
with salients reaching out along the railroads, conforming
in general with the densely populated areas. In every case
these map patterns are definitely focused on the central
business district of Philadelphia.

The land-use maps of the Philadelphia City Planning

[2] Philadelphia City Planning Commission, Economic Base Study of the Philadelphia Area (Philadelphia, 1949). Map of Philadelphia Retail Trading Area,
Figure VII, p. 42. Another map of this study (Figure VI) indicates the following larger groups of counties as wholesale area: eighteen counties in the
Wholesale Grocery Primary Area, forty-five counties for Drygoods, and
forty-nine counties for Drugs.

Commission show that nearly all the main connecting
streets within the city (formerly main streets of towns or
roads between them) are taken up by business, while industrial uses occupy all the waterfront as well as many locations adjacent to the railways. In fact, transportation itself
(railroad yards, waterfront facilities, taxi and trailer lots)
accounts for a great deal of the industrial area. In the
northern part of the city, population and business and industry are fairly well interspersed, and it is here that the railroads form the most complete network. Elsewhere in the
interior, away from the Delaware River, industry is quite
scattered except in the older centers such as Norristown
or Bristol. In general, industry occupies the lower ground
along stream beds, while the highest ground is taken up by
the high-rent, low-density residential areas, such, for example, as Germantown and Chestnut Hill in the northwest
of Philadelphia and the "Main Line" suburbs outside the city
to the west.

The concentration of commercial and industrial uses
along the main arteries has made them inadequate for
present-day traffic. Philadelphia is at present executing
a comprehensive construction program of expressways
which will by-pass the congested street system and serve
to bring vehicular traffic into the city center and also will
give through traffic easy passage. The same sort of adaption has already been performed by the railroads by means
of a few freight cut-offs which by-pass the city and free the
local yards and tracks of through freight traffic. The rail-
freight network inside the city has many grade crossings
and even many places where tracks and trucks and pedestrian traffic are all in competition for street space.

## GROWTH OF THE CENTER

The original survey of 1682 covered all of the present
central area from South Street to Vine Street between the
Delaware and Schuylkill Rivers in a regular grid of streets
with two wide central streets forming central axes and with
five symmetrically placed squares reserved for public use.
The original settlement, however, did not develop around its
formal axes but clustered around the sheltered harbor
formed by Dock Creek (Figure 7A). This inlet formed a

broad irregular diagonal across three or four blocks and
then continued in two small streams, the main one running
westward to a duck pond at Washington Square and the
smaller stream running southwest. The inlet was crossed
before 1700 by a drawbridge at Front Street. This and
several bridges over the smaller streams provided connections between the different parts of the town until the
need for access to the developing commercial properties
fronting on Dock Creek brought about the gradual filling in
of all the waterways during the eighteenth century, so that
today Dock Street remains one of the few wide streets in
downtown Philadelphia.

Figure 6 illustrates two stages in the growth of the
built-up area, from early days until the city broke out of
its original boundaries. The higher ground south and west of
Dock Street was from the first predominantly residential in
use, and much of this area has remained so to the present
day with many fine houses which have survived since the
time of the Revolutionary War. The early commercial
development was mainly along the Delaware waterfront
north of Dock Street. Water Street served as access to the
wharves which formed an irregular line corresponding
roughly with the west side of Delaware Avenue, the present
waterfront street. A steep bank along the river, occupied
by the very narrow block between Water Street and Front
Street, separated the dockside level from the higher ground
of the town behind.

The large regular blocks of the original survey, averaging about 400 by 600 feet between street lines, soon proved
unsuited to the needs of the crowded commercial town near
the waterfront. It was necessary to provide access to the
many activities which were vying for space in the midst of
the town. The blocks were soon modified by the addition of
minor streets and courts and alleys, all parallel to the
street lines but spaced apparently at random. The lots, however, are almost invariably narrow (less than twenty feet
wide as a rule, with many less than fifteen feet wide) and
usually have frontage on two streets. Nearly all of the
original blocks were broken up in this manner into as many
as seven subblocks which differ greatly as to proportions and
orientation. A notable exception is the block on which the
State House (later Independence Hall) was built. This was

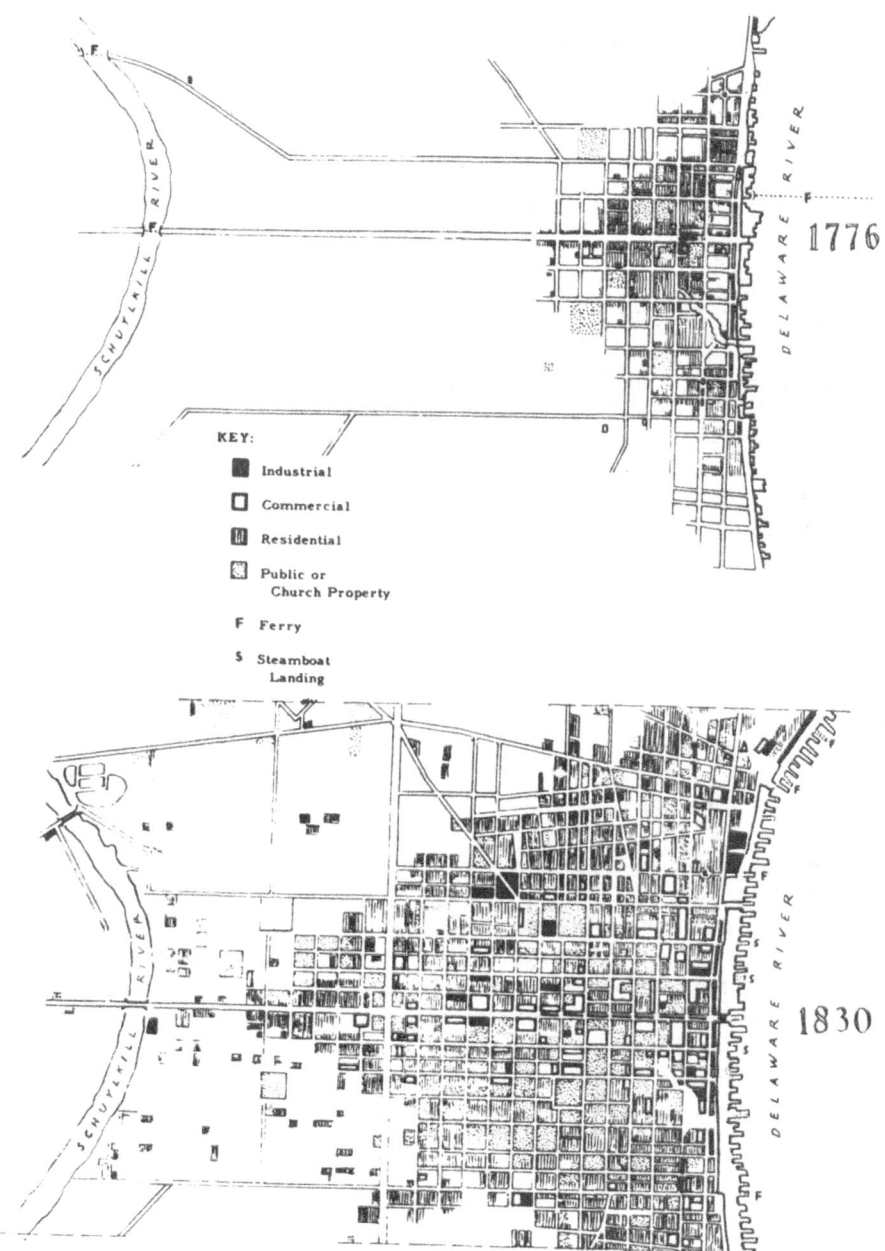

KEY:

■ Industrial

□ Commercial

▥ Residential

▨ Public or
Church Property

F Ferry

S Steamboat
Landing

Figure 6.   OLD PHILADELPHIA: 1776 AND 1830

added to the public squares in the mid-eighteenth century.

Since its earliest days Philadelphia has experienced
a constant shifting of activities, some migrating as the town
expanded, others succeeding to the vacated space, while
additional space has been provided continually by construction of larger buildings or conversion of residences
to commercial use. Yet the shifts were never complete,
and many traces remain of the succession of activities in
different parts of the entire central area. Sometimes a few
business firms remain in an area from which the remainder
of the "line" has migrated; sometimes distinctive buildings
remain as reminders of former activities, such as isolated
churches or fine residences now surrounded by commercial establishments, or former bank buildings now used as
offices or stores. The old buildings are never completely
supplanted except in very small areas of intense development; there is probably not a spot in the entire downtown
area which is much more than a block from several cen-
tury-old buildings.

The present business district grew out of the colonial
town early in the nineteenth century, while all of the close-
in vacant land was being filled up by residential or industrial
uses. The general drift of the center has been continually
westward from the Delaware until now the predominantly
residential expanse of the city has been invaded by a fairly
continuous area of higher building density extending roughly
from Locust to Race Streets and from Front to Eighteenth
(Figure 7B).

The progressive accumulation of business functions
was soon accompanied by development of mass transit,
making it possible for greater numbers of people to congregate in comparatively small central areas and also making it possible to get about easily between different parts
of that central area as it proceeded to expand. Horse cars
appeared very early in the nineteenth century. Steam power
dates from 1832 on the Philadelphia and Germantown Railway, for Germantown, then as now, was a major residential
suburb. ("Old Ironsides," the first locomotive, did not at
once supplant the horses; it had insufficient traction for
rainy weather, when the horses were again hitched up to the
cars.) The street railways continued to be horse drawn until

the 80's, when most of the lines were electrified. The location of these transit facilities inevitably affected the patterns of development of the entire central business district and of the concentrations of population adjacent to it. (The chief concentrations of population grew up directly north, south, and west of the central district, along the trolley and bus lines, Figure 7A).

The present focus around City Hall was set by the Pennsylvania Railroad's Broad Street Station in 1881 and the Reading Station at Twelfth and Market soon after. These terminal stations made strong anchors for those activities which require the most central locations, but the very bulk of these facilities constricted further development. Only recently the area west of City Hall has been freed for redevelopment by the demolition of the old Broad Street Station and its tracks—the "Chinese Wall" that divided the area for so long.[3] The new Penn Center group of office buildings, now under construction on the site of the old station tracks, will supply the increasing demand for centrally located space.

Some idea of the westward movement of the "core" of the business district which preceded the present location may be gained by glancing at the movement of some of the financial institutions (Figure 7B). In 1754 the first group of bankers and brokers began holding meetings in Bradford's Coffee House on the corner of Front and High (now Market) Streets, moving later to the Merchants' Coffee House on Second Street near Walnut. The Bank of Pennsylvania, first in the country, set up by Robert Morris to finance the Revolutionary War, was located on Front Street, north of Walnut (1780-84). The next, the Bank of North America, was on Chestnut, west of Third. On Third Street, south of Chestnut, is the earliest bank building (1789) which still remains, the Bank of the United States, later the Girard Bank. The brokers continued on Second Street until they moved into their newly constructed Merchants' Exchange at Second and Walnut in the early 1830's. In 1888 they moved to the Drexel Building on Independence Square, at that time the city's

[3] The main line traffic of the Pennsylvania was diverted from Broad Street in the 1930's by construction of the new station at Thirtieth Street and the new Suburban Terminal with tracks underground, adjacent to the old Broad Street Terminal.

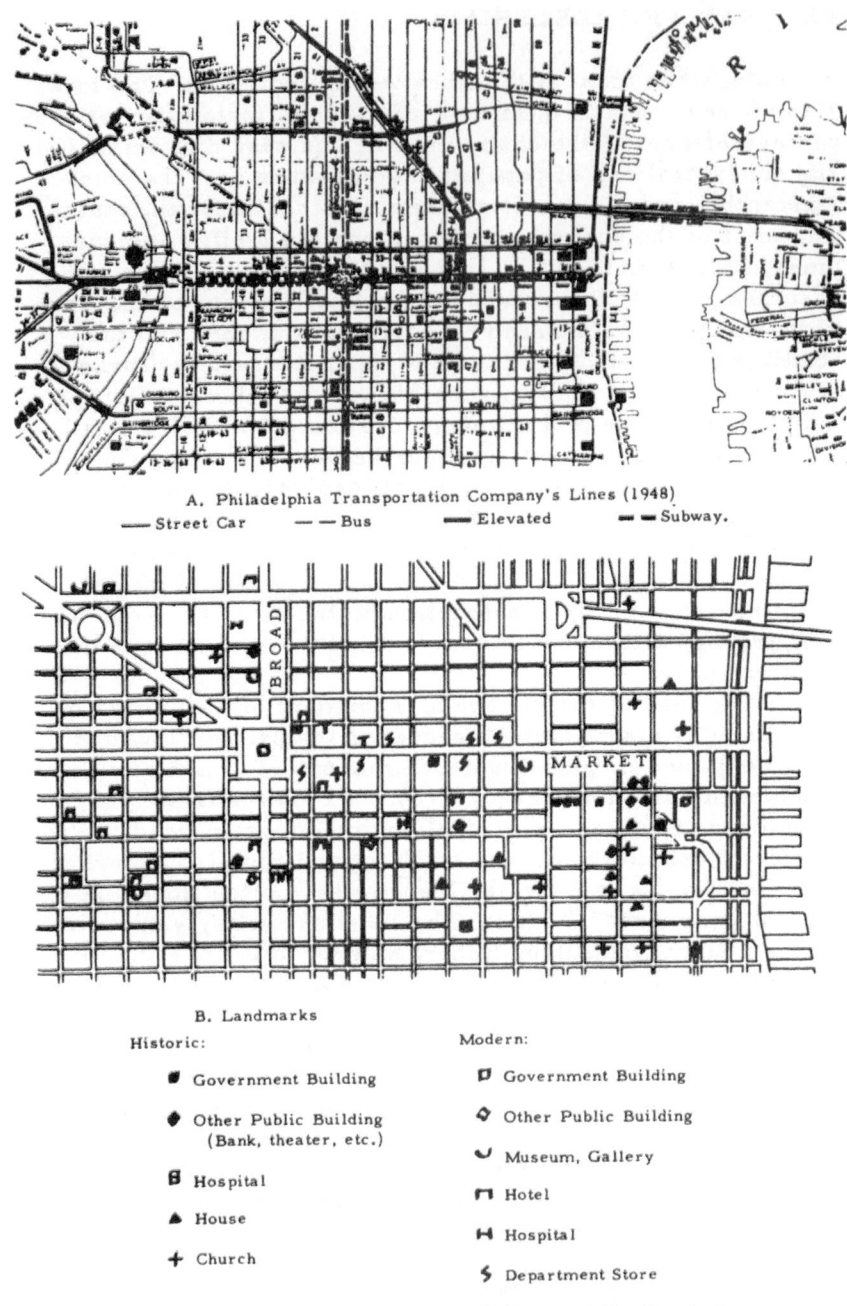

A. Philadelphia Transportation Company's Lines (1948)

——— Street Car    — — Bus    ▅▅ Elevated    ▬ ▬ Subway.

B. Landmarks

Historic:                Modern:

◗ Government Building      ▯ Government Building

◆ Other Public Building      ◊ Other Public Building
   (Bank, theater, etc.)

B Hospital                    ∪ Museum, Gallery

▲ House                         ⊓ Hotel

+ Church                      ⋈ Hospital

                             $ Department Store

                             T Transportation Terminal

Figure 7.    CENTRAL PHILADELPHIA TODAY

largest office building, and then to their present quarters on
Walnut, west of Broad, in 1913. Banks and insurance companies grew up around Independence Square in the mid-
nineteenth century, making the leap to the newer Broad
Street center in the early years of this century. Several of
them retain their older buildings in "Bank Row," Chestnut
between Fourth and Fifth, merely as a storehouse for
records. One, the Philadelphia Savings Fund Society, main-
tains its central office at Walnut and Seventh where it moved
in 1869, but it serves the bulk of its customers in its new
midtown branch at Twelfth and Market Streets.

This movement of the banks was by no means steady
and it is not typical of other kinds of business. Manufacturing, for example, was originally a central function but is
so now only for comparatively small firms. The Baldwin
Locomotive Works may be cited as typical of the "giants."
The first locomotive for the Philadelphia and Germantown
Railway was built in 1828 by Baldwin and Mason in their
shop on Sansom Street (between Chestnut and Walnut), west
of Second, a block or so from the Merchants' Exchange and
the Girard Bank; the works were for many years at Broad
and Spring Garden Streets, less than a mile north of City
Hall; when the plant outgrew that location, it was moved
outside the city to the heavy industrial area along the Delaware near Chester.

The space vacated by firms which have moved elsewhere in the central city or beyond it is usually taken up by
comparatively small, new firms which tend to locate in
"trade" groups. Nearly all of this succession of uses takes
the form of adding to an existing group. Sometimes the
group as a whole remains quite stable over a long period of
time, even though most of its constituent firms may be
short-lived. Sometimes the entire group will "follow the
leader" to a new location. The inevitable result of these continuing changes is that all locations are shared by several
different kinds of business, even in those areas which appear to be dominated by a single business group.

## CENTRAL PHILADELPHIA TODAY

The following sketch of present-day central Philadelphia is intended to serve as background for the next few

chapters of this study, in which methods will be developed
for analyzing central activities and their locational relationships. The area to be described is a broad one, extending more than two miles from the waterfront (Delaware
Avenue) to the railroad yards along the Schuylkill and more
than a mile from north to south. Within this general area
can be traced the development of several specialized areas
and the widespread succession of uses that have occurred.

The central area is well served by public transportation, and, in general, the more highly developed parts are
the better served. This is to be expected, since it is mass
transport that makes the central district possible by pump-
ing in its daytime population; it is the network of transportation lines, reinforcing and supplementing the original street
system, that ties the center to the rest of the city and to the
region and that laces together the various parts of the central area itself (Figure 7A). The location and importance of
the railroad terminals have been noted. Suburban bus lines
from New Jersey and the rapid transit lines (Market Street
Subway and Broad Street Subway) also converge at the center, the former feeding into a terminal on Thirteenth Street,
north of Market and adjacent to the Reading Terminal, the
latter having a number of stations at City Hall and nearby.
In addition to these major channels of mass transit there is
a rather complete bus and trolley network serving the entire
central area. The north-south lines of this network run through
on every street from Second to Sixteenth, while west of Sixteenth the lines turn into Arch or Market and run the full
length of these streets, doubling back from loops at Front
Street. All of the north-south streets are one-way except
Broad. The central area is strongly tied to West Philadelphia by the lines which cross the three bridges over the
Schuylkill at Market, Chestnut, and Locust Streets. The lines
entering at Market Street have the advantage of running underground, returning from a loop under City Hall, and the others
run on one-way streets so that east-west traffic is speedier
on Market and below than it is along Arch. The South Street
Bridge seems too remote to serve the main center, but South
Street itself does serve as a nucleus for commercial and industrial uses, although it is quite run-down and resembles
an outlying "string street" rather than a central location.

Beyond the central area the trolley and bus lines fan

out and make good use of the diagonal streets which were
once country roads connecting the original villages in Philadelphia County. And of course the entire surface transportation system is further extended by the subways, which
tap outlying areas by bus and trolley feeder lines to the
subway terminals. It would be extremely interesting to
trace the parallel development of mass transit facilities
and the spreading residential areas and outlying suburbs
that were successively brought within easy reach of the
center as the transit facilities expanded. Such a study would
add to our understanding of how parts of the central area
developed, but it would serve chiefly to illuminate the history of various outer areas, including the decay of many of
them as they became congested and as more attractive new
suburbs became accessible. Such studies must be set aside
as peripheral to our main objective: comprehension of the
present functioning of the city center.

The general effect of the existing pattern of mass transit facilities is that some parts of the central area are
readily accessible from several outlying areas, while others
are easily reached from only a few. A further effect is that
some parts of the central area are more strongly tied together than others. The migration of the banking center has
already been noted. The movement was entirely to the westward along Chestnut and Walnut Streets. (The countermove-
ment, whereby the vacated spaces have been occupied by
other activities, will be discussed later.) Fashionable residential areas have experienced a parallel movement extending all the way from the area southeast of Independence
Square to the vicinity of Rittenhouse Square. Retailing has
followed a somewhat similar development, with its presently most active areas strung out along Market and Chestnut Streets, east of Broad, with the dominant department
stores located along Market Street from Thirteenth to
Eighth. A host of high-style specialty shops has sprung up
west of Broad on Chestnut and Walnut and the side streets,
many of them located in remodeled one-family residences.
In this vicinity is also found the chief nucleus of medical
offices in central Philadelphia. A large area of fine residences survives west and south of Rittenhouse Square.
Frontage on the square itself has been largely taken over
by large, high-rent apartment houses.

All of these groupings seem to demonstrate the influence of easy movement along a band of east-west streets —a sort of transportation axis for the movement of people. A factor in this ease of movement is undoubtedly the consistent character of the entire area along this axis, at least during the course of its development, with "good" residential neighborhoods continually giving way to other uses. There is still a fairly continuous residential area south of Locust Street, all the way from the Schuylkill to Second Street, which appears to give the more central commercial uses room for further expansion.

Two broad areas dominated by wholesaling and manufacturing developed rather coherently, the former in a band about three blocks wide along the Delaware and the latter mainly between Market and Vine Streets, east of Broad. Movement of goods is a predominant factor in wholesaling, for which the rail and heavy trucking facilities along the waterfront provide the necessary transportation axis. In manufacturing (and especially in the light manufacturing which predominates in the center) the movement of both persons and goods is important; this area is very well served by mass transit and well enough served by the network of streets which provides access by truck.

None of the above groups of activities is confined to a single area, of course. Both manufacturing and wholesaling, for example, are found in many locations beyond those described, and especially along the railroads: the Reading across the north and the Baltimore & Ohio to the west bordering the Schuylkill (Figure 7A). The main axes (Market Street and Broad Street) have well-developed commercial or light industrial uses along their entire lengths, varying in character with the contiguous areas. Some housing, usually of poor quality, is found in small scattered pockets throughout the commercial and industrial areas, except in their most congested parts. In some places this "reserve" of decaying residential areas is fairly extensive—north of Franklin Square, for example, or in the triangle west of Broad and north of Parkway.

The patterns of activities sketched above were described in general terms as they might appear to any attentive observer who is not concerned with detail. Any observation is conditioned by its point of view, however, and

the description so far has been mainly in terms of movement—that ever present factor in the allocation of activities
among urban locations.[4] Other observations might begin
with the physical improvements and the succession of uses
to which they are put and the conditions in which they are
maintained; in other words, in terms of growth and obsolescence. From this point of view, the most obvious patterns
are seen in the buildings themselves. It is also possible to
build up a general picture out of the separate descriptions
of a number of activities. An observer interested in a particular kind of business would see the patterns of establishments which are directly engaged plus connected patterns of
related or linked establishments. A fairly complete picture
would require the piling up of a number of such partial descriptions, like a group of transparent overlays on the map,
any one of which can be picked out for close attention with
the rest serving as background.

Description of urban relationships has been set forth
here in two phases: comprehensive, taken from some generalized viewpoint, and detailed, based on the active relationships of a particular group of establishments. The comprehensive picture is necessary to give shape to the whole,
but it is likely to be oversimplified, since activities are
everywhere intermingled, with entirely unrelated establishments side by side (except in residential areas or in very
limited locations such as a single building). The set of
detailed pictures, on the other hand, can be confusing or
overly specialized. Both types of approach will be pursued,
therefore, since neither is adequate by itself.

The physical setting has not been stressed in this general picture of the downtown area and its various centers
of activity. The entire description might be repeated with
primary emphasis on the physical setting in each location,
that is, in terms of the buildings utilized, their type, age,
fitness for use, surroundings, and so on. The resulting picture would be rather more complex than that sketched above,
largely because of the succession of uses which occurs
inevitably, sooner or later, within each building. Description

[4] The relationships between land-based activities and the daily movement of
persons and goods among urban locations are thoroughly treated in Robert B.
Mitchell and Chester Rapkin, Urban Traffic (New York, 1954).

of the present scene, based on physical structures, might
well begin with the most recent construction or with its
counterpart—the deterioration of structures in well-located
"old" areas which are ripe for rebuilding.

The most active "new" center is the site of the old
Broad Street Station, demolition of which cleared the way
for expanding the major concentration of office buildings
around City Hall. Near Rittenhouse Square is another active
center of new construction, in a number of high-rent apartment houses. In older locations the picture is complicated
by the succession and consequent mixture of different activities, with the result that there is often scant consistency
between type of structure and present use. The availability
of residences for conversion has been mentioned frequently.
In areas of mixed activities where low rent is a prime consideration, there seems to be almost no limit to the variety
of uses to which old buildings are put, especially by small
establishments.

In the "Old City" east of Seventh Street, for example,
the buildings are predominantly old and narrow, many of
them structurally unsound, most of them nonfireproof. Yet
the location has excellent advantages and the old buildings
are very actively utilized by a great mixture of different
kinds of business establishments. This is the center for
shipping offices, tied together by linkages with each other,
with the Customs House at Second and Chestnut, and with
the warehouses along the waterfront. Here are found numerous specialized groups of wholesalers: those dealing in
foods are near lower Dock Street, wool just to the north,
apparel mostly north of Market and west of Third, and
metals to the north of Arch. All are intermingled with other
wholesale groups and manufacturers and retailers. Most of
these overlapping groups of activities are residual, dating
from the past development of the city when the entire commercial activity of Philadelphia was contained within this
area, its center drifting no more than half a mile in two
centuries, from the waterfront to Independence Square, until
the "leap" to the present nucleus near City Hall was ac-
complished in the decades around 1900. A strong secondary
center remains at Independence Square, anchored by large
insurance firms, but much space was left vacant all over
the "Old City" area, especially in its eastward parts, and

much of this space has been taken over by new firms, attracted by the low rent that goes with over age buildings in
run-down environments.

A generous portion of Philadelphia's rich heritage of
historic buildings is found in the "Old City": fine houses,
churches, and public buildings dating from the mid-eighteenth and early nineteenth centuries. This area is a living
museum of commercial building types from the timber-
framed warehouse of Ben Franklin's day to the latest plate-
glass and stainless steel shop front. Examples remain from
each successive wave of boomtime construction, each in
the "high style" of its own period: formal Georgian in hard-
burned red brick, the headers shiny black, with classic detail at entrances and windows: Greek fronts, their wide
openings framed in massive granite, with severely elegant
moldings, as a rule, but sometimes vigorously crude as if
demanding a bigger setting than the narrow, bustling street;
granite fronts increasing in vigor at the mid-century, taking
on Gothic detail; the "General Grant" with its bulgy orna-
ment, much like the ornate furniture of that day; cast iron
fronts, first as more economical substitutes for hewn
granite posts and lintels, then as entire facades in any desired style; the bank architecture of the 70's and 80's,
striving for individuality of expression in no style at all;
big loft buildings in the Roman-arch brick masonry of the
80's and 90's; and then the "correct eclectic" detail that
swept the country after the Chicago Fair in 1893.

The entire eastern end of downtown Philadelphia (the
"Old City") has been declared a Redevelopment Area by the
Planning Commission, with extensive changes projected,
first of which is the clearing of two malls opening out the
blocks north and east of Independence Square. These new
open spaces will greatly enhance the value of frontage on
the adjacent streets, but they will also become barriers to
the free shifting of land uses. The mixture of activities
crowding the old buildings east and north of the malls will
become relatively isolated from the more central area. It
will be interesting to observe which activities will tend to
remain and which will migrate in the near future.

"The Triangle" (between the Parkway and West Market
Street) has also been declared a Redevelopment Area, with
a mixture of activities in obsolescent buildings in its western

part somewhat similar to that in the eastern part of the
"Old City." What to do about the confusion of activities and
accommodations in such areas is a question for which there
is no easy answer. The Penn Center project opposite City
Hall comes on the crest of a wave of demand for centrally
located space, and it will dominate its own surroundings by
further intensifying the present high concentration of busi-
ness-office activities nearby. The surrounding areas of
mixed activities will remain much the same, no doubt, but
puzzling as before.

### OBJECTIVE MEASURES

The foregoing descriptions of central Philadelphia have
been brief and sketchy, but spinning them out at length would
only add descriptive detail; the objective basis would still
be lacking for comparing the advantages of different locations or comparing the importance of different activities.
Subjective impressions gained from direct observation are
valid enough, but they need to be bolstered (and they may be
contradicted) by quantitative measures. As an example of
the enrichment which even the crudest measurement can add
to description, the following illustration is derived from
figures on daytime population in central Philadelphia.

It was estimated that more than half a million persons
per day enter the area between Vine and South Streets.[5] Of
these, about two-thirds use the bus and trolley and subway
lines of the Philadelphia Transportation Company; nearly
one-fifth enter by auto, truck, or taxi, and the remainder
(about one-seventh of the total) by railway or interurban bus.
The majority (69 percent of the total) come into the intensely built-up central rectangle bounded by Arch, Seventh,
Locust, and Eighteenth Streets, an area approximately one-
fifth of the total. Of the number entering the more concentrated core area, the proportion using the Philadelphia
Transportation Company's lines is still about two-thirds of
the total; automobiles account for somewhat less, and railroads and interurban buses a somewhat higher proportion.

[5] Philadelphia City Planning Commission Chart, 1950. Sources: Preliminary
Estimate from Origin and Destination Survey, 1947; also information from
railroads and Philadelphia Transportation Company, 1949.

In the surrounding areas the bus and trolley lines are by far
the most important and automobiles are much more important than in the center, while subway and interurban buses
become almost negligible. The comparative figures are as
follows:

| | Total | Percent-age | Core | Percent-age | Re-mainder | Percent-age |
|---|---|---|---|---|---|---|
| P.T.C. bus or trolley | 194,800 | 37.5 | 88,500 | 24.8 | 106,300 | 61.6 |
| P.T.C. subway | 157,500 | 30.5 | 146,400 | 41.2 | 11,100 | 6.4 |
| Auto, truck, taxi | 101,100 | 19.6 | 48,000 | 13.5 | 53,100 | 30.8 |
| Railroad | 43,000 | 8.4 | 43,000 | 12.1 | .. | |
| Interurban bus | 31,700 | 6.0 | 29,700 | 8.4 | 2,000 | 1.2 |
| All | 528,100 | 100.0 | 355,600 | 100.0 | 172,500 | 100.0 |

Table I.    TRIPS TO CENTRAL BUSINESS DISTRICT

These figures suggest some general observations regarding the relative importance of different modes of travel in
different parts of the downtown area. In the congested center
the subway is most effective; in the surrounding areas, the
more dispersed bus and trolley lines play more important
roles and the automobile is also utilized more freely. Some
idea of the distribution of the daytime population is also
given by these figures; the concentration per unit area in
the congested core is more than eight times as great as in
the surrounding parts.
    The importance of the railroad stations to the central
city, frequently mentioned in foregoing pages, does not
seem to be borne out by the daytime population figures. It
may be that the importance of the stations is residual, deriving from an earlier time before other means of travel
were so fully developed as they are now, or it may be that
the explanation lies in the relatively more important roles
played by those who come by train compared with those who
come by other modes of travel. In any case, the center

around Broad and Market Streets is an area where banks
and business offices predominate and executives abound.
The point to be stressed here is not that the railroads are
less important than might have been anticipated on the
basis of general observation, but that possession of the
numbers themselves enables us to raise the question "why"
and direct our further observations toward achieving a
firmer explanation.

Another general measure of concentration in the central area can be stated in terms of the bulk of the buildings.
In a study made in 1949, an equivalent floor area ratio for
all nonresidential uses was computed for each block. The
space per block was nearly three times as great in the central rectangle (Arch, Seventh, Locust, Eighteenth) as in the
surrounding blocks between Vine and South Streets.[6]

The combination of these figures showing average concentrations (of daytime population and of floor space) in itself indicates that space is used very differently in different
parts of the downtown area. In the center the daytime population per unit of floor space is nearly three times as high
as it is in the surrounding parts. In other words, the center
is an area used intensely by people. The converse of this—
that the prevailing activities in outer areas are those requiring the handling of goods—is not directly apparent from
the figures. The fact is, however, that wholesaling and
manufacturing and shipping facilities, all activities with
much space devoted to goods handling, account for a considerable share of the outer area.

Differences between the central and outer parts of the
downtown area were depicted in the boldest strokes in the
foregoing example. More detailed description could be
achieved readily enough by further subdivision into smaller
units, revealing further contrasts and relationships as the
different characteristics of subareas are compared. Of
course, contrast is enhanced as smaller units of area are
examined. For example, the daytime population per unit
of floor space is undoubtedly much greater in the few blocks
around City Hall than the average for the entire central
area. And since many of the largest buildings are also

[6] Philadelphia City Planning Commission, Philadelphia Central District
Study (Philadelphia, 1950).

located here, pedestrian traffic is extremely heavy and retailing is also a flourishing activity. Further examination
of the activities and structures which occur in this area will
reveal as many characteristics as may be desired.

The differentiation of characteristics for each location
can become an enormous undertaking, but it is only by systematic measurement of activities in each subarea and relationships among them that the entire organism of the city
center can be described in terms that will bear analysis. To
locate the establishments constituting any given kind of business and to trace the linkages which make up its important
activity patterns would be relatively easy. But this connotes
a total background against which each particular description is set. The difficulty consists in building up a comprehensive description out of individual activities of all sorts
while giving each its due value.

It will be the task of the next few chapters to build up
methods for quantitative description and comparison of all
the land-based activities that occur over the entire central
area. The basic data for these methods will consist of
block-by-block listings of establishments, classified as to
kind of business.

## SUMMARY

The picture of changing land uses in central Philadelphia which has been presented in this chapter is anything
but complete. Only enough detail has been supplied to show
that the arguments of previous chapters can be tested in an
actual situation; only enough background has been given to
relate the center to its region, historic and at present.
These few examples suffice, however, to demonstrate that
patterns of physical accommodations (streets and open
spaces and buildings and public improvements) are by no
means fixed, but that they are built up in different locations
in response to the changing needs of urban activities as these
develop.

There is a natural lag in the response of physical improvements to the demand which brings them about, since
buildings take some time to plan and construct. New buildings, moreover, are usually provided in response to clear
demand from strong business firms well able to pay the

price, and also free to shift locations. It is very common for buildings (and their neighborhoods as well) to become obsolete long before their physical usefulness has been impaired. Run-down localities are those from which the more vital activities have moved; only after income falls off is the building itself allowed to deteriorate.

The interplay of activities and their accommodations in the various locations of central Philadelphia which has been briefly described here might be spelled out in much more detail, throwing light on many questions concerning urban resources and their utilization. Before proceeding with more description and analysis, however, methods will be devised for measuring and locating patterns of activities as they occur on the map. Only then, with quantitative descriptions which can be evaluated and compared objectively, will analysis of the interplay of activities and their accommodations be resumed.

# VII

## MEASURES OF LAND-USE PATTERNS

A VERY rich mine of basic information on the down-town activities of a large city was opened up by a study made recently in Philadelphia.[1] The Institute for Urban Land Use and Housing Studies of Columbia University collaborated in the design and execution of this study, which had for its immediate objective the answering of these planning questions:

1. What is the difference between the present inventory of land, building space, and street frontage in the central district of Philadelphia and the future requirements thereof in 1960 and 1980?

2. What kinds of patterns and relationships exist among establishments using space in the central city, and how can these patterns be expected to change by 1960 and again by 1980?

3. What may be anticipated as to the geographical distribution of types of establishments by subareas within the central city, taking into account both the present pattern of land use and the probable effect of public improvement and redevelopment projects?

In the course of answering these questions, an inspection census was conducted in the spring of 1949, in which each establishment was listed by location and by kind of business. Data from the commercial and industrial survey made in 1934-35 by the Works Progress Administration were also tabulated as a basis for charting changes in land-use patterns. These tabulations formed the groundwork of that study, which is largely a presentation of findings that bear on the three questions.

The same data will be used in the present study as a basis for developing measures of locational characteristics of central district establishments of different kinds. Such characteristics as degree of concentration and location and

---

[1] Philadelphia City Planning Commission, Philadelphia Central District Study (Philadelphia, 1950)

distribution over the map of a given kind of business or
functional activity will be developed in this chapter. Later
chapters will treat of such relationships as the proportions
of different kinds of business at each location or the extent
to which they are found together in the same map units and,
perhaps most important, the changes occurring in these
measures at different times.

Patterns of locational arrangement of establishments
will be studied for the present without much regard to the
underlying forces which have resulted in these patterns.
Causes will be touched on only tentatively as they may il-
lumine relationships or as they may suggest applicability
for our measures. For example, the existence of two different kinds of business in close proximity may be in itself
a strong indication or reflection of underlying causes. But
whether proximity is a result of linkages or has come about
by chance, or whether the activities themselves are actually
in conflict, all these possible situations can be more fruit-
fully studied with the aid of definite measures by which numerical comparisons can be made.

Comparative measures of the patterns of locational arrangement (concentration, dispersion, proximity, and the
like) can, by their very differences, point the way for ex-
ploring those relationships between activities in which location is a factor. They can lead to understanding the processes which will lead to further changes.

## THE PHILADELPHIA
## CENTRAL BUSINESS DISTRICT

The unit of location in the Philadelphia Study[2] was the
"standard block" of the Philadelphia City Planning Commission ("C.P.C. Block") which has been used for years by the
city as a convenient map unit for recording data. These
blocks all have streets as boundaries, but they usually have
intermediate streets or alleys within them. The central
district was delimited to include whole tiers of blocks between the Delaware and Schuylkill Rivers, about two miles
apart. 'The north and south boundaries were determined by
taking a sample of establishments from the listings in the
classified telephone directory, noting their block locations
and the total numbers in each tier of blocks. The lines were

[2] Ibid.

drawn where these numbers fall off sharply (see Figure 8A).
So defined, the central district encompasses a somewhat
broader area than the popular "downtown" conception, which
is generally limited to the most concentrated area of commerical structures. The broader definition of the central
district gives scope for the more concentrated central activities and for others not so concentrated and not quite so
centrally located. It includes the entire "Old City" area of
Colonial times and ample space for further expansion of
the present concentrated core of commercial buildings.
Within it may be traced the shifting of central activities
from the first settlement near the Delaware to the center
at Independence Square and to the new Penn Center development west of City Hall.

Land-use patterns can be analyzed most effectively on
the basis of equal areas—on a rectangular grid for example.
The C.P.C. Blocks which form the groundwork of this study
are, with a few exceptions, rectangular, but they vary considerably in area. Much of the difficulty is removed, however, by consolidating a few tiers of the smaller blocks.
This was done in the present sudy by combining four narrow tiers of blocks into two tiers of average width. The
north and south boundaries were also modified slightly to
conform with census tract boundaries. The resulting diagrammatic map (Figure 8B) shows a total of 284 blocks outside of parks, as against 377 in the original study. The
blocks are all shown as equal squares, which is not strictly
true, but the discrepancies have at least been relegated to
the outlying blocks, where they will have little bearing on
land-use patterns. All data in the present study are related
to this key map. Some descriptive detail is thus lost, but
this is more than offset by the gain in simplicity and ease
of comprehension—especially when comparisons are to be
made between different activities and their combinations.
In Figure 8C the position of the central district is shown,
relative to the entire city and a few outlying centers.

## MAP DISTRIBUTIONS

The relative importance of different kinds of business
within each block is readily seen in a tabulation, by blocks,
of establishments and floor space. For showing relation-

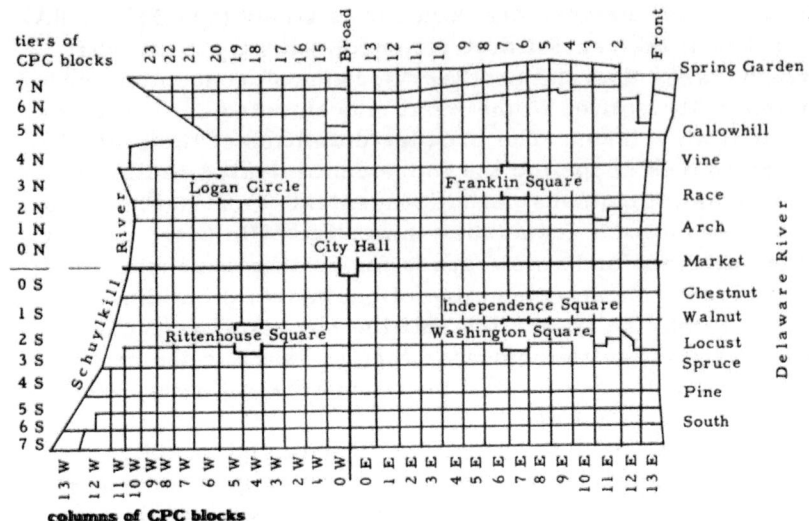

A. Map of the Philadelphia Central Business District showing
"Standard Blocks" of the City Planning Commission (CPC)
(from <u>Philadelphia Central District Study</u>, 1951)

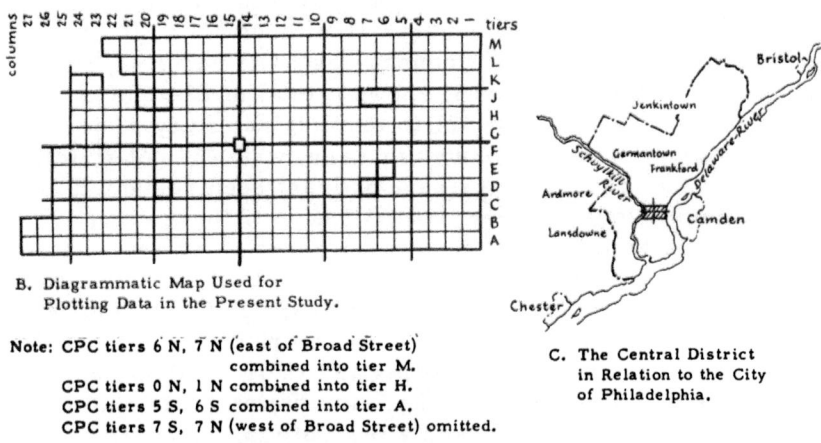

B. Diagrammatic Map Used for
   Plotting Data in the Present Study.

Note: CPC tiers 6 N, 7 N (east of Broad Street)
                              combined into tier M.
      CPC tiers 0 N, 1 N combined into tier H.
      CPC tiers 5 S, 6 S combined into tier A.
      CPC tiers 7 S, 7 N (west of Broad Street) omitted.

C. The Central District
   in Relation to the City
   of Philadelphia.

Figure 8.   THE PHILADELPHIA CENTRAL BUSI-
            NESS DISTRICT

ships between blocks, however, or relationships between the different locational patterns taken by different kinds of business, it is necessary to make use of maps, since maps can show at once not only "how much" but "where."

In Figure 9 a portion of the tabulation of establishments is spread out over the diagrammatic map (Figure 8B) to show the total number of establishments in each block. The full tabulation of establishments in this form would require a separate map for each kind of business. The tabulation of floor space would require another complete set. Indeed, any characteristic or measure which can be shown block by block may be plotted on such a map.

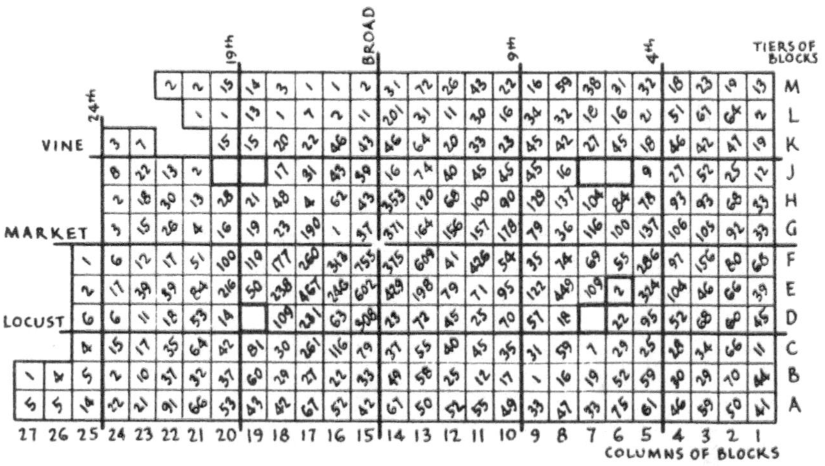

Figure 9. MAP DISTRIBUTION OF ESTABLISH-
MENTS, NUMBER IN EACH BLOCK, ALL
KINDS OF BUSINESS, 1949

Note: There are 285 occupied blocks, including Independence Square (E6) with its public buildings.

This map (Figure 9) conveys several definite impressions regarding location and distribution of establishments. Blocks with the greatest number of establishments, for example, are mostly concentrated near the intersection of Broad and Market Streets, while a minor concentration is seen near Independence Square (Block E6). A fairly high level (roughly 100 per block) is maintained across the middle of the map from Rittenhouse Square (Block D19)

almost to the Delaware River, and the locations of lower
density levels can be sensed by poring over the numbers.
A full set of maps showing distributions of establishments
and floor space will be found in Appendix A.

But study of Figure 9 by itself can reveal only impressions of density at best—impressions much like those which
result from a general familiarity with the concentrating of
business activities in the central district. What is required
is a standard basis for deriving expressions of location,
concentration, etc., for a given kind of business so that
characteristics of business groups can be adequately described and systematic comparisons can be made between
them. Of course mere numbers of establishments cannot
suffice for explaining urban activities and relationships, but
the establishment count does provide a ready beginning.
When expressions for measuring mapped distributions are
developed on the basis of the data shown in Figure 9, then
other attributes may be brought into the picture, such as
gross sales, number of persons employed or served, and
volume of goods handled. Any of these might be appropriate
for a location study of a particular business group for which
these data are available, but for the present aggregative
study we shall be content with estimates of numbers of establishments and amounts of floor space alone.

## Levels of Density

Numbers of establishments per block in Figure 9 range
from 1 to 755. A beginning toward organized grouping will be
made by picking out the most concentrated blocks and successive "layers" of lesser concentration in regularly descending
order: over 400 per block, 400 to 201, 200 to 101.... The number
of blocks in each group in given in Table IIA; the accumulated
total number of blocks at each level is given in Table IIB and
Figure 10A shows this grouping of blocks plotted on the map.

This table (also Figure 10A) reduces the mass of numbers in Figure 9 to manageable proportions by telling how
many blocks occur in various groups. But the divisions are
arbitrary and would not apply to other distributions unless
the range of numbers happened to be much the same as this
one. For systematic description and comparison of various
groupings of establishments and of various other attributes

| A. Distribution of Establishments by Blocks | | B. Cumulative Distribution of Establishments by Blocks | |
| --- | --- | --- | --- |
| Number per Block | Number of Blocks | Number per Block | Number of Blocks |
| Over 400 | 7 | More than 400 | 7 |
| 400 to 201 | 14 | More than 200 | 21 |
| 200 to 101 | 25 | More than 100 | 46 |
| 100 to 51 | 63 | More than 50 | 109 |
| 50 to 26 | 84 | More than 25 | 193 |
| 25 and under | 92 | 1 and over | 285 |

Table II.    DISTRIBUTION OF ESTABLISHMENTS,
ALL KINDS OF BUSINESS, 1949 BY
NUMBERS PER BLOCK

of location it will be necessary to have simple expressions, methodically derived. What rational basis for groupings of blocks will answer these purposes effectively?

### Distribution Diagrams

The most fruitful approach is first to consider the full distribution of establishments among all of the blocks in the central district. In Figure 11 the numbers of Figure 9 are plotted on a percentage basis, starting with the block having the greatest number and adding less dense blocks in turn. Each point on this curve represents a single block, except that where two or more blocks have the same number of establishments the intermediate points are omitted. Thus the vertical spacing of points is at equal intervals while the horizontal spacing decreases continually—in this case from 755 per block (3.5 percent) to 1 per block (0.005 percent). The full calculation for this distribution curve is described in Appendix C. Of course no such degree of detail as this will be needed in the simplified expressions which are sought. The complete distribution curve is used here to show the basis for the abbreviated expressions.

The fullness of the curve is an indication of the degree of concentration, for if all blocks had the same number of establishments the curve would become a straight line along

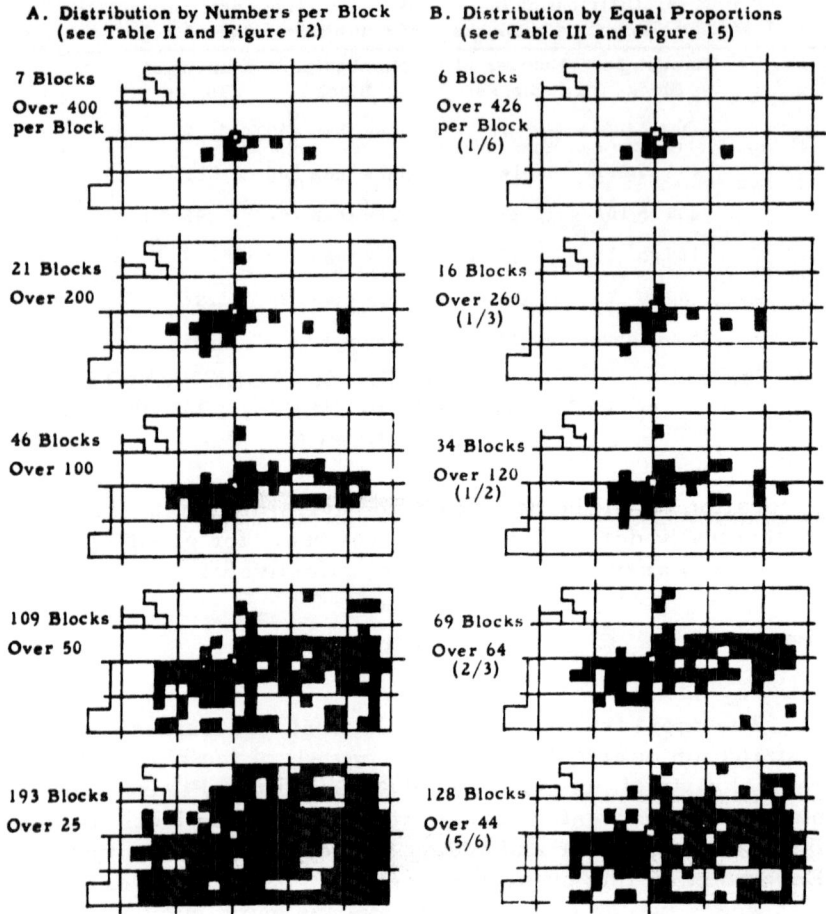

**A. Distribution by Numbers per Block**
(see Table II and Figure 12)

**B. Distribution by Equal Proportions**
(see Table III and Figure 15)

7 Blocks
Over 400
per Block

6 Blocks
Over 426
per Block
(1/6)

21 Blocks
Over 200

16 Blocks
Over 260
(1/3)

46 Blocks
Over 100

34 Blocks
Over 120
(1/2)

109 Blocks
Over 50

69 Blocks
Over 64
(2/3)

193 Blocks
Over 25

128 Blocks
Over 44
(5/6)

Figure 10.    MAP DISTRIBUTIONS AT SUCCESSIVE
              DENSITIES, ALL KINDS OF BUSINESS,
              1949

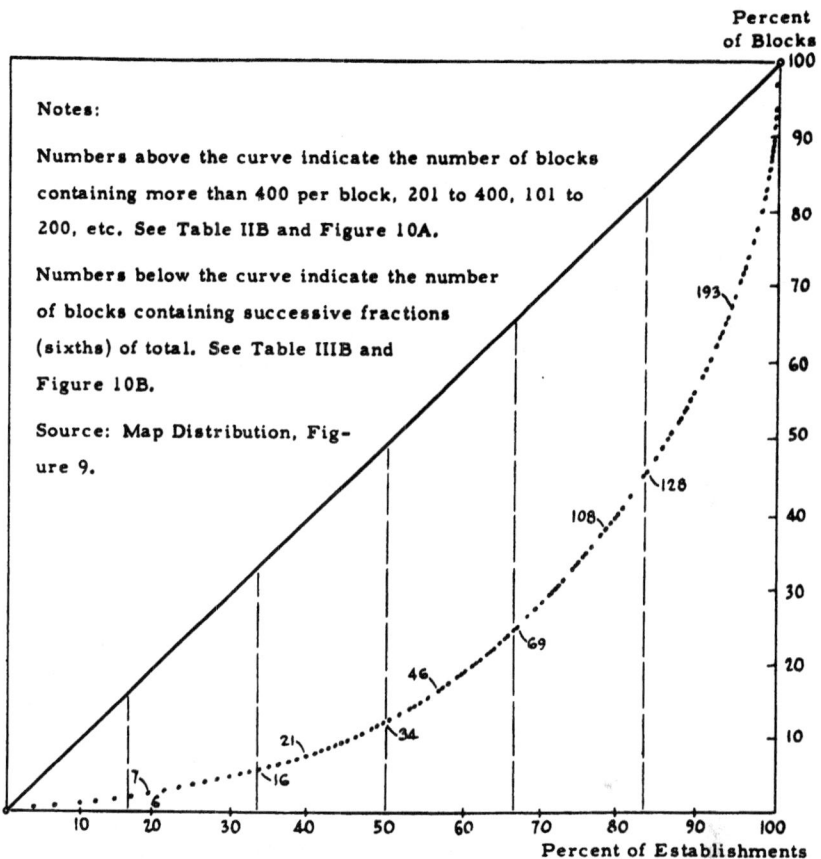

Figure 11.    DISTRIBUTION CURVE: CUMULATIVE
              PERCENTAGES OF ESTABLISHMENTS
              AND OF BLOCKS, 1949

the diagonal from 0:0 to 100:100. Along this line 10 percent
of blocks would contain 10 percent of establishments, 10 percent of blocks would contain 20 percent of establishments,
and so on. Unequal distribution appears as a curve below the
diagonal, with the area between diagonal and curve indicating the degree of concentration.
    The shape of the curve, i.e., successive changes in
slope, indicates the nature of the distribution in its various
parts. Thus for a very heavy concentration in a few blocks

the lower end of the curve would be nearly horizontal; for
a large group of nearly equal blocks the curve would be near
to a straight line; if there were vacant blocks they would be
indicated by a vertical line at the right. In the present case
the upper end of the curve is very nearly vertical, since the
last few blocks contain very few establishments. This curve
would not be appreciably different, in fact, if there were 28
or 29 entirely vacant blocks, that is, if the curve terminated
at 90 percent of total blocks. This particular curve is re-
markably smooth and regular, since it represents the distribution of all kinds of business over a wide area. Curves
representing the separate components (Manufacturing,
Retailing, and the rest) which together make up the full
distribution will show a number of vacant blocks and more
concentration, as a rule, than this aggregate curve.

　　The degree of concentration for any given area, as indicated by the fullness of its distribution curve, will be con-
tingent upon the extent of the area itself. Thus, if a distribution curve were drawn for only the more concentrated central portion of Figure 9, it would be flatter (nearer to the
diagonal) than the curve in Figure 11, indicating a lesser
degree of contrast within the smaller area. Conversely, if a
larger area had been taken in, with more low-density blocks,
the distribution curve would be somewhat fuller. In other
words, the degree of concentration is a measure of con-
trasting density within an area, not an absolute measure.
This measure provides the means for comparing component
groups of establishments within an area, but it does not

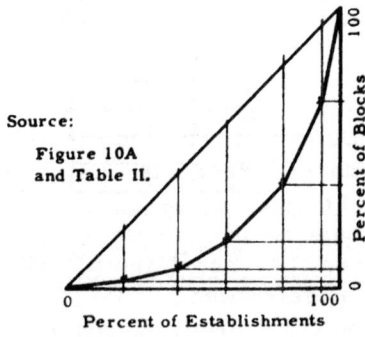

Figure 12.    SIMPLIFIED DISTRIBUTION CURVE,
              BASED ON NUMBERS PER BLOCK

allow for comparisons between different areas unless these
are somehow "standardized" as to size.

For comparative study of mapped distributions, the full
curve is not required; a few points will reveal its shape
well enough. Thus the divisions of Table IIB and Figure
10A are indicated on Figure 11 at the points representing
the 7th, 21st, 46th, 109th, and 193d blocks and repeated on
the simplified curve of Figure 12.

But these divisions are still arbitrary. A systematic
arrangement is needed; for example, the division of total
establishments into equal groups. This is simple to manip-
ulate and gives comparable results for different groupings
regardless of the numbers involved. The only question is,
how many divisions should be made?

### Concentration Groups

The simplest division of the distribution curve is into
two groups. In the present case (reading from the curve of
Figure 11), half of the establishments are contained in 12
percent of the blocks. This one measure (the ordinate of the
curve at its mid-point) gives a good basis for comparing different concentrations, while the corresponding group of
blocks picked out on the map states in the simplest terms
where the more concentrated blocks are located. In this
study such a group of blocks is called a median concentration group (Figure 13).

For many purposes the most useful division is into
three groups. This is the simplest basis on which the
"shape" of the distribution curve can be measured (by ordinates of two points) and groups of blocks at successive
levels of density can be located on the map. In this study
such groups of blocks are called one-third concentration
group and two-thirds concentration group (Figure 14).

These maps, Figures 13 and 14, show where the concentrations are located, and they also measure, by percentage, the degree of concentration—thus expressing both
where and how much.

These groupings by halves and by thirds are extended
in Table III to six equal divisions of establishments and are
set out again in the simplified curve of Figure 15. Maps
corresponding to all these divisions are given in Figure

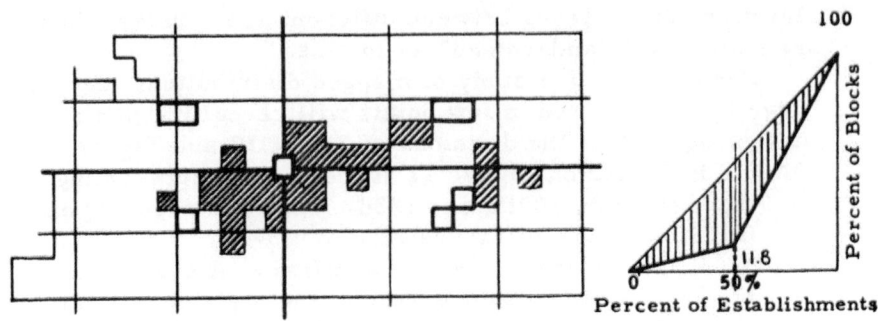

34 Blocks, 11.8% of Total.

Figure 13.     MEDIAN CONCENTRATION GROUP
                (CONTAINING HALF OF TOTAL ES-
                TABLISHMENTS) FOR ALL KINDS OF
                BUSINESS, 1949

10B on page 92, parallel with the original arbitrary grouping of Table II and Figure 10A.

This grouping by sixths (in Table III and Figures 10B
and 15) is as simple as the first arbitrary groupings (in
Table II and Figures 10 and 12). In fact it amounts to little
more than a respacing of the original divisions on an equal
basis so that each group of blocks contains an equal number
of establishments, as may be observed by comparing Figures 12 and 15. Moreover, a regular grouping, whether by
sixths or by thirds or by halves, has considerable advantages: standard application to various kinds of map distributions, easily derived measures of concentration, relative

| A. Distribution of Establishments by Blocks | | B. Cumulative Distribution of Establishments by Blocks | |
|---|---|---|---|
| Groups of Blocks Containing | Number of Blocks | Groups of Blocks Containing | Number of Blocks |
| Up to 1/6 | 6 | 1/6 | 6 |
| 1/6 to 1/3 | 10 | 1/3 | 16 |
| 1/3 to 1/2 | 18 | 1/2 | 34 |
| 1/2 to 2/3 | 35 | 2/3 | 69 |
| 2/3 to 5/6 | 59 | 5/6 | 128 |
| 5/6 to Total | 157 | Total | 285 |

Table III.     DISTRIBUTION OF ESTABLISHMENTS,
                ALL KINDS OF BUSINESS, 1949 BY SIX
                EQUAL DIVISIONS

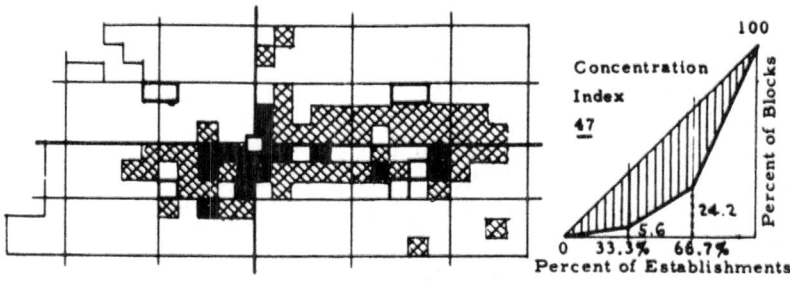

1/3: 16 Blocks, 5.6% of Total
2/3: 69 Blocks, 24.2% of Total

Figure 14.   ONE-THIRD AND TWO-THIRDS CON-
CENTRATION GROUPS (CONTAINING
ONE-THIRD AND TWO-THIRDS OF
TOTAL ESTABLISHMENTS) FOR ALL
KINDS OF BUSINESS, 1949

ease of statistical treatment, and so on. And of course the
comparative measures are more readily derived and applied when the grouping is by thirds or by halves.

One or the other of these simplified groupings, whichever best suits the case in hand—by thirds as in Figure 14
or by halves as in Figure 13—will be used throughout this
study for describing and comparing the distribution patterns of different kinds of business and relating them to

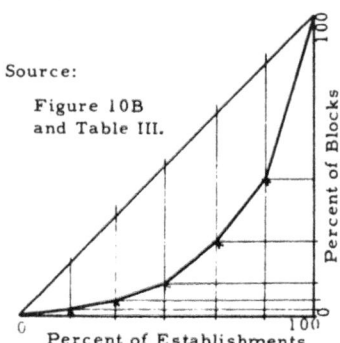

Figure 15.   SIMPLIFIED DISTRIBUTION CURVE,
BASED ON EQUAL DIVISION OF ES-
TABLISHMENTS

various characteristics of the different locations in the central business district. In somes cases it will be necessary to consider the most concentrated or the least concentrated locations, and for these the groups at the one-sixth level or the five-sixths level will be used.

In any case, it is to be noted that the simplified expressions derived from equal groupings represent two distinct phases of the reality behind the distribution of establishments: the spread of establishments among locations, as shown on the map, and the characteristics of the distribution without regard for location, as shown in the curves.

### Index of Concentration

It has been seen, in Figures 13 and 14, that the number of blocks in each concentration group, expressed as a percentage of total blocks, is an ordinate of the distribution curve. In this study the index of concentration is computed from the ordinates for the third points (as in Figure 14) as follows:

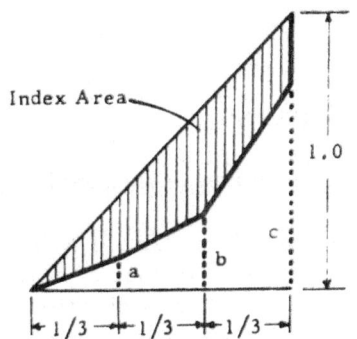

Figure 16.    INDEX CURVE

In the simplified curve of Figure 16, its degree of concentration is indicated by the shaded area, and this may be expressed as a fraction of the area of the entire triangle, which is half of a unit square or .5.

The area below the curve, made up of a triangle and two trapezoids, all having a base of 1/3, is:

$$1/3 \times a/2 + 1/3 \times \frac{a + b}{2} + 1/3 \times \frac{b + c}{2} = a/3 + b/3 + c/6.$$

The index area, between diagonal and curve, is:

$$.5 - (a/3 + b/3 + c/6).$$

The index of concentration is the "index area" divided by .5, or:

$$1 - 2 (a/3 + b/3 + c/6).$$

For the distribution of establishments on which this discussion is based (Figures 9 through 15) there are no vacant blocks, so that ordinate "c" in Figure 14 is 100 and the index of concentration, expressed as a percentage, is:

$$100 - 2 (5.6/3 + 24.2/3 + 16.7) \text{ or } 46.8$$

This index, which represents the area of the full distribution curve of Figure 11, is of course only a crude measure of that area. However it is readily set up in connection with concentration groups by thirds, which will be among our chief tools for analysis and therefore always at hand. For the purpose of comparing the relative concentration of different distributions this index is entirely adequate, as indeed the index derived from a single measure (as in Figure 13) would be.[3]

Comparison of Two Groups<br/>Establishments and Floor Space

Up to now the distribution based on number of establishments has been studied. How does the distribution based on floor space compare?

Map distributions, by sixths, of establishments and floor space are given in parallel columns in Figure 17 together with the simplified distribution curves in which each successive point represents the number of blocks in the corresponding map. The maps and the curve in the establishments column are repeated from Figures 10B and 15 for easier comparison with the distribution in the floor-space column. The latter distribution was computed directly from the mapped data (similar to Figure 9) by selecting in turn

---

[3] When measuring the curve at a single point, the middle ordinate, "m," is derived from the median concentration group and the index area (diagram at right) becomes a triangle. The area of this triangle is $1/2$ (.5 - m). Dividing by the half square gives .5 - m for the index of concentration. In the present case, (see Figure 13), the index of concentration is .5 - .118 or .38

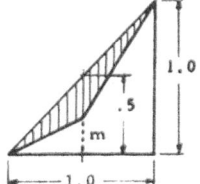

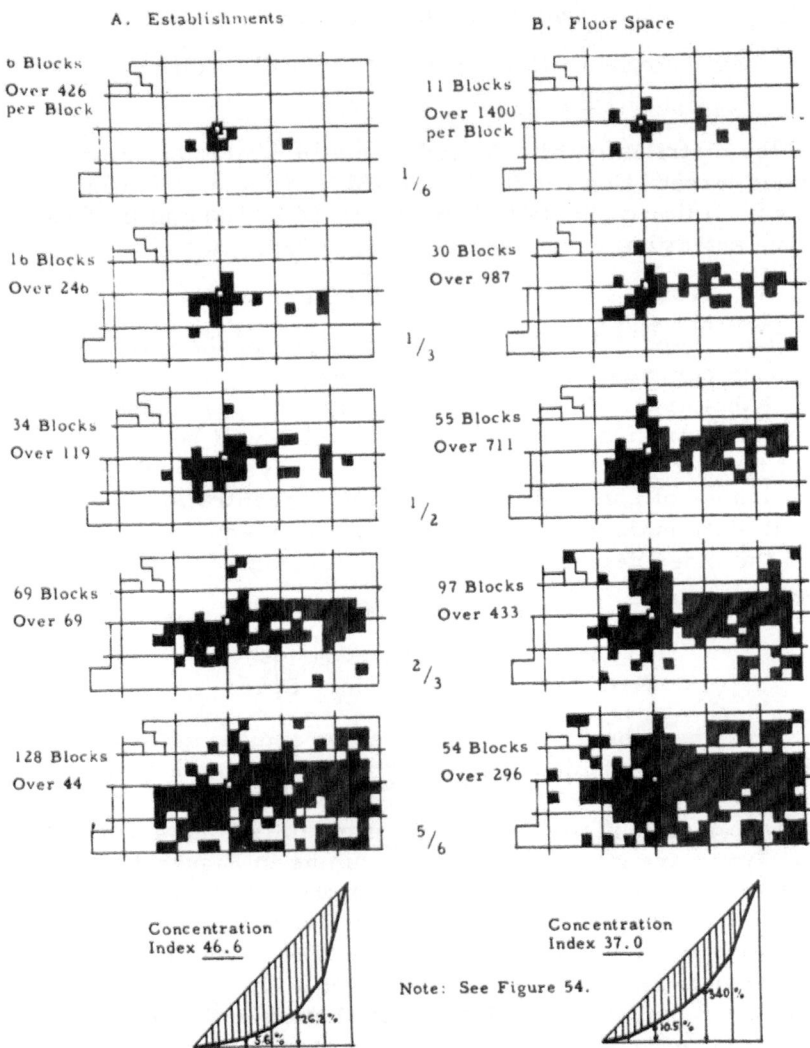

Figure 17.    MAP DISTRIBUTION BY SIXTHS, ALL
              KINDS OF BUSINESS, 1949

the blocks having the greatest floor space up to each designated level, that is, one-sixth, one-third, one-half, etc., of
total floor space for all blocks.

It is at once apparent from Figure 17 that the distribution based on establishment count is considerably more concentrated, in other words, that more blocks are required
at each level of concentration to make up the requisite fraction of total floor space than are required for the corresponding fraction of the total number of establishments. These
differences in concentration are expressed by their indexes,
shown on the distribution curves at the bottom of Figure 17,
that is, 46.6 for establishments and 37.0 for floor space.

It also becomes apparent, when the groups at each level
are matched, that their location patterns are quite different.
Much of the difference is caused by the lower concentration
on the "floor space" side but in no case are all of the "establishment" blocks included within the "floor space" group.
Before analyzing these differences it will be necessary to
develop some techniques for measuring and comparing the
mapped distributions.

## MEASURES OF LOCATION

The diagrammatic maps in this chapter can be used to
form an impression of where the major concentrations and
successive levels of concentration are to be found. And, as
always with data of any intricacy, the firmer impressions
are gained from simplified statements. Thus the detailed
numbers for each block in the central district (see map,
Figure 9) can reveal only a general impression at best,
while the most simplified version (the median concentration
group depicted in Figure 13) is most definite. The sequence
of maps at successive densities by sixths (Figure 17) contains more detail than will be needed, as a rule. A single
map showing two levels of concentration (one-third and two-
thirds concentration groups, Figure 14) is sufficiently detailed for all except the most refined analysis.

The position and extent of any one of these groups of
blocks can be estimated fairly well by eye. However, for
purposes of analysis it is important to standardize, to use
systematically derived measures, wherever possible,
rather than to depend on subjective judgments. Several

definite measures will be developed in the next few paragraphs.

## Center of Gravity

Each block in an assemblage can be located readily
by measuring from coordinate base lines. The "standard
blocks" of the Philadelphia City Planning Commission, for
example, are all numbered in relation to Broad and Market
Streets. (See Figure 8A on page 88.) A more convenient
origin for measurement, however, is a point one-half block
south and one-half block east of the lower right corner of the
map. The center of the first column of blocks as numbered
for the present study (see Figure 8B) is thus one block to
the left of the origin, the second column is two blocks distant, and so on. The distances of the tiers of blocks also
agree with their numbers, starting with the lowest. This is
illustrated in Figure 18, which pictures the median concentration group for floor space, the central map of Figure 17B.

The sum of any group of blocks may be represented by
an equivalent mass located at the center of gravity for the
group. On the assumption that all blocks in the group are
of equal weight, the distance to their aggregate center is
found by dividing the number of blocks into the sum of their
distances from the origin.[4]

Thus the shaded square in Figure 18, with an area of
5.5 square blocks, represents the entire group of 55 blocks;
and its center is at the center of gravity for the entire group.
But partial groups can also be represented separately. The
entire group of Figure 18, for example, is made up of two
virtually separate subgroups, and the center of gravity for
the entire group falls in the relatively empty space between
them. A more realistic picture of this situation might be
given by designating the subgroups separately. These are

---

[4] A more refined method of determining the center of gravity of this group
would be to assign suitable weights to the separate blocks, those occurring
in the first sixth being weighted most heavily, and so on. Thus in Figure 18,
the total weights for three groups of blocks might be taken as equal: the 11
blocks comprising the first sixth (Figure 17B), the 19 additional blocks making up the first third, and the 25 additional blocks making up the entire median concentration group. The position of the center of gravity, on this
"weighted" basis is somewhat west and south of the "unweighted" result,
coordinates 10.8 and 6.0.

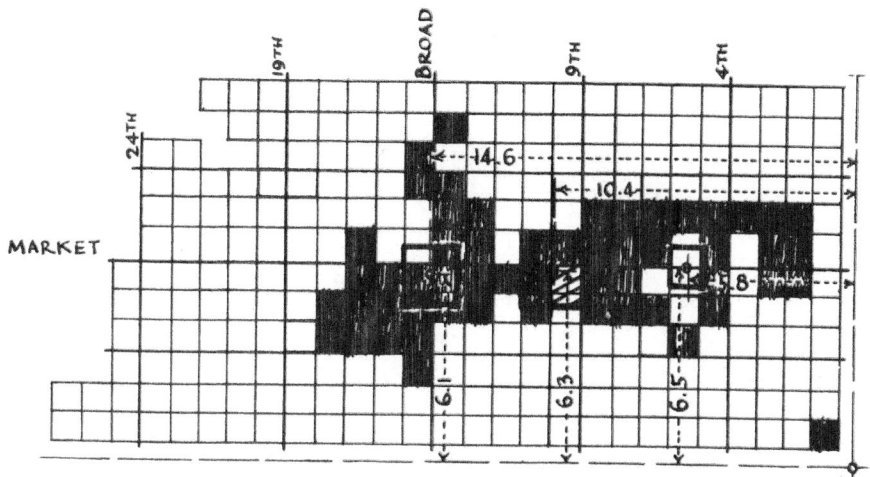

Figure 18.    CENTER OF GRAVITY, MEDIAN CON-
              CENTRATION GROUP FOR FLOOR
              SPACE, ALL KINDS OF BUSINESS, 1949

represented in Figure 18 by the open squares with areas
proportional to the 29 blocks and 26 blocks in the subgroups,
divided at Tenth Street.

### Density Profiles

In the course of computing the center of gravity for a
group of blocks, the number of blocks in each column is
counted; likewise the number in each tier. These numbers
along the baselines of the map, when represented graphically,
become profiles showing the density of the entire group as
measured along each axis. This is illustrated in Figure 19.
It is as though all the blocks shown in the diagram had slid
down, piling up on the baseline to form a west-east profile
and again (starting with their original position on the map)
that they had been slid to the right like the beads on an abacus
to show a profile along a north-south line.

### Radius of Dispersion

One comparative measure of map distributions remains
—a measure of the average extent of the pattern of blocks
constituting a concentration group. This may be defined as

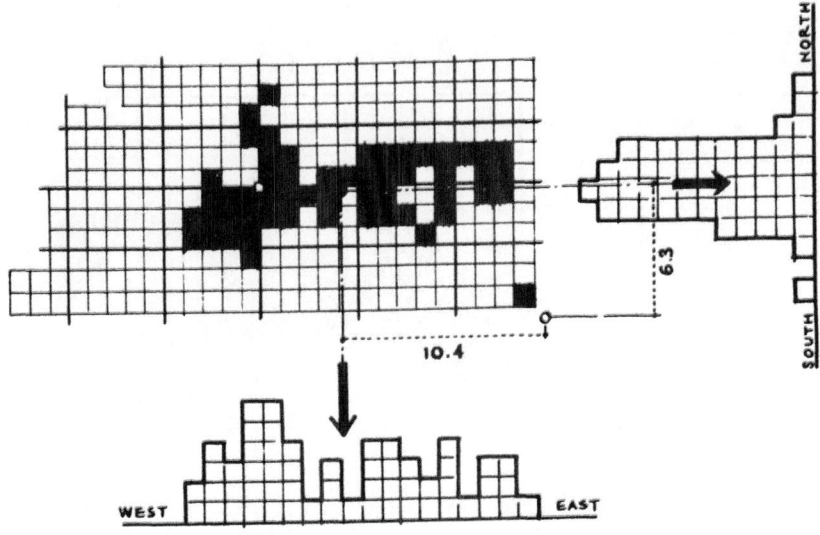

Figure 19.   DENSITY PROFILES, MEDIAN CON-
CENTRATION GROUP FOR FLOOR
SPACE, ALL KINDS OF BUSINESS, 1949

the average distance of all blocks in the group from the
center of gravity for the entire group. It is a measure of the
scatter or spread of a group of blocks at a given level of
concentration taken around their center of gravity.

The density profile of Figure 19 provides the data for
this measure, the calculation for which begins with the location of the center of gravity itself. The average distance is
obtained by computing separate components from each profile. The horizontal (west-east) conponent $\underline{H}$ is the sum of
the products of blocks in each column times their horizontal
distances from the center of gravity divided by the total number of blocks. The vertical (south-north) component $\underline{V}$ is
similar, taking the number of blocks in each tier times its
vertical distance from the center of gravity, and again dividing the sum by the total number of blocks.[5] The radius
of dispersion is the diagonal of a rectangle having these

---

[5] These same components could be determined with a fair degree of accuracy
by looking at each half of each density profile (Figure 19) and making a careful estimate by eye of each partial center of gravity. Such a visual determina-
tion will be sufficiently accurate for most purposes. Where greater refinement is desired, the relative weights of blocks can be taken into account as
mentioned in footnote 4, page 102.

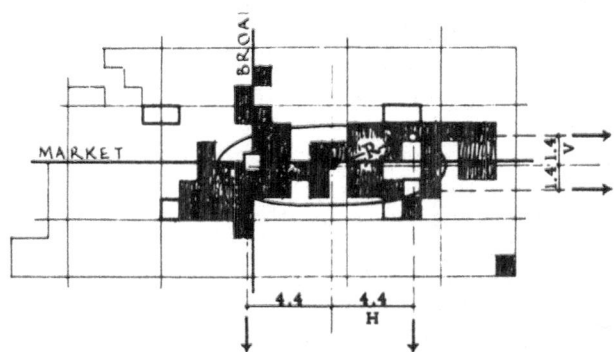

Figure 20.    RADIUS OF DISPERSION, MEDIAN CON-
              CENTRATION GROUP FOR FLOOR
              SPACE, ALL KINDS OF BUSINESS, 1949

horizontal and vertical components as sides. This radius
provides a simple measure for making comparisons among
various groups. Moreover, when the components are taken
into account, a simple measure of the shape is also provided
by the ratio of V to H. An ellipse is used here to represent
this shape, as it is more clearly distinguished against the
background of horizontal and vertical lines. Both radius and
ellipse are illustrated in Figure 20 for the same group of
blocks used in the two previous figures.

The ellipse might be related to the horizontal and verti-

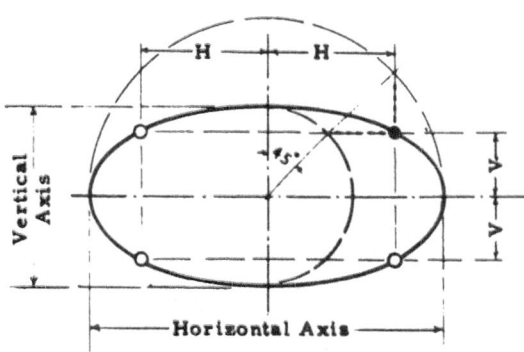

Figure 21.    CONSTRUCTION OF CIRCUMSCRIBED
              ELLIPSE

cal components of the radius of dispersion by inscribing it within the rectangle of dimensions 2H and 2V, or it might be circumscribed. The circumscribed figure was chosen as neater, in that the ellipse passes through the point which defines the radius of dispersion. Construction of circumscribed ellipse is illustrated in Figure 21.

Representation of a scattered group of blocks by a single shape (rectangle or ellipse) is a rather extreme abstraction in which all individual details wash out and only a size and an idealized shape remain. In Figure 20, for example, the virtual separation into two groups and the different shapes of these are disregarded. If the two groups were treated separately, as suggested above at Figure 18, the left-hand group would be seen as a squat ellipse with its major axis vertical, and the right-hand group would appear as a spread-out ellipse along Market Street.[6]

## ALTERNATIVE MODES OF MEASUREMENT

The techniques developed in this chapter for dealing with survey data have been predicated on a grid of equal-sized blocks. The resulting diagrams are quite detailed and will enable comparisons to be made between groups of blocks representing different kinds of activities, such, for example, as different kind-of-business groups, discussed in Chapter III, or the two ways of recording activities which are illustrated by Figure 17, that is, number of establishments and amount of floor space.

For some purposes, however, the block is too large a unit for analyzing location; for other purposes the block data are overly detailed and a bolder picture based on groups of blocks will be preferred. Moreover, it is frequently impossible to allocate data to regular grids. But where the survey units are irregular as, for example, in census tracts, it is possible to derive satisfactory measures by suitable modifications in the techniques already described.

The block as a unit is not sufficiently detailed in the case of a group of closely linked establishments, which tend

[6] The approximate dimensions of ellipses representing the subgroups in Figure 20, estimated visually from the profiles (see footnote 5), are as follows: for the left group, $V/H = 1.7/1.5 = 1.1$ and for the right-hand group $V/H = 1.0/2.5 = 0.4$.

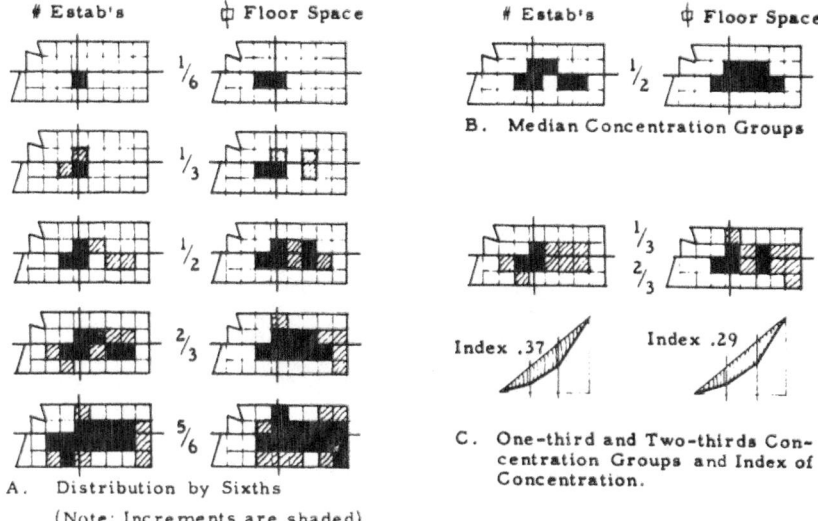

A.  Distribution by Sixths
    (Note: Increments are shaded)

B.  Median Concentration Groups

C.  One-third and Two-thirds Con-
    centration Groups and Index of
    Concentration.

Figure 22.    CONCENTRATION GROUPS ON A GRID
              OF NINE BLOCKS PER UNIT, ALL
              KINDS OF BUSINESS, 1949

to locate side by side or across the street from each other
rather than back to back in the same block. A concentration
of such establishments located along two or three blocks of
a single street would be "diluted" by the other establishments in the four to six blocks in which they occur. Pairs
of opposite block fronts would be preferable as units of
location in such cases, but this is equivalent to a diagonal
grid with twice as many units of area as our maps. Such
fineness of detail is best reserved for study of local areas
rather than for the general statements that are being sought
in this study.

Large-Scale Grids

For a quick general view of location within a fairly wide
area, a map unit somewhat larger than a single block will
provide a more satisfactory picture. Thus the simplified
statement made by Figure 17 is further simplified in Figure 22, where the block-by-block numbers of the original

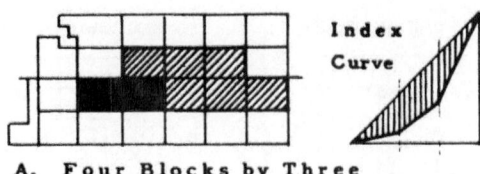

A. Four Blocks by Three

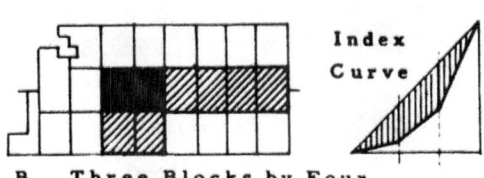

B. Three Blocks by Four

Figure 23.     ONE-THIRD AND TWO-THIRDS CON-
CENTRATION GROUPS AND INDEXES
OF CONCENTRATION ON GRIDS OF
TWELVE BLOCKS PER UNIT, BY NUM-
BER OF ESTABLISHMENTS, FOR ALL
KINDS OF BUSINESS, 1949

data are grouped into a grid having nine blocks to the unit,
a total of 32 map units compared with the 280-odd blocks
of the basic map.

Figure 22A gives the distribution at six levels as before and also gives the location of the increment at each
level. Much of the detail which was glossed over in Figure
17 is lost entirely in Figure 22, but the latter is easier to
compute and much more readliy comprehended.

In Figure 22B the median concentration groups are
singled out, comparable with the middle pair of maps in
Figure 17. The general expression embodied in the right-
hand diagram of Figure 22B (the "floor space" column) is
seen to conform quite well with the ellipse in Figure 20. The
degree of concentration, however, shows up quite differently
when using the larger grid. As always when numbers are
grouped, the contrasts are diminished and so the indexes
of concentration in Figure 22C are considerably lower than
those in Figure 17.

Fine differences are not caught on coarse screens. At
the same time, the simplified version is largely shaped by
the positioning of the screen itself. This is illustrated in

Figure 23 where the establishment count has been regrouped twice into grids having twelve blocks to the unit, once with the screen units positioned horizontally and again vertically. The somewhat different results are caused by the positioning of the grids and depend on whether certain concentrated groups of blocks fall within a single map unit or between two of them. Even the indexes of concentration work out differently.

The shift to a large-scale grid is roughly equivalent to the use of <u>grouped averages</u> in graphs representing time series, where a sequence of five-year averages, for example, can give a simpler picture by eliminating yearly fluctuations. In either case, whether data are spread out on a two-dimensional map or plotted as a line on a chart, the shape of the simplified version is largely determined by the arbitrary position of the dividing lines. This arbitrariness can be overcome by applying moving averages to mapped data, by methods to be described in the following paragraphs.

Smoothing of Mapped Data

The successive levels of concentration with which we have been dealing (as in Figures 17 and 22) suggest contours on the map to represent them in a more generalized form.

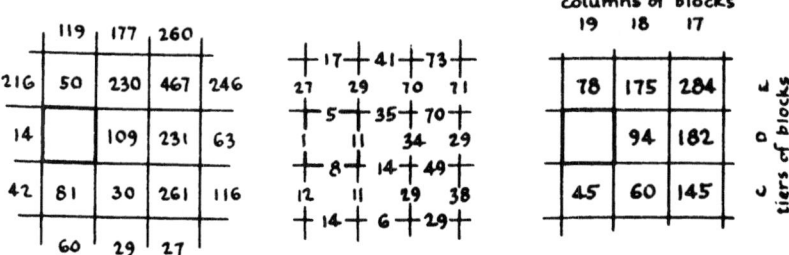

A. Numbers per Block (from Figure 9).

B. Averages between Blocks (one-tenth of sum of adjacent numbers, from A).

C. Adjusted Block Numbers (sum of averages, from B).

Figure 24.   ADJUSTMENT OF BLOCK NUMBERS, TAKING ACCOUNT OF FOUR ADJACENT BLOCKS

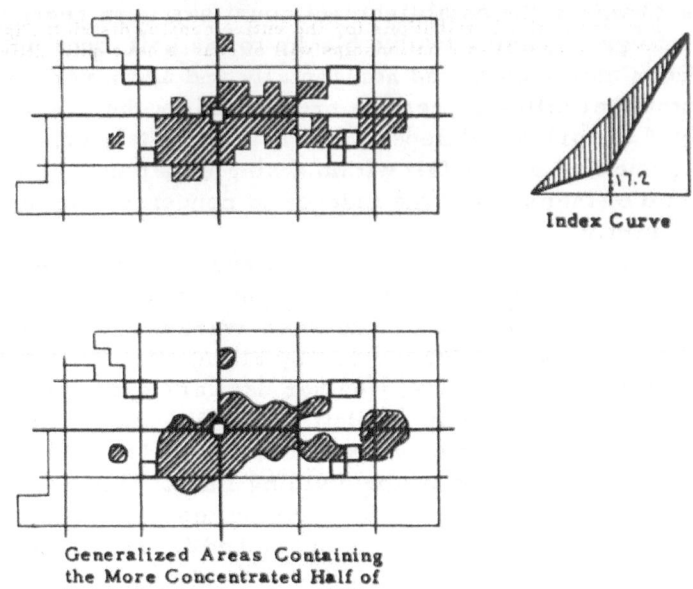

Index Curve

Generalized Areas Containing
the More Concentrated Half of
Total Establishments, 1949

Figure 25.    ADJUSTED MEDIAN CONCENTRATION
                    GROUP

However, the numbers vary so considerably from block to
block and the resulting outlines of concentration groups are
so broken that some method of smoothing must be worked
out before contours can be drawn. A basis for this averaging is suggested by the across-the-street relationship noted
above on pages 106 and 107.

The establishments in any single block might be located
on any one of its four sides, and some of them are likely
to be closely related to establishments across the street.
But our data are not recorded for individual block fronts.
If they were, each total block value would be derived from
the sum of the numbers on its sides. However, the recorded
values can be adjusted in a manner consistent with the ideal
situation. The process is described in Figure 24 for nine
blocks in the southwestern part of the central district,
centering on Block D18 (see Figure 9, page 89). The number in each block (Figure 24A) is averaged with the numbers in each of the four adjoining blocks (Figure 24B) and

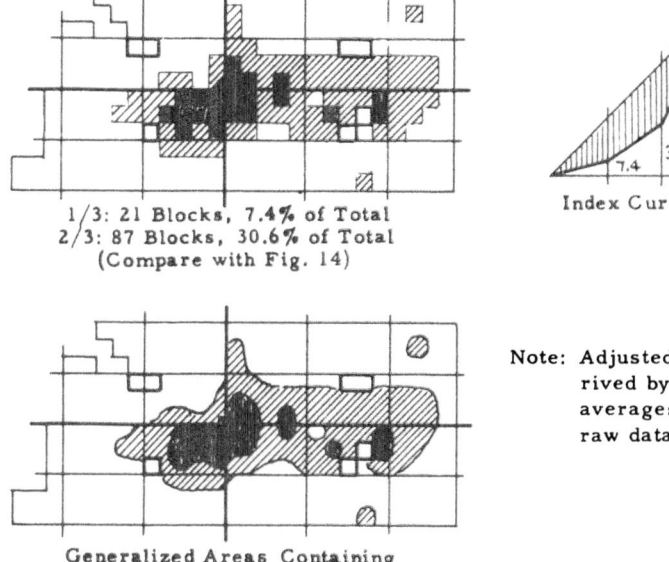

1/3: 21 Blocks, 7.4% of Total
2/3: 87 Blocks, 30.6% of Total
(Compare with Fig. 14)

Index Curve

Generalized Areas Containing
the More Concentrated Establishments, by Thirds, 1949

Note: Adjusted areas are derived by "two-dimensional
averages" applied to the
raw data.

Figure 26.    ADJUSTED CONCENTRATION GROUPS,
              BY THIRDS

the adjusted block number (Figure 24C) is derived from
the sum of the four averages. Thus, in adjusting the number for a given block, the original number is counted four
times, the number in each adjoining block once. The empty
park blocks, as D19, are left empty. Along the north and
south borders of the central district, the number for each
adjoining block across the line is assumed to be equal to
the block which is being adjusted.

    This entire process of smoothing irregular numbers
over a rectangular grid may be rationalized in terms of
moving averages applied to fluctuating line diagrams; in
the present instance, the lines would be profiles plotted
from the sequence of numbers in each tier or column of
blocks. The adjustment described in the paragraph just
above and in Figure 24 is tantamount to applying two-cell
averages to each profile, in each direction, and averaging

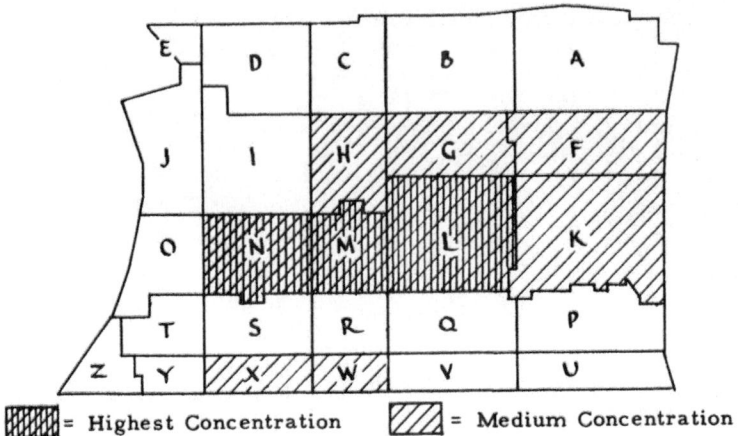

= Highest Concentration        = Medium Concentration

Note: These 26 Areas were used in the analysis of space re-
      quirements made for the Philadelphia City Planning Com-
      mission in 1949.

Figure 27.    IRREGULAR GRID AREAS

the results at each block. Or, by analogy, the adjustment
can be explained in physical terms as the process which
would take place on a three-dimensional model wherein
each block is represented by a prism of damp sand, with
heights proportional to numbers. On weathering, the sand in
the higher piles would slump into adjacent lower piles and
the hollows would be filled in to some extent. On such a
physical model the adjustment could not, of course, be confined to the across-the-street blocks; there would be adjustment across corners as well. Such an adjustment in
all directions can be matched arithmetically by setting down
the averages at each intersection of the surrounding blocks
and again averaging the four corners of each block to arrive
at the adjusted block figure. By this method each block in
question is counted four times, the across-the-street blocks
twice, and the corner blocks once. The general result[7] is

[7] The four-block process applied to the numbers
in Figure 24A would result in the set of adjusted
numbers to the right, instead of the numbers in
Figure 24C.

| 85 | 156 | 224 |
|----|-----|-----|
|    | 113 | 167 |
| 39 | 70  | 104 |

an even greater smoothing of irregularities than that pictured in Figure 24; the peaks are more blunted, the hollows
more filled in. The former method is preferred, however,
because the across-the-street relationship is considered
most important and also because the computation is simpler.

The process described in Figure 24 was repeated for
the entire central district, and new groups of blocks at
successive levels of concentration were picked out (as described at page 95, "Concentration Groups") to derive the
generalized areas containing one-third, one-half, and two-
thirds of all establishments, as pictured in Figures 25 and
26. These adjusted concentration groups are naturally more
coherent and continuous than the original concentration
groups depicted in Figures 13 and 14 (page 97). The very
compactness of the adjusted groups makes it possible to
draw contours to represent levels of concentration. The
index of concentration is also diminished when the block
numbers are smoothed; that is, more blocks are required
at each level to contain the given fraction of total establishments.[8]

The shapes of the concentration groups in these figures
are somewhat generalized, but not in the broad, oversimplified strokes of Figures 22 and 23. Rather they convey much
the same sense of reality, although with less confusing
detail, as do Figures 13 and 14.

### Irregular Map Units

Systematic measurement of land-use patterns has been
greatly facilitated throughout the present study by the regular grid on which the data were recorded. But subdivision
of maps into irregular units is rather more common. Census tracts, for example, with their invaluable data, and the
political divisions (such as precincts and wards) used in
many cities as statistical units are usually quite irregular.
In fact, it is frequently desirable to set up unequal groups
of blocks as study units, these groups conforming to the
locations taken by activities of various kinds. This was done,

[8] Had the second method of smoothing been followed (see footnote 7), the concentration index would have been even lower and the concentration groups
slightly larger, with somewhat more compact outlines.

for example, in the original field study made by Alderson
and Sessions for the Philadelphia City Planning Commission, where a grid of 26 units (containing from 6 to 28 blocks
each) was set up for comparing locations of land uses and
their changes.[9]

The concentration group technique developed in this
chapter can be applied to irregular subdivisions by taking
account of average densities, that is, the number per unit
area for each subdivision. Thus in designating the one-third
concentration group, the map unit with the highest density is
taken first and others are added until their total number
comes as near as possible to one-third of the total for the
entire central district. When the data by grid areas is
processed in this manner, the one-third and two-thirds concentration groups appear as in Figure 27. By this method
both large and small map units are properly accounted for.

## SUMMARY

Means have been developed in this chapter for describing and analyzing the whole interweaving fabric of urban
activities in terms of land use, as patterns of establishments on the map. Measures of these patterns have been
devised for comparing their locations, their degrees of
concentration, or the extent of their dispersion. With these
devices for empirical measurement it will be possible to
test hypotheses as to locational relationships among activities and to verify subjective impressions. Thus the measurement of mapped survey data—the chief concern of this
chapter—can be tied in with key locations in the geographic
history of the central district, with the transit network,
with areas of new or outworn buildings, and as many more
as may help to explain the workings of the central district
as a whole. These methods of measurement are facilitated
by regular blocks of the Philadelphia central district, but
they are not dependent on regular map units. The concluding section of this chapter deals with modification of techniques to suit irregular map units.

The block data used in this study are, of course, abstracted from the full reality which they somehow repre-

[9] Philadelphia Central District Study, Figure 4.

sent. The processing of these data for analysis requires further abstraction and the choice of method will therefore depend on the purpose of the analysis. Any number of attributes of urban activities might be taken as bases for study of location. In the present study, however, all the measures to be used will be developed from block-to-block distributions of establishments and floor space.

# VIII

## LOCATIONS OF BUSINESS GROUPS

This chapter will be concerned with making comparisons
between groups of blocks. These may be either groups
representing different kinds of business or groups representing different attributes of a single kind of business.

### OVERLAPPING OF TWO GROUPS

Some of the measures developed in Chapter VII may be
compared directly. These are expressed as a definite ratio
(index of concentration), position on the map (center of
gravity), or distance (radius of dispersion). These measures express certain locational characteristics of irregular
groups of blocks, concentration groups, for example. In addition to these comparative numerical measures, concentration groups can also be compared by observing the extent to which they coincide or overlap. As before, measures
both of degree and of position will be derived.

#### General Case

Comparison of locations taken by two different groups
may be expressed in terms of the blocks in which both are
found together and those in which each is found by itself.
The general case of two overlapping groups is stated diagrammatically in Figure 28, where "Group A" and "Group
B" represent blocks in which characteristics "A" and "B"
are counted as important. The cluster of blocks common to
both groups is called "Product" and designated "(AB)." Uncombined blocks are designated "A alone" or "B alone".
The entire combination of blocks is called "Sum."
    The extent of overlap can be variously expressed as
ratios between the various terms of this diagram. Two extreme cases are to be noted, however, in which some terms
of the diagram may disappear or become identical. One extreme occurs when the groups are entirely separate, with
no overlap (no product). In this case all of the blocks in

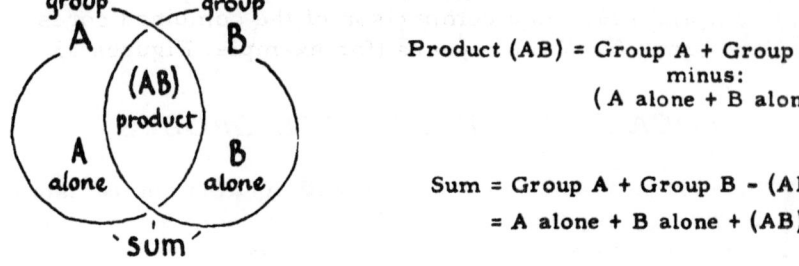

Product (AB) = Group A + Group B
minus:
( A alone + B alone )


Sum = Group A + Group B - (AB)
= A alone + B alone + (AB)

Figure 28.    TWO OVERLAPPING GROUPS, GEN-
ERAL CASE

each group are designated "alone". At the other extreme, all of
the blocks in the smaller group are contained in the larger (sum
equal to larger group and none of the blocks in the smaller group
occurring alone). The ratios between the various terms are
best illustrated by an actual case (Figure 29).

An Illustration of Overlapping Groups
(Establishments and Floor Space)

The two overlapping groups in Figure 29 are taken from
the map distributions by sixths (Figure 17). The median
concentration group by establishment count (the middle diagram of Figure 17A, 34 blocks) is substituted for "Group
A" of the general case depicted in Figure 28 and the corresponding group by floor space count (Figure 17B, 55 blocks)
is substituted for "Group B." The 30 blocks common to
both groups, containing all but four of the "establishment"
group and a little over half of the "floor space" group, show
the location of a high concentration per block on both counts.
The blocks left out of this common group are at a comparatively high level on one count and low on the other. The
blocks designated "alone" are therefore not merely marginal to the common group but strongly characteristic of those
activities which show up as large numbers of comparatively
small establishments, on the one hand, or as a comparatively small number of large establishments on the other. The
purely numerical relationships embodied in this situation
can be expressed in the form of Figure 28 by substituting
the numbers from Figure 29. This is done in Figure 30.

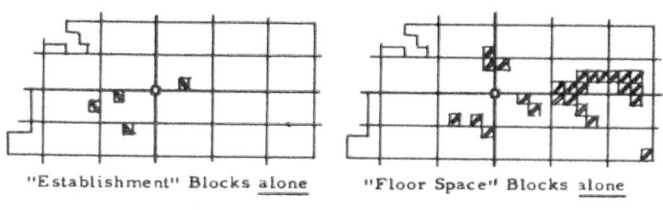

"Establishment" Blocks <u>alone</u>          "Floor Space" Blocks <u>alone</u>

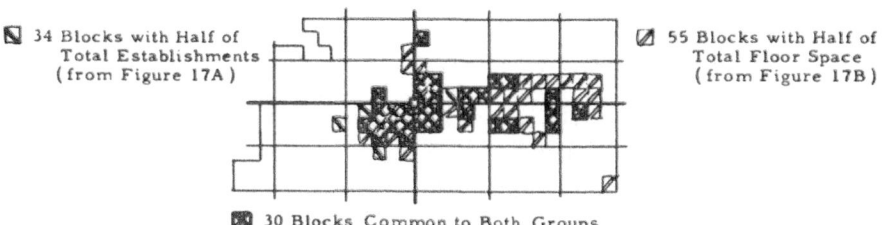

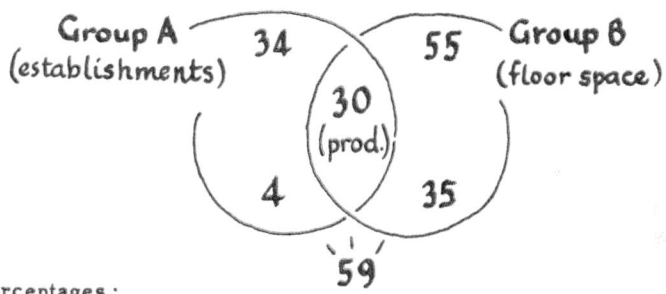

30 Blocks Common to Both Groups

Figure 29.   OVERLAPPING GROUPS OF BLOCKS,
ESTABLISHMENTS AND FLOOR SPACE,
1949

Group A          34          55          Group B
(establishments)                         (floor space)

30
(prod.)

4          35

59

Percentages:

Product = 88% of Group A        A alone = 12% of Group A
        = 55% of Group B        B alone = 45% of Group B
        = 51% of Sum              Sum = 66% of (Group A
        = 30% of (Group A                      + Group B)
                  + Group B)

Figure 30.   MEASURES FOR OVERLAPPING GROUPS,
FROM FIGURE 29

Questions of location of the blocks represented by the
various terms of this diagram must be referred to the
mapped data.

This method for comparing establishments and floor
space will serve as an example, to be repeated later in
comparing other map groupings. The situation depicted in
Figure 29 itself will now be utilized to express the general
location of a business group's main concentration.

### Combined Core (Establishments and Floor Space)

The two component groups in Figure 29 may be taken
as expressing two phases of locational needs of establishments: A, the need for proximity to other establishments
or essential services, and B, the need for relatively large
floor space. In the superimposing of both groups we have
a complex expression embodying both phases. To summarize this situation, that is, to illustrate the effect of both
the establishment count and floor-space distribution, either
the 30 blocks common to both groups (product) or all 59
blocks (sum) could be used. The 30-block cluster gives a
compact expression of relatively high concentration, but it contains quite different proportions of the two participating groups:
a fairly high proportion of the establishment blocks, but only
about half of the floor space blocks. The 50-block cluster, on
the other hand, contains all of both groups, although it is
strongly shaped by the floor-space configuration.

The larger cluster of blocks—the sum of concentration
groups representing distribution of activities by number of
establishments and by floor space—will be termed combined
core in this study. Thus the entire cluster of 59 blocks in
Figure 29 represents the locations utilized by all kinds of
business at the median level. Similar combined cores can
be set up for each kind-of-business activity. These might
be taken at any level (see Figure 17). The median level is
chosen as sufficiently inclusive without being unwieldy. But,
whatever the level, the combined core has the inherent limitation that it expresses primarily the component group with
the lower concentration and, therefore, the large number of
blocks. Thus in the present example the floor-space group
predominates, while the establishment group merely adds a
few additional blocks.

So long as this limitation is kept in mind, the combined core concept will be extremely useful in making comparisons between different kind-of-business groups. For analyzing the characteristics of individual kinds of business, however, the discrepancies between the components (establishment and floor-space groupings) become important, since it is these discrepancies that highlight the special characteristics of each particular kind of business.

## COMPARISON OF COMPONENT GROUPS

The method of comparison developed above and illustrated in Figures 29 and 30 will be applied to a number of different activity groupings in order to evaluate relationships between them; to answer, for example, such questions as these: To what extent does the concentration for a particular kind of business fall within the corresponding group of blocks determined by all kinds of business? Do the locations of two different kinds of business overlap strongly or do they tend to locate separately? Within a given kind of business, what are the different locational characteristics of establishments at different levels of concentration? And for all of these, where do the concentrations and their combinations occur?

### Relationship of Each Group to the Aggregation

Application of the method to the first of the above questions is illustrated in Figure 31, which shows, in the right-hand column, the combined cores for six major kinds of business and, in the middle column, each of these superimposed on the combined core for all kinds—the 59 blocks of Figure 29—the reference core. In the left-hand column are shown the blocks for each kind of business which fall outside of the reference core. The underlying data for this set of maps are, of course, the tabulation of establishments by number per block and by floor area which was mentioned at the beginning of this chapter. Up to this point the maps and tables are all based on the summation of all business establishments. With Figure 31 we are beginning to deal with the separate business groups and with functional relationships between these various members of the central

district anatomy—relationships which we shall examine more
carefully in later chapters.

The set of maps in Figure 31 gives a rather full picture of the disposition of major activities in the central
district of Philadelphia. For example, the right-hand column shows the relative locations of each major business
group and (by the number of blocks in each) a simple measure of their degree of concentration. The central column
shows the degree of conformity of each of these major
groups with the aggregation of all of them. This is expressed (at the right of each map) as the percentage of
blocks in each major group which fall within the reference
core for all kinds of business. The maps in the left-hand
column, by showing the blocks which fall outside the reference core, point up those locations which are especially
characteristic of each separate activity. These are generally scattered, but some fairly coherent areas show up,
especially in Manufacturing and Wholesaling with Stocks.

Certain broad similarities between groups are also
revealed, especially in the combined blocks of the middle
column. Thus Manufacturing and Wholesaling with Stocks
occupy much the same area, and so do Business Services
and Consumer Services, while Wholesaling without Stocks
appears to fall almost entirely within both of the latter
latter groups.

The percentages in Figure 31 express one numerical
relationship between each major business group and the
entire aggregation of them, that is, blocks in each product
as percentage of blocks in each group. Another useful relationship is: blocks in each product as percentage of blocks
in the reference core. These two sets of percentages are
compared in Table IV, lines 3 and 4. (The first three lines
of Table IV are, of course, repeated from Figure 31.) The
percentages in line 3 express the degree of conformance of
each group with their aggregation: the percentages in row
4 express the relative importance of each group in the makeup of their aggregation. Thus, for example, Wholesaling
without Stocks (W-) is entirely within the core but occupies
a relatively small part of it (100 percent and 22 percent)
while Wholesaling with Stocks (W+) has only about half of
its blocks within the core, but these account for nearly one-
third of it (52 percent and 31 percent).

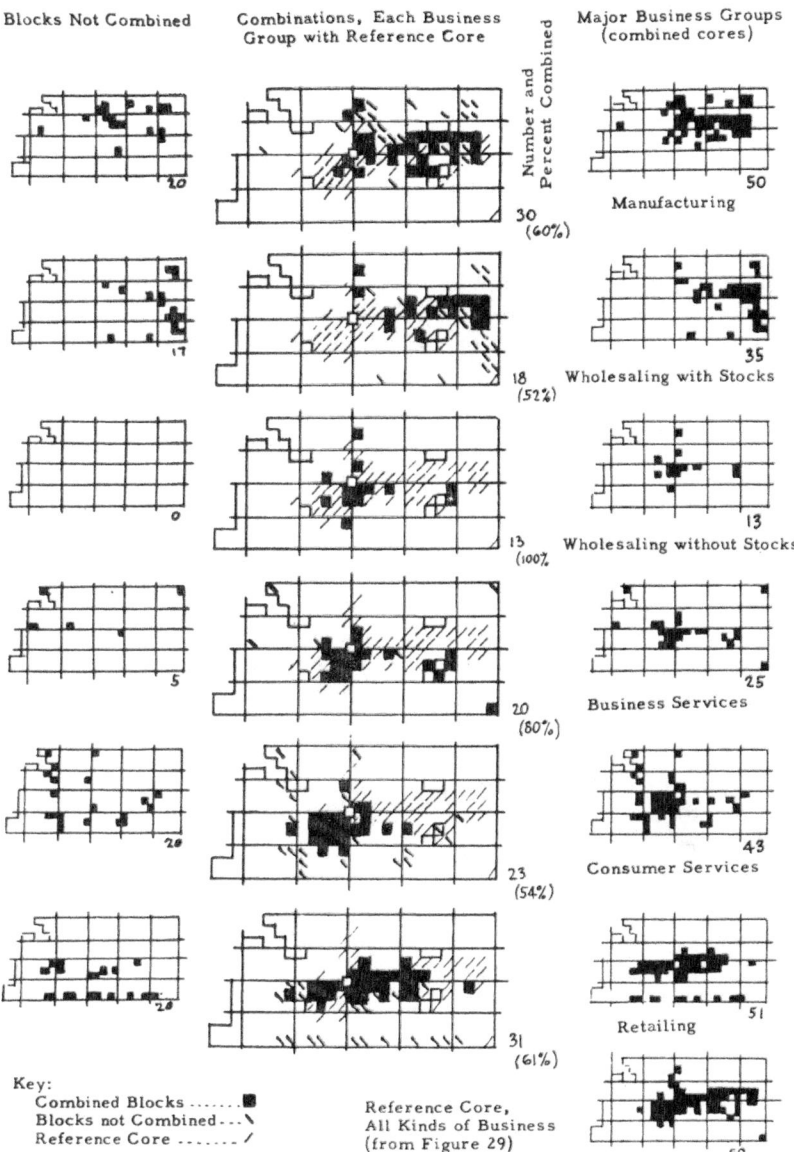

Figure 31.    RELATIONSHIPS OF SIX MAJOR BUSI-
NESS GROUPS TO AGGREGATION OF
ALL KINDS OF BUSINESS, 1949

| Number of blocks:                              | M  | W+ | W-  | B₈ | C₈ | R  |
|------------------------------------------------|----|----|-----|----|----|----|
| 1) Total in each group                         | 50 | 35 | 13  | 25 | 43 | 51 |
| 2) Combined with core                          | 30 | 18 | 13  | 20 | 23 | 31 |
| Percentages                                    |    |    |     |    |    |    |
| 3) Each group (line 2 divided by line 1)       | 60 | 52 | 100 | 80 | 54 | 61 |
| 4) Aggregation (line 2 divided by 59)          | 51 | 31 | 22  | 34 | 39 | 53 |

Table IV.   COMBINATIONS, SIX KINDS OF BUSI-
NESS WITH AGGREGATION OF ALL
KINDS (reference core of 59 blocks)

The same procedure followed above and illustrated by
Figure 31 and Table IV could be used for comparing any
single group of blocks with others. For example the manufacturing group might be compared with each of the major
groups or each of its component subgroups might be compared with manufacturing as a whole. Each single comparison is, of course, a specific application of the general
case diagrammed in Figure 28, and the numerical expression of each comparison may be stated as one or more ratios
between suitable pairs of symbols in this figure. A fairly
complete list of possible ratios is given in Figure 30, while
the ratios most suitable for comparing several groups si-
multaneously are those listed in Table IV.

Centers of Gravity and Density Profiles

The map at the top of Figure 32 shows the reference
core (for all kinds of business, repeated from Figure 31)
with its center of gravity. Also plotted are the centers of
gravity for each of the six business groups pictured in Figure 31. The density profiles for the reference core are
drawn adjacent to this map, while below are the six profiles
for each kind of business group, together with the positions
of the center of gravity of each. The position of the center
of gravity for the reference core is also repeated at each
group and a smoothed profile (two-cell moving average) for
the reference core is superimposed on the individual profiles.

In Figure 32, therefore, the six major groups are again
compared with their aggregation, but now the comparison

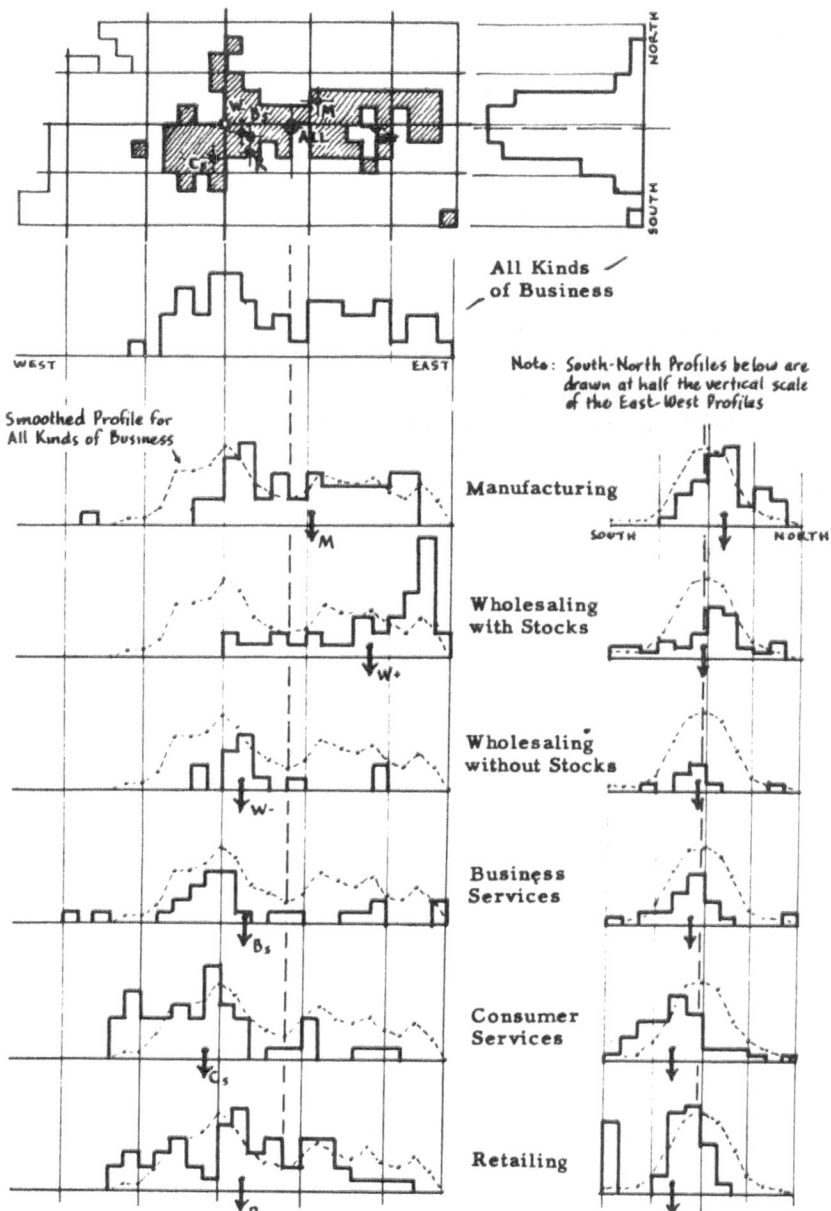

All Kinds
of Business

WEST       EAST

Note: South-North Profiles below are
drawn at half the vertical scale
of the East-West Profiles

Smoothed Profile for
All Kinds of Business

Manufacturing

SOUTH      NORTH

Wholesaling
with Stocks

Wholesaling
without Stocks

Business
Services

Consumer
Services

Retailing

Figure 32.    CENTERS OF GRAVITY AND DENSITY
PROFILES FOR SIX MAJOR BUSINESS
GROUPS COMPARED WITH AGGREGA-
TION OF ALL KINDS OF BUSINESS, 1949

is concerned with location rather than with the degree of
conformance between groups. Certain major concentrations within groups become especially clear in the west-
east profiles. In Wholesaling with Stocks, for example, a
heavy concentration in a few columns of the easternmost
blocks (not a high area in the reference profile) appears
much more important than the low density of the remainder
of the profile for this group. A glance at the characteristics for this group as displayed in Figure 31 will confirm
the impression that this locality (a warehouse district)
might well be considered separately from the remaining
locations in which wholesaling with Stocks is concentrated.

Major concentrations within groups are also to be observed in Wholesaling without Stocks and Business Services
but these fall within the reference profile and to a large extent their map positions conform with the aggregation (the
reference core, see Figure 31). Rather noticeable "outside
groups" appear in the south-north profiles: Manufacturing
to the north and Consumer Services and Retailing to the
south. These may also be inferred from the maps of blocks
not in combination, the left hand column in Figure 31.

In the density profile technique we have a simple means
for discerning gross relationships which may be described
in detail and analyzed by studying the overlapping on the map
of the participating groups.

| Kinds of Business | Components | | | Radius of Dispersion |
| | Horizontal (H) | Vertical (V) | Ratio (V/H) | $\sqrt{H^2 + V^2}$ |
| --- | --- | --- | --- | --- |
| Aggregation (all kinds) | 4.55 | 1.39 | .30 | 4.75 |
| Manufacturing | 3.83 | 1.49 | .39 | 4.22 |
| Wholesaling with Stocks | 3.35 | 2.07 | .61 | 3.94 |
| Wholesaling without Stocks | 2.78 | 1.13 | .41 | 3.00 |
| Business Services | 4.51 | 1.48 | .33 | 4.75 |
| Consumer Services | 3.33 | 1.89 | .57 | 3.83 |
| Retailing | 3.80 | 2.12 | .56 | 4.35 |

Table V.   RADIUS OF DISPERSION, WITH HORIZON-
TAL AND VERTICAL COMPONENTS FOR
AGGREGATION OF ALL KINDS OF BUSI-
NESS AND SIX MAJOR BUSINESS GROUPS

### Radius of Dispersion

The radii for the groups with which we have been dealing are shown in Table V together with their horizontal and vertical components, also the ratio between them. These numbers give dimensions to both the size and shape of each corresponding group on the map—the same groups which are illustrated by the right-hand column of maps in Figure 31.

The size of a group in terms of its radius of dispersion is not necessarily correlated with the number of blocks in the group. The latter is a measure of concentration and, in general, the radius will be smaller for the more concentrated groups (those with fewer blocks), but when the blocks comprising a concentration group are scattered, the radius, as a rule, will be large.

| Concentration Index[a] | | | | Radius of Dispersion[b] | |
|---|---|---|---|---|---|
| | .29 | Aggregation | | 4.75 | |
| high | .45 | W− | W− | 3.0 | low |
| | .41 | $B_s$ | $C_s$ | 3.8 | |
| | .38 | W+ | W+ | 3.9 | |
| | .35 | $C_s$ | M | 4.2 | |
| | .32 | M | R | 4.35 | |
| low | .32 | R | $B_s$ | 4.75 | high |

[a] As indicated by number of blocks in combined core, Figure 31. The computation is described on page 99, note 3.
[b] From Table V.

Table VI.   RANK COMPARISON OF GROUPS: CONCENTRATION AND DISPERSION

When the six groups are listed in rank order by both measures (concentration and dispersion, Table VI) only Business Services is very much out of line, since it has high concentration and also a large radius, due to its widely dispersed blocks. Consumer Services is also out of line, with relatively low concentration and low radius. That is, although there are many blocks in this group, most of them are located in a compact group.

### SUMMARY

Methods have been developed in this chapter for combining and comparing the concentration groups which are

used to characterize activities of various kinds. Thus, for
example, the inherently different patterns for a single kind
of business as derived from an establishment count versus
a floor space count are compromised by using a combined
core of blocks in which both counts are represented.

Whether for comparing separate attributes of a single
kind of business (e.g., number of establishments and floor
space per block as revealed by survey data) or for comparing two different kinds of business, the overlapping of
blocks in each group can be analyzed numerically, (Figures 29, 30) or part-whole relationships can be stated by
comparing component groups of activities with their aggregations (Figure 31). Thus groups of blocks for each
kind of business can be compared by determining the percent of each that is contained in the corresponding group for
all kinds of business (Figure 31) or by comparing locations
of their centers of gravity (Figure 32). Any number of comparisons can be made—depending only on the purposes of
analysis.

These techniques for comparing locations could, of
course, be applied to any group of blocks whatever, for comparing them and relating them to specific locations such as
custom house or bank, railway station or freight terminal.
They may be used to relate traffic and land use as described
in Urban Traffic by Mitchell and Rapkin.[1] Perhaps their
most useful application is in giving a quick summary picture
of change between successive time periods by comparing,
for example, the patterns revealed in Figures 31 and 32
based on data for 1949 with similar figures based on 1935
data.

[1] New York, 1954. See Chapter VIII.

# IX

## MULTIPLE COMPARISONS

PATTERNS of central district establishments as they appear on the map are results of a sorting process in which specific needs of each establishment for space and location are matched against the available accommodations. The underlying activities change continually during this process, with corresponding changes in establishments and their linkages. The physical setting is also modified but more slowly, since its structures are fixed and relatively permanent.

The continually shifting panorama of land uses may be considered static at a given time—at the time, for instance, when a new establishment is set up and its location relative to other establishments and to transportation is determined. Each new establishment fits as best it can into a known pattern of several related establishments which are interspersed among many others having the same general requirements for location. But the older establishments may have had different requirements and linkages, even different kinds of activities, at the time when they were formed, and their locations may be no longer suitable. The resulting aggregation of related and unrelated land-use patterns, some fairly stable, others shifting, is inevitably jumbled.

How are the actors to be identified in this continuing play of ever-changing activities among ever shifting groups of establishments? What is it that can be traced through the continually forming and dissolving sets of relationships which lie behind the changing patterns and land use?

### REALIGNMENT OF MAJOR GROUPS

The establishment, as unit for analysis, is most readily classified by major business groups; but, when the character of functions performed by establishments is examined, it may become necessary to seek new principles of classification. Broad categories of land use tend to separate into subgroups which have more in common with other subgroups than with their own parents. A department store, for example, as its business expands, will set up a separate warehouse from which bulky items are delivered to the customers. Or a wholesaler dealing in, say, household equipment will set up a salesroom for taking orders, apart from the main warehouse establishment. Both warehouses are much alike as far as handling of goods is concerned, and the wholesaler's display room is much like the corresponding space in the department store as far as taking orders is concerned. Both branch establishments might be classified as business services, that is, serving other units of the same business, but one handles goods and the other deals with people. Facts such as these will have to be taken into account for identifying and understanding the changing roles of establishments in the interplay of central district activities.

During the data-gathering period of the Philadelphia study it became apparent that Wholesale Trade was actually composed of two separate groups of establishments: those maintaining stocks on the premises and those operating without stocks. These two groups were found to be located separately and, in the course of the study, each was treated as a major group. But the Wholesaling without Stocks category, as expressed by its combined core, is located almost entirely within the Business Services concentration of blocks (see Figure 31 on page 123). In fact, Wholesaling without

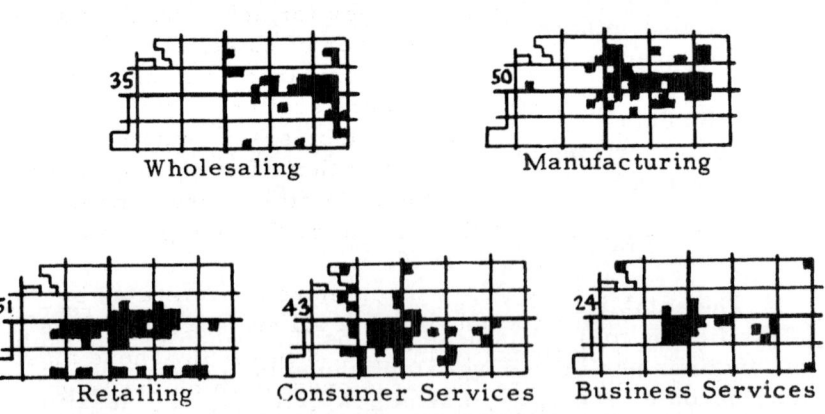

Figure 33.    FIVE MAJOR BUSINESS GROUPS, 1949
(COMBINED CORES)

Stocks might better be classified as a subgroup of Business
Services instead of being set up as a separate category.
When this is done the Business Services group is modified
but slightly, and the over-all relationships become an interplay between five groups instead of six. These five groups,
shown in Figure 33, are identical with those in Figure 31
with the exception of Business Services, which now includes establishments classified as Wholesaling without
Stocks.

This realignment will form the basis for further analysis in the present study. The entire arrangement provides
a somewhat more balanced set of components and relationships than was the case with six groups. The new combinations are summarized in Table VII, derived in the same
manner as Table IV on page 124.

### Combinations: Five Business Groups

The picture of major activities in the central district
of Philadelphia presented so far has been largely concerned
with concentrations of establishments classified by different
kinds of business, their disposition on the map, and their
relationship to a corresponding concentration for all establishments taken together. Up to this point there has been
little comparison of the different groups with each other,
although it has been noted that the methods outlined are
entirely appropriate for making such comparisons. The
relationship of each kind-of-business concentration with each
of the others can be studied more readily, however, by

| Number of blocks: | M | W | B | C | R |
|---|---|---|---|---|---|
| 1) Total in each group | 50 | 35 | 24 | 43 | 51 |
| 2) Combined with core | 30 | 18 | 21 | 23 | 31 |
| Percentages: | | | | | |
| 3) Each group (line 2 divided by line 1) | 60 | 52 | 88 | 54 | 61 |
| 4) Aggregation (line 2 divided by 59) | 51 | 31 | 41 | 39 | 53 |

Table VII.   COMBINATIONS, FIVE KINDS OF BUSI-
NESS WITH AGGREGATION OF ALL
KINDS (reference core of 59 blocks)

means of a single map on which each group is indicated by
a distinct symbol.

In Figure 34 the five business groups of Figure 33 are
superimposed. The paired relationships of each group with
the others can be counted on Figure 34 as readily as they
could on the set of ten maps which would be required to show
each pair separately (that is, combinations of the five maps
of Figure 33, taken two at a time). Moreover this map shows
at once the locations characterized by a single activity
(blocks having only one symbol) or by several, and from it
can be derived spatial relationships between the various
activity groupings.

The majority of the blocks in Figure 34 (79 out of 129,
or 61 percent) can be ascribed to one single group or another. The fact that a block is uncombined indicates that

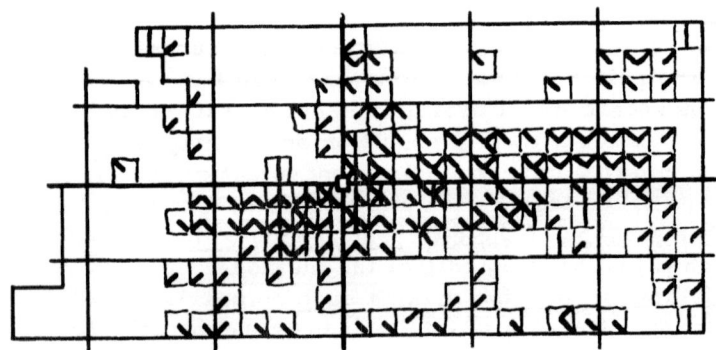

Key to Groups, with number of blocks in each:

50 🔲 Manufacturing    35 🔲 Business Services
                                                    51 🔲 Retailing
35 🔲 Wholesaling     43 🔲 Consumer Services

Figure 34.    FIVE MAJOR BUSINESS GROUPS SU-
              PERIMPOSED, 1949

it is clearly dominated by a single activity. The locations
of these separate blocks are shown in Figure 35.

The remaining blocks of Figure 34, those showing two
or more kinds of business, do not represent all possible
combinations, but each kind is found associated with each
of the others at least once. The more important combina-

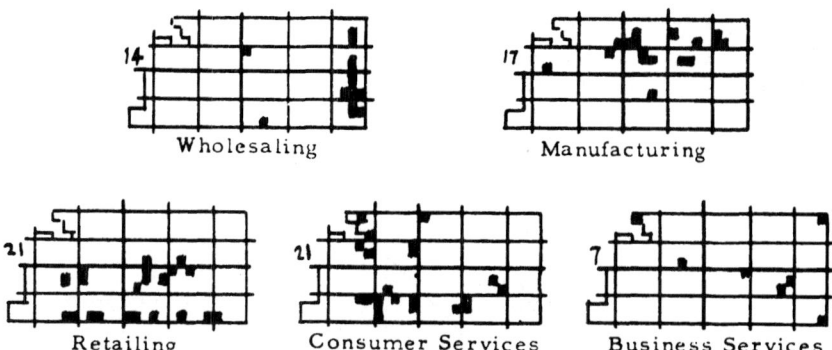

Figure 35.     BLOCKS WITH A SINGLE KIND-OF-
               BUSINESS CONCENTRATION, 1949

tions are shown in Figure 36: the closely related pairs in
Figure 36A and the most central group of three (B-R-C) in
Figure 36B. This latter group of blocks virtually pinpoints
the most active area in the central district.

The overlapping ellipses on each map in Figure 36 are

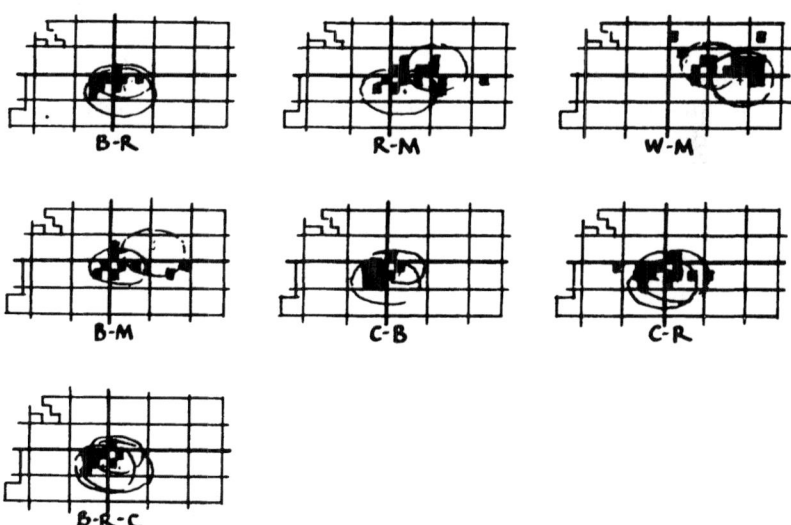

Figure 36.     BLOCKS COMMON TO VARIOUS COM-
               BINATIONS OF ACTIVITIES, 1949

| Total Blocks | Number Combined | Group | | M | W | B | C | R | Total Combinations |
|---|---|---|---|---|---|---|---|---|---|
| 50 | 33 | Manufacturing | (M) | ⑰ | 20 | 9 | 8 | 17 | 54 |
| 35 | 21 | Wholesaling | (W) | 20 | ⑭ | 1 | 1 | 8 | 30 |
| 24 | 17 | Business Services | (B) | 9 | 1 | ⑦ | 12 | 11 | 33 |
| 43 | 22 | Consumer Services | (C) | 8 | 1 | 12 | ㉑ | 18 | 39 |
| 51 | 30 | Retailing | (R) | 17 | 8 | 11 | 18 | ㉑ | 54 |

Table VIII.   TOTAL  COMBINATIONS,  FIVE  MAJOR
GROUPS,  1949

not sketched at random but are drawn to scale, propor-
tioned to the spread of each major concentration as described in Figure 21, p. 105, with dimensions from Table V
on page 126 (see "Radius of Dispersion," page 127). In a
very general way the actual overlappings of the major activities are approximated by these ellipses, which may be
taken as symbolizing the actual situation.

## MEASURES  OF  PROXIMITY

Numerical expressions for comparing relationships
between different kinds of business are derived from a
simple count of blocks in which the different combinations
are found. Such a count is presented in Table VIII. The
total numbers of the blocks in which each kind occurs is
given at the right of this table: the total number of blocks
in each group and the number of each in which combinations
occur appear at the left: the numbers of each kind standing
alone (not combined) are circled. These last represent the
same blocks as are shown in Figure 35.

The total number of combinations in Table VIII is considerably greater than the number of blocks in which combinations occur, since three or more are found together in
many cases. This multiple overlapping is particularly noticeable near the center at Broad and Market Streets (see
Figure 34).

The percentage of blocks, for each group, in which each
kind of business occurs by itself and the percentage of blocks
in which the various combinations occur, are shown in Table
IX. The first percentage is the ratio, in each case, of the

|                   | Percentage Alone | Percentage Combined with Others |
|-------------------|:----------------:|:-------------------------------:|
| Manufacturing     | 34               | 66                              |
| Wholesaling       | 40               | 60                              |
| Business Services | 29               | 71                              |
| Consumer Services | 49               | 51                              |
| Retailing         | 41               | 59                              |

Table IX.   PERCENTAGES, BLOCKS ALONE AND
            COMBINED WITH OTHERS

circled number in Table VIII and the total number of
blocks for the group; the remaining blocks, represented by
the percentages in the second column of Table IX, contain
all of the combinations for each business group.

The number of combinations occurring between any two
business groups, as shown in Table VIII, will have a different
significance to each member of the pair depending on the
number of blocks in each group. As a basis for drawing
comparisons, these numbers might be taken as: (1) the total
number of blocks in each group, (2) the total number of combinations in which each group participates, or (3) the total
number of combined blocks in each group. Each basis will
result in a different set of percentages. Taking the eleven
blocks in which Business Services and Retailing occur together as an example, these blocks represent: (1) about
two-fifths of the total number of blocks for the one and about
one-fifth for the other (42 percent and 22 percent). On the
basis of (2) the total number of combinations in which each
group participates, the same eleven blocks represent one-
third for Business Services and one-fifth for Retailing (33
percent and 20 percent). One the basis of (3), the total
number of combined blocks in each group, the same eleven
blocks represent two-thirds for Business Services and one-
third for Retailing (65 percent and 37 percent). Comparisons might be made on any of these bases; there appears
to be little to choose between them as to their relative
significance to the groups being compared. However, the
second will be used, since we are concerned with combinations rather than with the number of blocks in which combinations occur or do not occur. Thus in Table X the combinations are restated as percentages of the total combina-

tions in which each group participates (that is, the percentages are based on the right-hand column of Table VIII).

Each horizontal line in this table expresses the relative
strengths of the relationships between each group and the
other four, in so far as these relationships take the form of
two groups occupying blocks in common. The reciprocal
relationship within each paired group is seen in the diagonally opposite pairs of percentages, in ratios varying from
1 : 1 to nearly 2 : 1. Thus, for example, the pair Manufacturing and Retailing; each has 31 percent of its combinations in common with the other. Wholesaling and the Services also share blocks in equal proportions, but the numbers
are low (3 percent in each case). More typical are the unequal proportions within pairs such as Wholesaling and Man-

|                    | M  | W  | B  | C  | R  | Total |
|--------------------|----|----|----|----|----|-------|
| Manufacturing      | -- | 37 | 17 | 15 | 31 | 100   |
| Wholesaling        | 67 | -- | 3  | 3  | 27 | 100   |
| Business Services  | 27 | 3  | -- | 36 | 31 | 100   |
| Consumers Services | 21 | 3  | 31 | -- | 46 | 100   |
| Retailing          | 31 | 15 | 20 | 13 | -- | 100   |

Table X.    PERCENTAGE DISTRIBUTION. COMBI-
            NATION OF EACH KIND OF BUSINESS
            WITH EACH OTHER KIND (Read Across)

ufacturing (67 percent and 37 percent) or Wholesaling and
Retailing (27 percent and 15 percent).

A measure of relative proximity among groups is
readily derived from the table showing the number of times
that each combination occurs. Thus, in Table XI, each combination is expressed as a percentage of the total number of
combinations (by dividing each number in Table VIII by the
total number of combinations, 105).

Proximity of groups may be caused by functional relationships (e.g., linkages) between their establishments or it
may result from mere suitability of location, such as the
existence of proper accommodations and facilities at economic rentals. But, whatever the underlying causes, the
percentages in Table XI do give an indication of the tendencies of various groups to locate together.

### Diagrammatic Relationships

It is at once apparent from Table XI that the strongest locational tie between groups is that of Manufacturing and Wholesaling (19 percent of all combinations, in the situation pictured in Figure 34). It is also apparent that the ties between Wholesaling and the Services are insignificant (1 percent each). Other strong locational ties are those of Retailing with Manufacturing and with Consumer Services (16 per-

|                    | W  | B  | C  | R  | Total |
|--------------------|----|----|----|----|-------|
| Manufacturing      | 19 | 9  | 8  | 16 |       |
| Wholesaling        |    | 1  | 1  | 8  |       |
| Business Services  |    |    | 11 | 10 |       |
| Consumer Services  |    |    |    | 17 | 100   |

Table XI.   RELATIVE PROXIMITY, PAIRS
OF BUSINESS GROUPS

cent and 17 percent). The five remaining pairs are all about average (around 10 percent).

The three strongest combinations may be represented as a string of connected pairs:

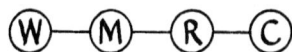

Continuing to add combinations in turn, the next two are those of Business Services with Retailing and Consumer Services:

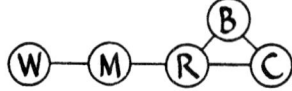

Adding the remaining combinations, excepting only the insignificant ties between Wholesaling and the Services, results in the diagrammatic framework of Figure 37. The dimensions in this diagram are roughly reciprocal to the percentages in Table XI and so represent the relative closeness of the relationships.

In Figure 37 as in the underlying tables it is seen that

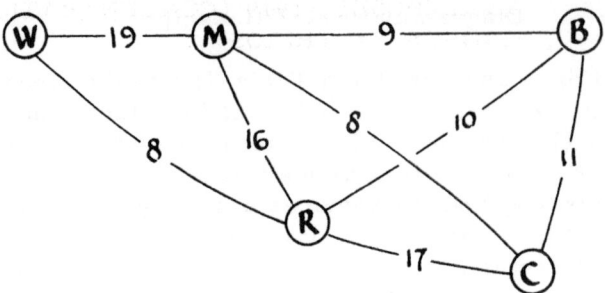

Note: Numbers represent proximity of pairs of activities, as in Table XI.
Distances between symbols are reciprocals of these numbers.

Figure 37.    DIAGRAMMATIC RELATIONSHIPS
AMONG FIVE MAJOR BUSINESS
GROUPS, 1949

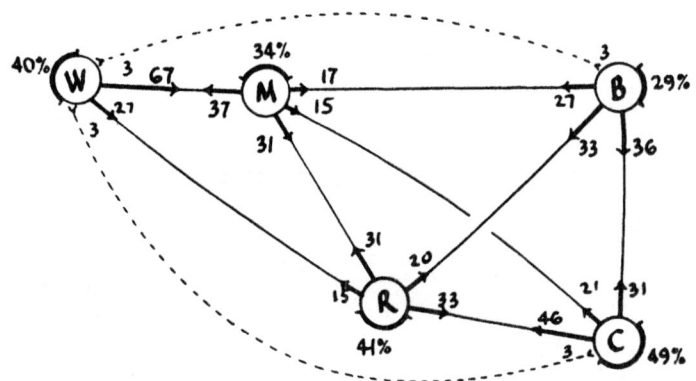

Note: Heavy segment of each circle indicates percentage of blocks "alone"
as in Table IX.  Lengths of arrows represent percentages of combined blocks shared with indicated partners, from Table X.  Distance between each pair of symbols is reciprocal to their proximity,
as in Figure 37.

Figure 38.    CONSISTENCY OF RELATIONSHIPS
AMONG FIVE MAJOR BUSINESS GROUPS

only Manufacturing and Retailing have significant ties with
all of the other groups, while each of the services (B and
C) relate to three and Wholesaling only to two. Of course,
the separate parties in each of these paired relationships
differ considerably in their degree of participation. This is
demonstrated in Figure 38, where the diagram is the same
but the numbers are from Table IX and X.

In Figure 38 it is seen that Business Services is the
most combined group with only 29 percent of its blocks
standing alone, but Manufacturing is not far behind. Retailing is the most uniformly distributed among the others, with
Manufacturing again a close second. Consumer Services is
the most isolated group in that it has the greatest percentage
of its blocks uncombined. Wholesaling is the least uniformly
distributed. When pairs are examined the most balanced
relationship is M-R. That is, each of these shares about the
same proportion of its combinations with the other or nearly
a 1 : 1 ratio. Almost equally balanced is the relationship
between the Services (C-B) while the remaining pairs coming together at the Services are less balanced (C-R in a
4 : 3 ratio and C-M, B-M, and B-R in ratios of about 3 : 2).
Those in which Wholesaling participates (M-W, W-R) are
least balanced, each in roughly a 2 : 1 ratio.

What can be said as to the meaning of the relationships
that are summarized in this diagram? Are they typical for
other central districts? How will this balance of relationships differ in subareas where one activity dominates? What
differences will be revealed by separate examination of the
components: distributions by number of establishments, and
by floor space. (It is to be remembered that illustrations
in this chapter are all based on combined cores, a meld of
the two kinds of distribution.)

Of course, the diagrams themselves can give us no more
for sure than statements of relative proximity, however
much we may be tempted to read underlying causes into
them. It remains to be seen how much these statements can
be accounted for by functional relationships between establishments or whether, in a given case, proximity is fortui-
tous. For the present our objective extends no further than
schematic description, both ample and flexible, for studying
various combinations of activities within the central district.
The figures and tables in this chapter can serve very well

as prototypes for statements of functional relationships between groups, whether for the entire central district, for a
small cluster of blocks, or for the establishments occupying
a short length of street (both sides) where a special kind of
business predominates, or even for stating relationships
among the establishments housed in a single commercial
building.

## SUMMARY

The methods developed in Chapters VII and VIII for
comparing business groups have been utilized in this chapter
for comparing each major group with the others. A realignment in major groups was first made, however, in which
their number was reduced to five. Locational relationships
(combinations) between these are stated both on the map and
numerically, in tabular form. The relative strengths of these
numerical relationships are also made the basis for diagrammatic statements which will be used for further study
of relationships between major activities, both in the central
district generally and in various localities within it.

# X

## SCHEMATIC RELATIONSHIPS

IN the course of developing measures of land-use patterns
in the preceding three chapters, the only data used were
the number of establishments and the floor area per block,
classified as to kind of business. But these measures comprise no more than the groundwork for describing and analyzing urban relationships, no more than the means whereby
activities of different kinds are located on the map in terms
that can be evaluated and compared. To build up on this
groundwork a more thorough understanding of activities and
relationships in the central district it will be necessary to
bring in other attributes of establishments, attributes relating to the functions actually performed, and to take account
of the pressures and limitations that make for changes in
land use or that inhibit change. In other words, the location
patterns of establishments which have been pictured in
Chapters VII, VIII and IX are to be reexamined in the light
of those activity systems and their accommodations which
were discussed in Chapters II, III and IV.

Before proceeding with detailed analyses of land-use
relationships and their changes, the subject of the concluding chapters of this study, the descriptive scheme already
developed will be elaborated somewhat further. The schematic diagrams to be set up in this chapter are extreme sim-
plifications of the actual complexities, but they will serve
as a sort of skeletal pattern, to be fleshed out later with
substantial data from real-life situations.

### RELATIONSHIP DIAGRAMS

Locational relationships between the five major business
groups have been traced by comparing their patterns of concentration (Chapter VIII) and measures of proximity between
each pair of groups (Chapter IX). These measures of proximity suggested restatement of relationships between activities in the diagrammatic form of Figures 37 and 38 . These
figures, together with the relationships which they symbol-

ize, will be taken as the starting point for this chapter.

## Multiple Relationships

The measures of relationship depicted in Figure 38 are abstracted from the data for the entire central business district. The same scheme, however, would apply to any specific location within this district, the difference in each case consisting merely in the relative strengths of the ties between groups. But when a limited location is investigated, no more than two or three of the groups are found to be concentrated there and several of the ties between groups are found to be insignificant. Thus, when studying specific locations, attention will be focused on the separate elements of the diagram—individual groups and ties between pairs of groups.

A general statement of relationships among five groups is given in Figure 39. Measures are disregarded in this diagram, or presumed to be all of equal strength.[1] Otherwise the scheme is the same as in Figures 37 and 38. Each kind-of-business group is seen to be related to the other four, making ten paired combinations. Each member of a pair of groups is related to the remaining three, but these other relationships may have little bearing when the prime focus of our attention is the connection between the members of each pair.

While the relationships between groups which were symbolized in Figures 37 and 38 had to do only with proximity, the same scheme would apply when expressing operating relationships such as linkage. Thus for the general case depicted in Figure 39, each connection (that is, each line between two groups) might represent the summation of linkages between all of the establishments in each pair. It would not be possible to equate all of the linkages for the ten pairs, however, since the same measures do not apply to all kinds of establishments.

A symmetrical diagram such as Figure 39 has little

[1] The sequence of groups in Figure 39 makes the adjacent pairs appear to be more closely related than the diagonal pairs, but this cannot be helped where equality of relationship among five groups is represented graphically.

merit in the representation of actual relationships; it serves
rather in a formal way, as a list of the relationships that
can exist. In practice each part of the diagram is treated
separately, with measures pertaining to specific relationships. (See "Elements" at the right of Figure 39). These
may be considered in two ways: first, as a cluster of dif-

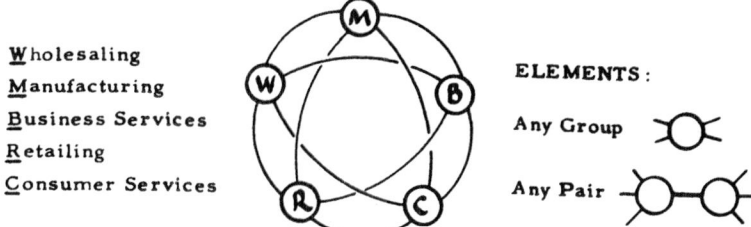

<u>W</u>holesaling
<u>M</u>anufacturing
<u>B</u>usiness Services
<u>R</u>etailing
<u>C</u>onsumer Services

ELEMENTS:

Any Group

Any Pair

Figure 39.    GENERALIZED DIAGRAM OF RELATION-
SHIPS AMONG FIVE MAJOR BUSINESS
GROUPS

ferent relationships pertaining to a single group or as those
relationships pertaining to a single group or as those relationships which are maintained between a pair of groups.[2]
Since some groups have little or no relationship with each
other, the "shape" in each part of the diagram will vary
greatly when measures are applied. This will be especially
true when the diagram represents a limited area dominated
by major concentrations of not more than two or three major
groups, such, for example, as a manufacturing-wholesaling
center or an area shared by retail stores and office buildings.
    There is no magic, of course, in the number of groups
which are taken as the basis for organizing a study of relationships between activities. Six major kinds of business
were distinguished in the original survey on which the
present study is based.[3] A much more elaborate classification might be required for some purposes, such, for example, as a study of linkages among all of the establishments concerned in the operation of the grocery chain de-

[2] The same elements might be used to represent linkages which converge at
a single establishment or the linkage between two given establishments.
[3] Including Wholesaling without Stocks, now merged with Business Services.

scribed in Chapter III. In any case the analysis is shortly
reduced to the units or elements designated in Figure 39:
either the group itself with its connections or a pair of
groups with its joint activities.

A further simplification for demonstrating the entire
set of relationships among activities of the central district
is achieved by treating Wholesaling and Manufacturing as a
single group. They are, of course, separate activities, but
they have a strong tendency to locate together. Of the remaining activities in the central district, only Retailing is
found together with Wholesaling to any extent and this occurs
almost entirely in blocks where Manufacturing is also concentrated (see Figure 38). Relationships among central activities can therefore be stated in the form of four groups,
equally disposed with regard to each other, as in Figure 40.

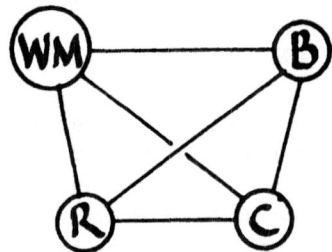

Figure 40.    A FOUR-PART GROUPING OF MAJOR
              ACTIVITIES

In Figure 40, as in Figure 39, the adjacent pairs appear
to be closer together than the diagonal pairs. But the grouping in Figure 40 is that of a regular tetrahedron, a three-
dimensional arrangement having each group equidistant
from the three others. This arrangement with four basic
groups enables us to consider the totality of relationships
very simply. It requires the least number of terms for developing the characteristics of the elements as they apply to different situations. Later study of more intricate arrangements
can be developed readily from these unit situations.

Unit Relationships

In the scheme of Figure 40 any group may be taken in
turn as central to the other three:

Or <u>any pair</u> may be considered as the primary unit with the others playing secondary roles to each primary pair:

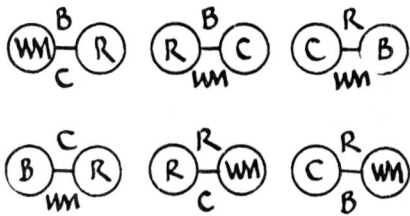

These relationships are all alike schematically, with all "dimensions" in balance, so that all possible combinations can be considered on equal terms, whether attention is focused on one of the four groups or on one of the six pairs.

When a case is taken for which measures exist, differences between groups or pairs of groups can be demonstrated. For example, the B group is most evenly distributed among the others and WM group is most uneven.[4] Or in graphic terms, with the length of arrows representing "strength" of relationships:

When a single pair is taken as primary, the relative importance of the secondary groups can be shown by their placing:

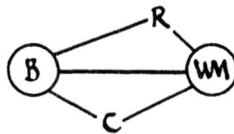

[4] This is in terms of the distributions for the entire central district, Figure 37. For selected areas these relationships will of course have quite different measures.

In this case R is shown to have a much closer relationship
to WM than it has to B while C is slightly closer to B than
it is to WM. Taking another pair (WM and R) as primary,
B is shown to be slightly closer to R, while C is close to R
but remote from WM:

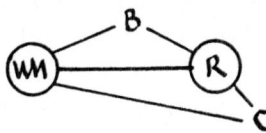

Diagrams like these, with as many units and dimensions
as each situation requires, could also be used for studying
individual cases, such as a single establishment and its
linkages, or a single linkage and its importance to the constituent establishments.

### Levels of Concentration

The patterns of business groups which have been presented in the two previous chapters are no more than general approximations showing relative locations of the groups.
They are based mainly on the "combined core"—a sort of
merger of blocks in which both floor space and number of
establishments take part (see page 120). These general approximations are enough for making a beginning, but more
refined statements of the patterns inherent in our data will
be required for effective analysis.

For analyzing relationships between business groups,
not only should patterns based on floor space and on establishment count be considered separately, but differences in
concentration should also be taken into account. Thus it will
be possible to look into different "centers" in which one
group or another predominates and, by tracing relationships among major and minor concentrations, to gain understanding of the different ways in which downtown space is
utilized. For this purpose the location of the one-third and
two-thirds concentration groups for various kinds of business will be taken separately (see page 95, "Concentration
Groups"). Diagrams very similar to those just described
will serve for demonstrating the various combinations
schematically.

### Changes over Time

All of the data pictured so far have been based on the 1949 survey. But similar data exist for 1934, and a comparison of the two years will show trends as to location, changing strength of relationship between various groups, and all the other measures that have been sketched in the two previous chapters. Again, the schematic diagrams of this chapter will serve as prototypes for demonstrating the various relationships and their changes.

The scheme of organization just outlined, with levels of concentration and changes over time added to the business group locations, is considerably more elaborate in detail than the material previously discussed. However, this scheme is still a massive simplification of the full range of phenomena which the data represent.

The concentration groups by thirds for each kind of business, counted by establishments and by floor space, will be pictured in Appendix A in sets of maps covering both years. The tables derived from these maps will be more intricate than those in Chapter IX since they will show locations of two levels of density. Maps derived from this appendix for showing detailed locations of blocks having various combinations of activities will be not unlike the maps in Figures 35 and 36. In any case, diagrams similar to those sketched in this section will serve for organizing detailed analysis so that attention can be focused in turn on selected elements.

## SOME GENERAL CONSIDERATIONS

Before beginning any detailed analysis of the five major business groups, some further speculation is in order concerning the general relationships between them and some typical characteristics of the groups themselves.

Each of the major business groups, taken as a whole, has a different set of locational relationships with the others, resulting largely from the totality of linkages which come together at the component establishments. But the establishments within each group are of various sorts, with different characteristics and balances of relationships. Thus, for example, Retailing is both a primary central activity and

accessory to other primary central activities. The first
is represented in the compact group of stores comprising
the main shopping district while the second is represented by the more scattered stores which serve the downtown working population. In like manner Wholesaling or
Manufacturing may be divided into those establishments
dealing primarily within the central district and those dis-
tributing goods over a much wider area. Consumer service establishments range from large institutions such as
schools or hospitals to the smallest barber shop or doctor's
office. The Business Service category is scarcely less
heterogeneous and presents a special difficulty in that it
includes transportation establishments which, for our purposes, might better be considered as part of the city's
mechanical plant along with water supply and public utility
installations.

### Accessibility—Persons vs. Goods

The location of individual establishments or of closely
related groups is affected by several broad considerations,
among which accessibility is surely the most important.
Thus activities which require contact with people tend to
cluster in areas which have the best mass transit facilities or where there is heavy pedestrian traffic, while activities characterized by handling of goods in bulk tend to
locate where they have access to heavy transportation facilities. In a broad way these different needs (of activities
where goods are handled and where people assemble) are
met in Philadelphia by the distinct areas characterized by
Wholesaling and Business Services (W and B in Figure 33,
page 130). Manufacturing requires access both for employees and for materials, both raw and finished, and its main
concentration is seen to overlap Wholesaling strongly and
Business Services somewhat less (Figure 36, page 133).
Retailing requires access for people primarily, but goods
are also involved—most heavily at the major stores where
movement of goods and crowds of people inevitably come into
conflict, for the main concentration of office buildings is in
the same location or near by. The Consumer Services group
is located opposite to Wholesaling on the map and also tends to
stand somewhat separate from other activities except where it

combines with Business Services and Retailing (Figure 36).

Street frontage is a prime consideration for all sorts
of establishments requiring direct access, all the way from
the smallest key grinder or watch repair shop on the side-
walk to the department store or printing establishment
occupying an entire building. Frontage connotes accessibility, whether for customers of for handling shipments
of goods. It is used for show windows and display in the
former case; in the latter, both sidewalks and streets are
often congested with goods and standing trucks. The two
purposes are not compatible; difficulties arise where both
must be served in the same location.

The persons-goods analysis of central activities and
their locations can be summarized diagrammatically in
terms of major business groups as follows:

persons - assembling

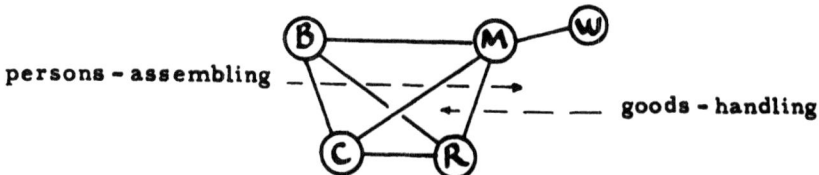

goods - handling

Figure 41.    THE PERSONS-GOODS BREAKDOWN

The arangement in this diagram is that of Figure 37 reversed, and by sheer coincidence it roughly approximates
the locations for the various groups (see maps, Figures
33 and 36). Of course no precise geographic lines can be
drawn, nor can any clear line be drawn between the persons
and goods sides of the above diagram, for the activities
are actually interspersed. And of course this summary diagram applies only to the whole central district in the broad
terms of major concentrations. In limited areas, perhaps
dominated by a single activity or a pair of them, or perhaps
mixed as to uses, the persons-goods breakdown might be represented more correctly by a somewhat different diagram.

Availability—Space vs. Location

In general, goods-handling establishments take up more
space than those dealing primarily with persons, both floor

space and the outside space required for access by transportation; and suitable locations are generally well distributed, since access by truck is relatively free. Persons-
oriented activities, on the other hand, are likely to pile up
where they are most accessible by mass transit. But only
those establishments whose activities can support relatively
high rents can pay for good central locations. Many desiring such space must go where they can get accommodations at prices they can afford. They find them in goods-
handling areas or they take over space vacated by firms
which have shifted their activities to more up-to-date buildings in the center or to more spacious, noncentral quarters. A
seemingly unending supply of space in small amounts is available in residential structures converted to commercial use. The
most desired locations, however, are necessarily few. Choice
of location is therefore restricted by the patters of space units
actually available for use by various kinds of activity.

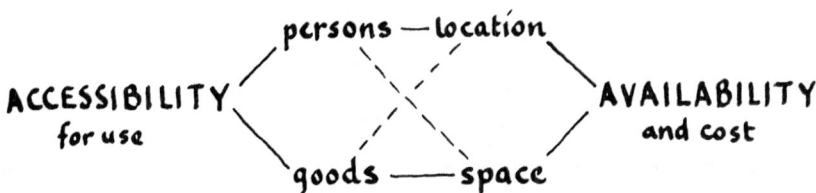

Figure 42.    ANALYTICAL DIAGRAM: AVAILABILITY
             AND ACCESSIBILITY

Accessibility is still prime in the ideal arrangement of
central district activities; availability largely explains how
such arrangements are modified. The elements concerned in
relationships between these factors are set forth in the above
diagram, which may be read somewhat as follows:
Urban space at given locations intended for various uses,
whether primarily for persons or for goods, is to be considered from the standpoints of both accessibility (for persons or goods or both) and availability (i.e., existence of
suitable space or the possibility of providing it at economic
rent). It may be further stated that the relationship between
accessibility and availability are reciprocal and dynamic,
that is—as accessible space is used more intensively, less
of it is available and its cost rises.

### Linkages—with Business and with Public

Accessibility is not only a matter of concern in the handling of goods and in easy transportation for people coming into the central district from outside; it has to do also with repeated contacts between business establishments themselves and with the public. Except for consumer services and retailing, no business establishments have any direct concern with the general public, yet all their employees are customers of the same downtown retail and personal-service shops. Some of the latter, especially those in the central shopping district, are directed toward the consumers of the entire city, but others are scattered throughout the central district wherever there is a working population to be served. The service shops are camp followers, as it were, of the forces engaged in the main campaign. They seek frontage where their customers can have access to them. A surprising amount of resident population is scattered throughout

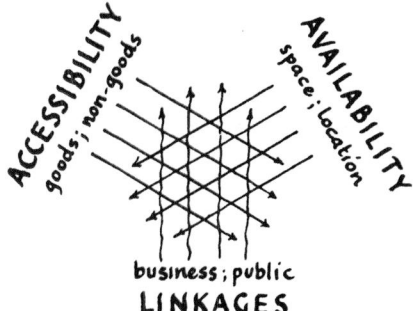

LINKAGES

Figure 43.    ANALYSIS OF LOCATION: THREE-
WAY SCREENING

the central district in Philadelphia, accounting for a considerable but undetermined proportion of the consumer-oriented establishments and blurring their relationship to the business-oriented community.

## SUMMARY

Two concepts are presented in this chapter:

First, the need for flexibility in classifying activities
so that the measures developed in the preceding chapters
can be applied effectively to the study of activities as they
operate on each other. A simplified scheme of relationships
was developed in which the separate elements can be examined systematically. Whole groups of categories can thus be
considered in their broad relationships over the entire central district or in a small study area. The same scheme can
be applied to the study of separate establishments and their
linkages.

Second, analysis of central district activities requires a
three-way screening in terms of: accessibility, availability,
and linkages. This process of screening serves as an outline for describing and explaining the interplay of central
district establishments of all kinds, both singly and in
groups. The working elements in that interplay are now to be
examined where they live. The question "what activities
belong together?" will be approached through investigation
of what activities are found together, giving a basis for
further investigation as to whether they function well together, or would be better separated.

# XI

## CONSTELLATIONS OF ACTIVITIES

GROUPINGS of activities, as found, are seen to vary greatly in different parts of the central business district of Philadelphia. A general view of the major groupings was presented in Chapter IX, expressed in two phases: as locational patterns (Figures 34, 35, and 36) and as measured relationships derived from these patterns (Tables VIII through XI, Figures 37 and 38). These groupings and relationships have all been based on amalgamation of two sorts of data: a count of establishments and a count of floor area, both for the year 1949, covering the entire central district. Only the most concentrated blocks (those containing half of all establishments or floor space) are considered in these tables and figures. Similar groupings and relationships for 1934 are given in Appendix A. Taken together, these two set of maps and tables and schematic diagrams provide the basis for a rough general description of changes taking place in the disposition of central district activities.

In later sections of this chapter, more detailed expressions based on each sort of count taken separately will be derived by the same methods and used as tools for analyzing that interplay between activities and their accommodations which is characteristic of central Philadelphia. Background for this analysis is provided by the discussion of schematic relationships in Chapter X and by the general descriptions in Chapter VI, especially the maps in Figure 7: "Philadelphia at the Present Day."

### GENERAL COMPARISONS OF LOCATIONS, 1934 AND 1949

Locations of business groups were much the same in both 1934 and 1949, as a comparison of the combined cores for each group for the two years (for example, Figures 33

and 75) will demonstrate.[1] Differences are minor except for
the services, which appear considerably more concentrated
in 1949, each of these groups occupying only about two-
thirds as many blocks as in 1934. Locations dominated by
a single kind of business (Figures 35 and 77) are also much
the same in both years. It is in the location of combinations
of activities as shown in Figures 36 and 78 that definite
changes in patterns begin to appear. These figures will
serve to illustrate the following discussion of the various
combinations.

The Wholesaling and Manufacturing combination (M-W)
has changed the least, although it does appear to have shifted
slightly to the west. Together these two groups dominate
the northeastern and eastern parts of the central district,
a wide crowded area with very heavy local truck traffic,
fairly well served by subway and trolley lines (Figure 7A).
Wholesaling, especially, occupies the oldest part of town, in
structures dating from every period of the city's history.
Whole blocks of mercantile buildings in Greek Revival style
along Front Street, dating from the boom days of the 1830's
and 1840's, are still used by the same type of establishment for which they were built, while a few blocks to the
west it is common to see a wholesaler in, say, textiles or
hosiery occupying a former bank building with ornate granite
front and elaborate interior trim of Civil War vintage. Access for deliveries and linkages with the trade together with
cheap rent are the prime requirements for establishments
in this area. Suitability of the structure itself seems to be
relatively minor in importance. Not that the tenants are
satisfied with their accommodations—in the entire area
east of Seventh Street, over one-third of the establishments
interviewed during the study made for the planning commission in 1949 expressed dissatisfaction.[2]

Combinations in which Retailing participates (R-M,
B-R, C-R) have all become more compact, occupying in a
close-knit group of blocks one or two blocks north and

---

[1] Only the most general comparisons can be made on the basis of these combined cores, since the degree of overlap between their components is ac-
cidental. Later, more detailed comparisons will be based on the separate
counts, by establishments and by floor area.
[2] Philadelphia City Planning Commission, Philadelphia Central District
Study, (Philadelphia, 1950), Figure 14.

south of Market and extending nearly a mile east and west, from about Eighth Street to Eighteenth Street. This is the area best served by mass transit, the destination area of two-thirds of the people who come into the central district each day (see Table I). The most concentrated part of this central area is that characterized by Business Services combinations: M-B, B-C, C-R. These are strongly centered near the junction of Broad and Market Streets, the chief focus of commercial activities during the past fifty years and more. These combinations have also become more compact in the fifteen-year interval between our survey dates. In this location there are no "single" blocks (Figures 35 and 77). That is, among those activities which demand the most central location, competition does not permit any one of them to predominate. This location is highlighted on the diagrammatic map by the very neat group of blocks in which major concentrations of Business and Consumer Services and Retailing are all three found together.

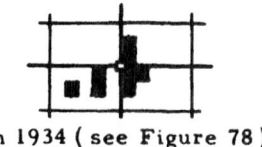

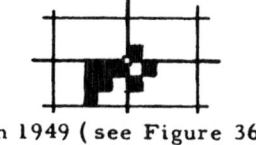

in 1934 ( see Figure 78 )              in 1949 ( see Figure 36 )

Figure 44.    BLOCKS COMMON TO RETAILING
              AND BUSINESS AND CONSUMER
              SERVICES

This is the location best served by mass transit: the railway and suburban bus stations, the chief crux of the subway system, the Market Street Subway with its trolley loop to West Philadelphia, and by the network of surface lines. The development of this area, anchored to Penn's original central square at Broad and Market Streets, has left the northwest quadrant largely vacant of business activities. The near corner of this quadrant is now in process of rapid development on the site of the old Broad Street Terminal. The central space blocked up by City Hall is scheduled to be opened again and restored to use as a public square when a new building to house the city offices is constructed.

Measures of locational relationships among the five
major business groups for 1949 have been expressed in
Tables VIII through XI. Similar measures for 1934 are given
in Appendix A, Tables XII through XV. These measures are
generalized expressions of tendencies for the various groups
to locate together. These tendencies for the two years are
most readily compared in terms of the last table in each set,
showing relative proximity of the five groups (Tables XI and
XV) or in terms of the diagrammatic equivalents of these
tables, Figures 37 and 79.

The five strongest relationship occur between the same
pairs in both cases: W-M, M-R, R-C, C-B, and B-R. However, the relative strengths of these relationships have
changed somewhat. Scant importance is to be ascribed to
changes of a couple of blocks or percentage points, one way
or the other, since these combined core groupings are
mixed in nature, but some major shifts appear to be significant, at least to the point of indicating where further
study of the underlying data is wanted. Thus, for example,
the strong relationship between Manufacturing and Wholesaling and the middling relationship between Business Services and Retailing have been much the same in both years,
so these may be taken for granted as relatively stable, at
least for the time being. But the other relationships (R-C,
C-B, B-R) changed considerably: the strongest in 1934, that
between Retailing and Consumer Services, fell off considerably, as did that between Consumer Services and Business
Services, while that between Manufacturing and Retailing
became much stronger. In view of the changing relationships among these three pairs, another look at the maps
showing their locations appears to be in order. (See Figures 33 and 75 for the groups themselves and Figures 36
and 78 for their combinations.)

The large R-C combination for 1934 seems to be a
function of the larger number of blocks in the Consumer
Services group for that year; seen most prominently in
the southern tier of blocks. The blocks common to both
groups in 1949 form a compact cluster. The relative
strengths of relationships for the two years are probably
realistic in this case. The indicated increase in strength of
the M-R combination also seems reliable, since there was
little change in total numbers for each group.

## CHARACTERISTIC LOCAL GROUPINGS

The sets of relationships among major business groups which are summarized by the schematic diagrams discussed above (Figures 37 and 79) were derived from the totality of proximity relationships for the entire central district, as mapped in Figures 34 and 76, etc. These generalized statements are good for a first approximation or summary of relationships for a wide area, but they need to be reexamined for each location (as in the preceding paragraph for the R-C combination). In the following discussion of locations and their characteristic groupings no differentiation is made between 1934 and 1949, since the relationships have remained much the same.

East of Fourth Street there are virtually no major concentrations other than Manufacturing and Wholesaling, with the latter predominant. Such Business Service establishments as occur here are mainly concerned with shipping and warehousing. Consumer Services and Retailing are distinctly minor. This entire area is strongly characterized as one where goods are handled. It may be symbolized as a coupling of Manufacturing and Wholesaling with its accessory Business Services.

Further west, say from Fourth to Ninth Streets, Manufacturing and Wholesaling are still most important, especially to the north, but Retailing has entered strongly into the picture. Business Service also plays an important part, chiefly in the form of banks or insurance company offices near Independence Square. Consumer Services, while relatively minor, are also beginning to count in this vicinity. There are really two kinds of grouping here:

(1) to the north, the Manufacturing-Wholesaling combination is still the main feature, with the former predominant, while Retailing plays a minor role. Many of the retail stores in this area handle bulk goods, such as household furnishings. The services do not seem to count here.

(2) To the south, all five groups appeared to participate on fairly equal terms in 1934, but in 1949 Wholesaling had become distinctly minor. This is a mixed central area with a symbolic grouping much like the four-part arrangement suggested in Chapter X, Figure 40, where Manufacturing and Wholesaling are considered as a joint group.

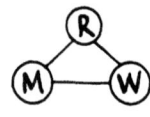

From Ninth Street to Broad, Retailing is the strongest group and the services stronger than before

(i.e., east of Ninth). Manufacturing is still strong north of Market;
Wholesaling is weak throughout. Here again a division at Market
Street is suggested by the relative predominance of Manufacturing
to the north:

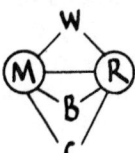

(1) North of Market, then, the important groupings from Ninth to Broad are Manufacturing and Retailing, with Wholesaling and Business Services secondary and Consumer Services minor.

(2) South of Market, Retailing and Consumer Services and Business Services are the important activities,
with Manufacturing secondary and Wholesaling very minor
indeed.

West of Broad, the predominant combinations are those between Consumer Services and Business Services and Retailing.
Manufacturing is of no importance here and Wholesaling is practically nonexistent. This area may be
characterized as one where only persons-assembly
is important.

Detailed study at locations will call for more refined
measures than those used so far, but the following constella-
tions of groups are already apparent:

The locations just considered have followed the sequence, east to west, of the historic development of the
city itself with its succession of activities and elaboration
of linkages in older parts and continuing encroachment of
residential areas by commerce. These locations include
only the more concentrated portions of the central district, approximately the area covered by the combined core
at the median level for each year as illustrated in Figures
29 and 74. The particular clusterings of activities in these
six locations, geared as they are to the existing physical
structures and linkages and levels of economic activity,
must be unique to the city of Philadelphia. And yet the
same types of combinations are to be found in one part or
another of any central city.

These locations are delimited rather arbitrarily by the
divisions of our diagrammatic maps. The schematic diagrams of local relationships are based on mere visual
inspection of the maps and are therefore to be considered

as tentative. Firm statements of normal relationships for
various local types of center would have to be based on a
careful grouping of blocks by combinations of activities, but
that would require a more detailed examination of locations
and activities than is justified by the crude data used for the
present discussion. However, these data will permit a broad
division based on goods-handling versus non-goods (or persons-assembling) activities, as suggested in Chapter X. In
three of the locations discussed above, Wholesaling or Manufacturing are prominent. In the other three the services are
considerable factors. Retailing is strong in both kinds of
area, concerned as it is both with persons and with goods.

### Goods-Handling vs. Non-Goods Activities

The combinations of activities in two broad areas are
now to be reexamined and the proximity relationships within each stated separately in Figure 45, as was done in Chapter IX for the central district as a whole. The goods area
is roughly that occupied by the combined core for Manufacturing: east of Broad and north of Market, also south of
Market to the east of Fourth. The non-goods area includes
both the old and new business centers, extending from
Fourth to Nineteenth, south of Market. Only the combinations within three blocks of Market Street were counted in
compiling the relationship diagrams for these areas. Combinations for both years were included in the calculation,
since the present purpose is a typical statement of relationships rather than the study of change. The latter will
have to await a more detailed processing of our basic data.

The diagrammatic relationships among activities in
goods-handling and non-goods areas, as depicted in Figure
45, are by no means "pure"—the areas which they represent
are far too large for that and the data far too spotty—but they
will serve as a preliminary statement of the combinations
most characteristic of these two general types of central
area. In the goods area, the M-W combination is by far
the most numerous; M-R has only about half as many
and W-R only a third. There are some combinations
of Consumer Services with Manufacturing and Retailing,
but Business Service combinations are scarce. The
outstanding cluster for this entire area is the M-W
combination with R as the main accessory, somewhat

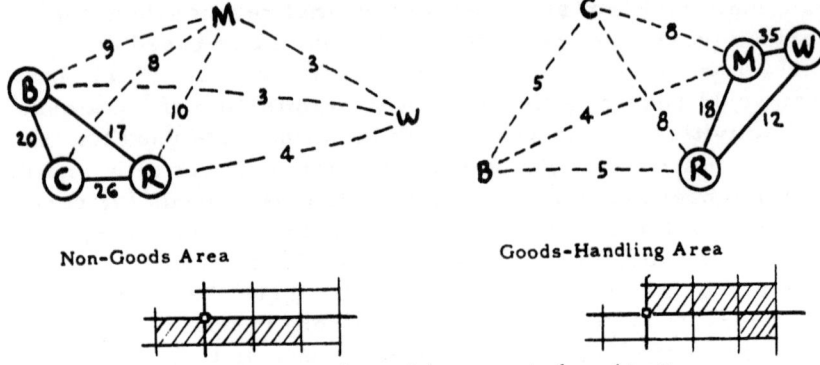

Non-Goods Area                                Goods-Handling Area

Note: Numbers are derived from count of combinations
in two key areas by the methods of Chapter IX

Figure 45.    RELATIONSHIPS AMONG FIVE BUSI-
NESS GROUPS IN GOODS-HANDLING
AND NON-GOODS AREAS

closer to M than to W.[3] The non-goods area is also dominated by a three-way cluster, the members of which are
more nearly in balance. The C-R combination is strongest,
with C-B and B-R not far behind. Manufacturing combines
rather definitely with all three, but wholesaling is virtually
out of the picture here.

These two general types of activity groupings may be
further summarized as follows:

1. Wholesaling and Manufacturing together form the
nucleus of goods-handling areas, with Retailing of bulk
goods in a secondary role and with a scattering of the services and miscellaneous retail establishments acting as ac-
cessories to the main groups of firms and to their employees.

2. The Business Services group forms the nucleus of
the more crowded commercial centers (persons-assembling or non-goods areas) with Retailing and Consumer Services playing secondary but important roles. Manufacturing
has some place here, but Wholesaling appears to be a mis-
fit.

[3] This cluster is almost completely dominant in the area north of Market
from Fourth to Ninth, as discussed and illustrated in the descriptions of the
six local groupings above.

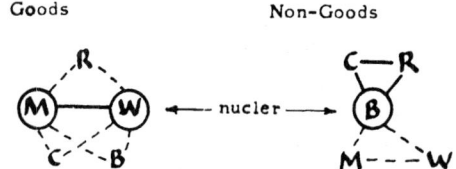

Figure 46.   SIMPLIFIED SCHEME OF RELATION-
SHIPS FOR GOODS-HANDLING AND
NON-GOODS ACTIVITIES

In the above summary, as in the measured relationships
of Figure 45, only the extreme highlights are picked out.
These are related in the simplest diagrammatic terms in
Figure 46. Actually, there is always a great deal of overlapping of contrary (unrelated) activities. There is scarcely a block in this central core of the central district where
any one of the five business groups is not represented by at
least a few establishments (see Appendix A, Figures 54
through 65). Nevertheless, by this grand division of activity
groupings a long step can be taken toward analyzing the
complexities of the central district. In the process, the
path to that major goal of urban studies—the more orderly
and efficient allocation of land uses—may become clearer.

### ESTABLISHMENTS AND FLOOR SPACE

The foregoing pictures of central district activities and
their interrelationships are fairly sharp, but they are rough
—no more than preliminary sketches made up out of the
amalgamation of two kinds of underlying data. It is time now to
deal with the separate elements of these data and to elaborate
on the sketches, perhaps to revise them in some instances.
In the comparison of establishments and floor space
(for all kinds of business in 1949) in Chapter VII it was
noted that establishments are relatively more concentrated
and floor space more spread out. It was further noted that
the concentration groups at any given level are located somewhat differently for the two kinds of count. Each of these
distributions reflects differences in the use of space by establishments, and each of them is worth study for the light it
can throw on the ways in which land uses are organized.
Comparison of the two distributions and differences between

them at various levels should reveal even more meaningful
relationships than those stated in the first sections of this
chapter.

The basic data for our comparisons consist in the
separate counts, block by block, of establishments and floor
space in 1934 and 1949 for all kinds of business and for the
five separate kinds. These are given in Appendix A, Figures
54 through 59 for 1934 and 60 through 66 for 1949.[4] These
distributions are put into workable form as concentration
groups in Figures 67 through 73, at six levels for the totals
(all establishments in Figure 67 and all floor space in 68)
and at three levels for the individual groups (Figures 69
through 73, each depicting a single kind of business).[5]

Much of the difference in location by the two counts is
due to the larger number of floor-space blocks at each level,
but always there are some blocks on the establishment side
which are not in the floor-space group. Thus in the first
pair of maps in Figure 17 (or the corresponding maps in
Figures 67 and 68) there are three such blocks out of the
six in the establishment group at this level: E-8, E-15, and
E-17. These three together have 1,518 establishments, about
average for this level of concentration. The other three
blocks, common to both counts, have 1,793. However, in the
eleven blocks in the floor-space group at this level, the total
number of establishments in the eight blocks outside of the
common group is only 1,658, roughly one-third as many per
block as the ones within the common group. The simplest
comparison is by average number per block for each group.
In the present case this is 552 in the establishment group
and 314 by floor space. The corresponding numbers for 1934
are 339 and 168, quite different in magnitude but in much the
same ratio, one to the other.[6]

These differences between the two distributions empha-

---

[4] The first of these maps, establishments in 1949, has already been given, in
Figure 9.
[5] In each of the latter figures, concentration groups by thirds are shown on
one map and the median group on another, together with the location of blocks
having no establishments. An index curve (see Figure 16 and accompanying
discussion, pp. 98ff.) is also given for each group. Thus, four sets of information are given for each: by establishments and by floor space for 1934
and for 1949.
[6] See Figure 54 for the numbers in 1949, and Figure 60 for 1934.

size a general fact and also point up its symptoms. The fact is that where the most establishments concentrate they are not large, or, in other words, the larger establishments are located somewhat apart from the most congested centers. Comparative measures of the differences between the two distributions show by how much and where significant differences occur.

A measure of the differences between concentration groups as counted by floor space and by establishments was described in Chapter VIII, "Overlapping of Two Groups," and was illustrated by Figures 27, 28, and 29. Full arrays of the overlapping groups for both 1934 and 1949 at three levels of concentration are displayed in Appendix A, Figures 80 and 81.

Strong similarities between the two distributions are inevitable. They are, after all, merely two phases or ways of counting a single phenomenon. The floor-space distribution itself is neither more nor less than a descriptive statement of the location of all business space in use. If all establishments were equal in size, the two distributions would coincide.

Both establishment and floor-space distributions became noticeably more concentrated in the interval from 1934 to 1949, with indexes of concentration increasing by 8 percent in each case. (See index curves in Figures 67 and 68, also Figure 66 where the four curves are superimposed.) Moreover, there has been a shift to the west in both groups; nearly two blocks for establishments, and more than a block for floor space. (See the locations of the centers of gravity at the one-half level in Figures 67 and 68.)

This general view of the two distributions needs to be extended to the less dense areas. These may be picked out as successively lower levels of density in Figures 67 and 68. In Figure 47 the increments alone are shown for both distributions in 1949. The center of gravity and average radius are also given for each increment, as well as the center of gravity at each successive level of density.

The "spread" of the successive increments occurs in a rhythmic sequence, as may be seen in the successive magnitudes of their average radii. These are plotted separately in Figure 48.

The average radius for each successive increment

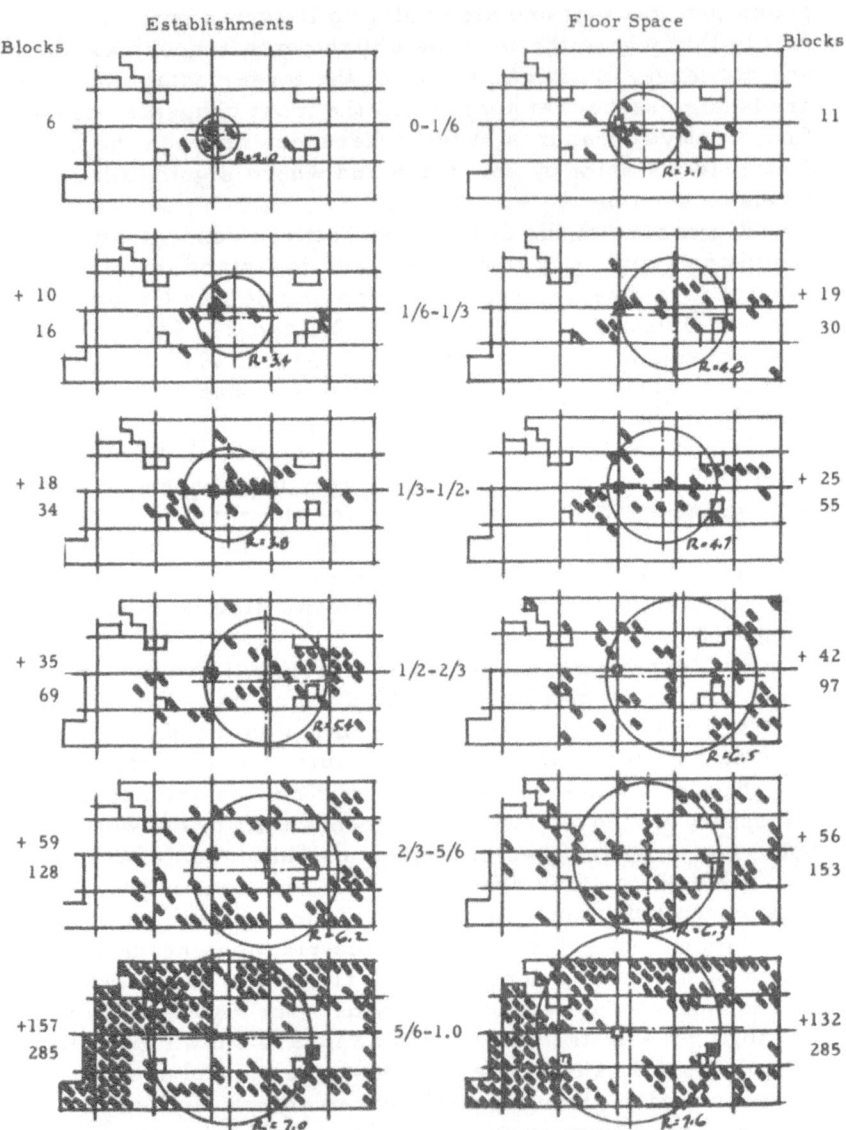

Note: R = Average Distance From Center of Gravity of Each Increment Group.

Figure 47.    DISTRIBUTION OF INCREMENTS BY
              SIXTHS, 1949

group increases rapidly at first and then levels off, and this
process is repeated once again. This is to say that as blocks
are picked out at uniformly decreasing densities, the increase in their average distance out from center is not uni-
form but advances in a sort of wave. Or the magnitudes in
Figure 48 may be read step by step thus: the most dense
location is compact; locations at the next level of density
tend to become dispersed; at the next level the spaces between tend to fill up; and so on through two cycles. This

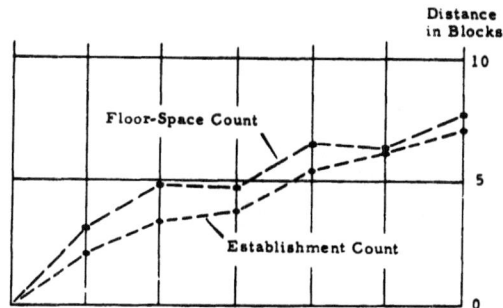

Figure 48.    AVERAGE DISTANCE OF BLOCKS IN
              EACH INCREMENT GROUP FROM
              CENTER OF GRAVITY FOR THAT
              GROUP

process of consolidation is more marked in the case of the
floor-space distribution, where the average radius actually
decreases at two levels. In both distributions the final increment is spread wide, the more central blocks having all
been taken. Thus, the lowest pair of maps in Figure 47 gives
a fair picture, in negative, of the shape of the central core.

### Variations among Business Groups

The variations in location between the two aggregate
distributions (by floor space and by establishment count)
which have been discussed in the foregoing pages may be
taken as standards against which to compare the variations
of the five separate groups. Only the locations can be taken
as standard, however; the indexes of concentration are quite
different for the separate groups and may be compared use-

fully with one another but not with the index for their aggregation.
(See Figures 69 through 73 for the concentration groups and indexes of concentration for the five kinds of business.)

The general increase in concentration from 1934 to 1949
noted above for the aggregation of all establishments and all
floor space is absent in the case of the components, and so is
the relatively higher concentration on the establishment side.
Changes among the separate groups show considerable minor
variation, frequently the reverse of the general trends noted
for their aggregations. The indexes of concentration are all
considerably greater for the separate groups—about the same,
on the average, for both counts and both years. Even higher
indexes would occur when the subgroups making up these
major business groups are examined separately (for example
Department Stores and Drug Stores).

As an extreme case the central department stores may
be taken as a special, highly concentrated group, located
along Market Street from Seventh to Broad. (Six of these are
noted among the landmarks of central Philadelphia in Figure 7.) Three of the smaller stores are located in a single
block, while each of the others is found in a separate block.
The larger stores so dominate the scene that it may be
assumed that two-thirds of the total space is to be found
in the three largest. The distribution curves for this very
concentrated hypothetical case, then, would be very flat,
since the entire concentration is contained in eleven blocks,
only 3.86 percent of the total number in the entire central
district. (See Figure 49 where the curves are plotted to
an exaggerated vertical scale.)

The curves in Figure 49 are very different from those
for Retailing as a whole (Figure 73), and yet the large stores
play so important a part that they strongly affect the more

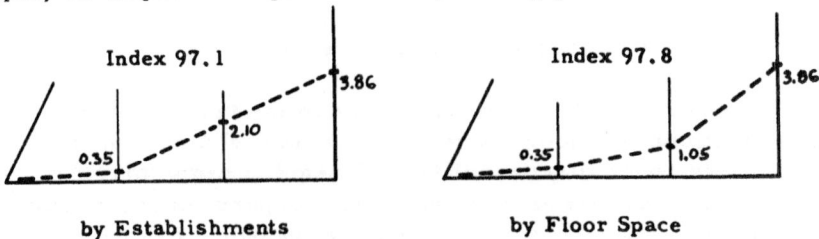

by Establishments                    by Floor Space

Figure 49.    INDEX CURVES FOR A GROUP OF
                       DEPARTMENT STORES

general distribution, as will be discussed shortly. The floor-
space distribution is the more concentrated here and would
be so in any retailing (or other) group where there are very
large establishments. These curves would have the same
appearance (indicating the same general relationship between the two distributions) if they were plotted against a
compact retail shopping center of, say, 30 blocks instead
of the 285 blocks used throughout this study. The indexes
of concentration would then become 72.3 and 80.0 instead
of the 97.1 and 97.8 shown in Figure 49. The distribution
of all retailing in so central a group of blocks would result
in a full curve, for there would be few, if any, blocks entirely devoid of retail establishments.

Detailed study of local relationships among business
groups will have to be studied on the basis of various kinds
of location and combinations of activities to be found in
them, in areas such as that suggested for Retailing in the
last paragraph. A beginning at analyzing different kinds of
central location was made earlier in this chapter for goods-
handling vs. non-goods areas, and some further suggestions
will occur in the remainder of the chapter. Systematic local
investigations, however, soon get beyond the scope of the
present study, which is limited to the outlining of general
relationships with some incidental pointing of the way to
more detailed studies and with some preparation of the
tools for the job. It is time now to return to the separate
groups as depicted in Figures 69 through 73.

Manufacturing, Figure 69, has a wide spread, its establishment distribution extending in a long rectangle, mostly north of Market and east of Broad, its floor-space distribution in the same general area but more extensive (less
concentrated). The latter distribution, in both years, may
be taken as the general extent of goods-handling activities.
The addition of Wholesaling to this general area would throw
its center somewhat to the east, but this would not greatly
modify the picture as it relates to the other kind-of-business
concentrations.

These brief sketches of the separate groups, their
characteristics and general locations in terms of their distributions by numbers and by floor areas, will serve as introduction to a more detailed study of locational relationships
than was given in the rough general picture in the first part

of this chapter, made up as it was from grosser data (i. e.,
combined cores at the median level for the five kinds of
business). In the next section this introduction will be
carried one step further by studying the occurrences together of the different kinds of business as seen in combinations of their one-third and two-thirds concentration groups.

Wholesaling, Figure 70, is virtually a group apart, with
its main concentrations occupying about the same area,
whichever way counted and in either year. Its one-third
concentration group by floor space was a more compact
group of blocks in 1949 and so was its corresponding group
counted by establishments, but the latter was largely a string
of blocks along Market below Seventh in 1949, where it had been
a string at right angles to Market in 1934. A closer look at this
area would seem to be in order, to see what changes took place
in the use of space in its buildings. Together with Manufacturing, the buildings used by much of the Wholesaling group
are old and have experienced a long succession of tenants.

Business Services, Figure 71, are more concentrated
by establishment count, virtually the reverse of the situation for Retailing. In fact, these two are the groups having
the greatest variation between the two kinds of distribution, a variation that is consistent for both years. On either
count, the grouping of the most concentrated blocks for
Business Services were more compact in 1949 than in 1934,
especially in the central concentration near Broad and
Market Streets. Whether counted by number of establishments or by floor space, Business Services crowd close
here, a good match for the most concentrated blocks for all
kinds of business (see first pair of maps in Figures 67 and 68).

Consumer Services, Figure 72, have also become more
concentrated in the same area, City Hall to Rittenhouse
Square. The combination of these groups here has already
been noted under "Characteristic Local Groupings" earlier
in this chapter, where it is illustrated by the overlapping of
the combined cores for each group in Figures 36 and 78.
In the earlier illustration, however, it was not possible to
analyze the combination in terms of the relative sizes of
establishments.[7]

---

[7] The combined cores already discussed, Figures 33 and A-75, are made by
superimposing the two median concentration groups (by establishment count
and by floor space) in Figures 69 through 73.

There was a considerable increase in concentration for
this entire group by establishment count from 1934 to 1949,
in fact, the greatest change of index for any group. This indicates a strong increase in number of establishments in
the more concentrated areas as compared with the increase
in space, which appears to be more scattered, since the
blocks in the one-third group by floor space count have
shifted away from this central location. The change in concentration on this count is slight. In other words, many
small establishments in the Consumer Service group were
flourishing in this area in 1949.

Retailing, Figure 73, is much more concentrated by
floor space count, with one-third of all space contained in
a mere handful of blocks (6 in 1934, 8 in 1949). These most-
concentrated blocks are the same ones in which the large
department stores are located. Rarely are they found in
the corresponding concentration group by establishment
count, which spreads over a much wider area. (There are
22 blocks in the one-third group by establishments in both
years as against the 6 or 8 in the floor-space concentration.)
There was little change in the index of concentration for
retailing from 1934 to 1949.

Gross changes are most readily seen in the median concentration group. The most noticeable change here is a
shifting to the west, mostly as a filling in of floor-space
blocks between City Hall and Rittenhouse Square. Reference
to the maps of concentration groups by thirds will show that
this area is in the first third by number of establishments
but in the second third by floor space. In other words, this
is an area of many small establishments. This area is also
adjacent to a large near-central residential area and a great
many of the small establishments here are quartered in
remodeled dwellings.

### TYPES OF ACTIVITY RELATIONSHIPS
### AND THEIR LOCATIONS

Since the use of space by different activities is reflected in patterns of establishments on the map, these patterns can be followed in turn for tracking down relationships
among the activities themselves. Just how far the relationships can be read from the map patterns is an undetermined

question. It will require further investigation to demonstrate how fully the vital relationships among activities do
relate to the proximity measures which have been used as
the basis of this inquiry. In any case, the measures already
dealt with have proved to be useful guides for outlining the
problem, and so their further refinement may still be trusted
for elaborating the outline in more detail without getting too
far away from reality.

The graphic data for this section consist in the superimposed concentration groups at one-third and two-thirds
levels for the five kinds of business, as mapped in Figures
50 (for 1934) and 51 (for 1949). Two maps are given for each
year: A) by establishment count and B) by floor-space count.
These maps are much like the superimposed groups of Figures 34 and 76, which were the subject of the first part of
this chapter, but those earlier maps and diagrams, and
the derived tables of combinations and schematic relationships, were simpler and cruder, derived as they were from
combined cores at the median level. In Figures 50 and 51
the one-third and two-thirds concentration groups are in-
indicated separately by symbols consisting of single and
double lines, and on each map the two-thirds concentration
group for all kinds of business is also indicated to serve as
a reference core. Thus, each of the four maps in Figures
50 and 51 contains data taken from six—the corresponding
maps in Figures 67 through 73. In sum, material shown
previously in twenty-four maps is recapitulated in four,
each showing distributions by one kind of count for one
year.

These maps can be used for deriving a great many
different statements about the separate groups, their
characteristics and relationships with the entire aggregation and with each other. The formal ringing out of all the
changes would be burdensome (and dull) and not, in itself,
very informing. These data are but the bare bones of the
activities which we seek to understand, but they do provide
a factual basis for testing hypotheses about the utilization
of urban land and improvements by different kinds of activities, as represented by our five kind-of-business groups.

In each of the maps in Figures 50 and 51, blocks comprising the one-third concentration group (the most concentrated blocks) are indicated by double lines, while the

additional blocks which make up the two-thirds group (medium concentration) are indicated by single lines. In the
discussion which follows, these two groups of blocks at
successive levels of concentration will be called "first third"
and "second third." Both together make up the two-thirds
concentration group.[8]

The full range of combinations among pairs of groups
(at two levels of concentration) is examined in Appendix B.
The tabular diagrams in this appendix, all derived from the
maps in Figures 45 and 46, provide measures of relationships between the various groups at different levels of concentration. This appendix serves as background for the discussion in the remainder of this chapter, but the materials
in it are not used directly in that discussion, which is referred to the maps in Appendix A. The following example
will demonstrate the possibilities inherent in taking account of combinations at different levels.

Consider Retailing in connection with both goods-handling and non-goods combinations of activities; the first is
exemplified by occurrences together of both Manufacturing
and Wholesaling, the latter by the services. These combinations are displayed in Figures 52 (for 1934) and 53 (for
1949), by establishment count and by floor-space count, all
abstracted from Figures 50 and 51.

The general locations of the major goods-handling combination (the left-hand maps in Figures 52A and 53A) were
much the same in both years and by both counts. However,
the relationship between the members appears closer in
1949, with a more extensive and coherent group of blocks
in which a first-third concentration of Wholesaling or Manufacturing, or of both, was represented. (These more concentrated blocks are indicated in black; blocks in which both
groups are represented by second-third concentrations are
lightly hatched.) For studying the conformation of the separate groups, the most convenient reference is the set of
maps in Appendix A, Figures 69 through 73.

The blocks, for each sort of combination, where Retailing also occurs are shown in the right-hand maps, Figures 52A and 53A, lightly hatched for blocks in which the

[8] See also Figure 18 in Chapter VII and Appendix A, Figures 67 through 73,
where the two levels of concentrations are designated by shading.

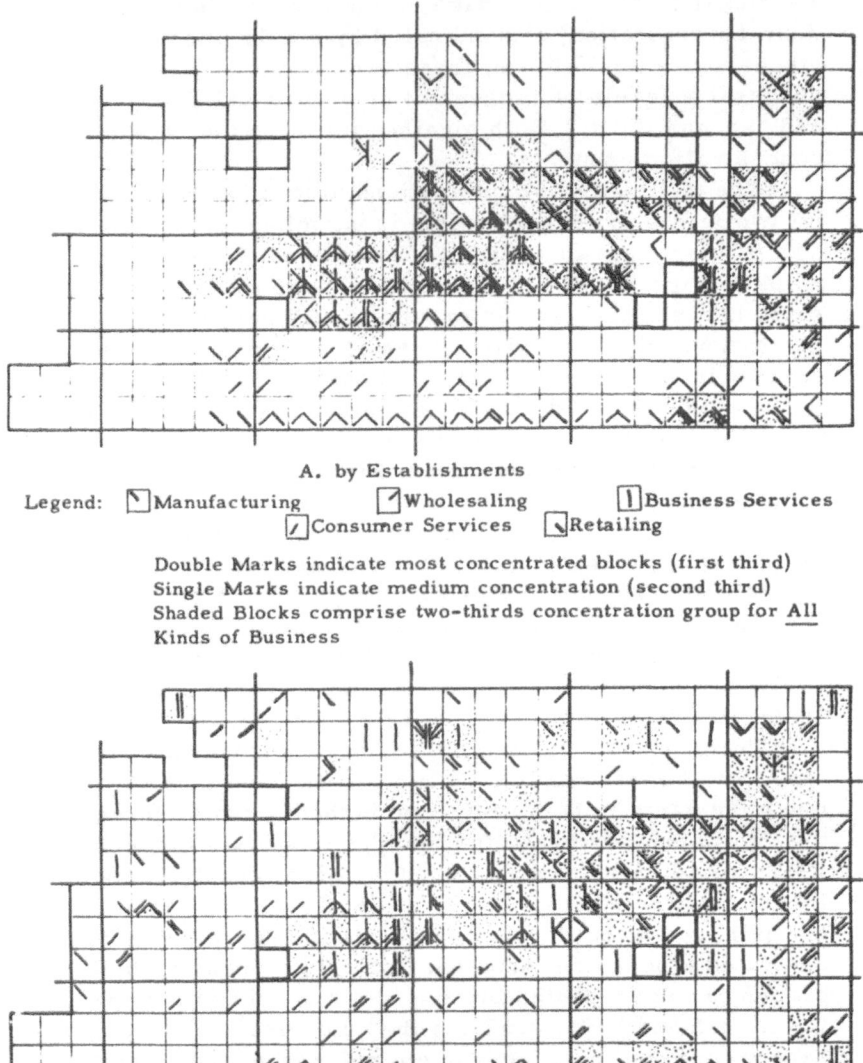

A. by Establishments

Legend:    Manufacturing       Wholesaling       Business Services
               Consumer Services    Retailing

Double Marks indicate most concentrated blocks (first third)
Single Marks indicate medium concentration (second third)
Shaded Blocks comprise two-thirds concentration group for All
Kinds of Business

B. by Floor Space

Figure 50.    FIVE MAJOR BUSINESS GROUPS SU-
PERIMPOSED, 1934 (CONCENTRATION
GROUPS BY THIRDS)

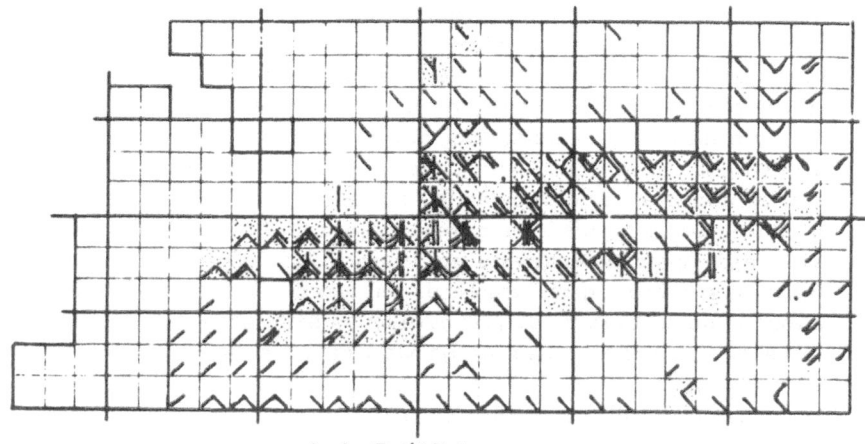

A. by Establishments

Legend: ◥Manufacturing　◥Wholesaling　⬜Business Services
◺Consumer Services　◺Retailing

Double Marks indicate most concentrated blocks (first third)
Single Marks indicate medium concentration (second third)
Shaded Blocks comprise two-thirds concentration group for All
Kinds of Business

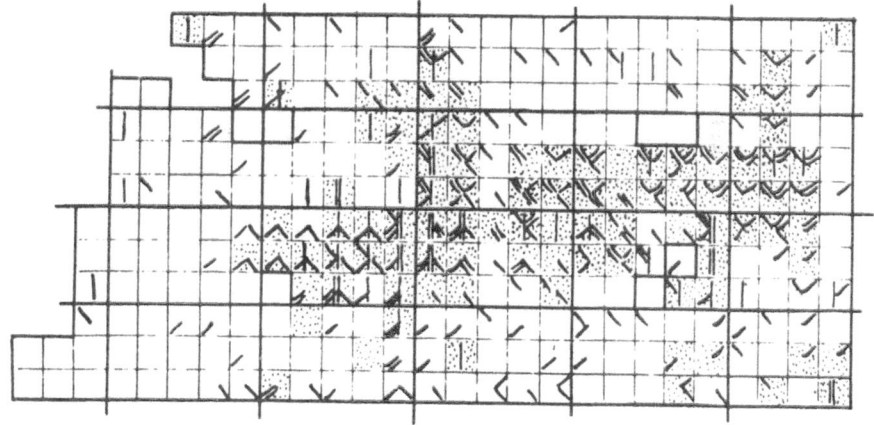

B. by Floor Space

Figure 51.　FIVE MAJOR BUSINESS GROUPS SU-
PERIMPOSED, 1949 (CONCENTRATION
GROUPS BY THIRDS)

second-third concentration is represented, solid black for
the first-third. These blocks are predominantly in the second-third, more so in 1934 than in 1949 and especially by
floor-space count. This is to say that Retailing, where it
occurs together with Manufacturing and Wholesaling, tends
to be a secondary activity. The blocks where Retailing is a
major partner in the combination (e.g., the five "solid" Retailing blocks in the establishment group for 1949, Figure
53A) may well be examined further to see whether the activities are indeed compatible—whether some goods-handling
should not be removed from these locations, in the interest
of better traffic conditions. It will be recalled that a major
junction of the transit system is located here—at Eighth and
Market Streets. Some conflict in persons-movement and
goods-movement is of course inevitable, especially in central manufacturing districts where large numbers of workers
are employed. The conflict is enhanced, however, by a
strong tendency for small manufacturing or wholesaling
firms to take over space in older buildings vacated by business firms which have moved to more up-to-date quarters.
When the goods involved are not bulky. little conflict results. No immediate conclusion can be drawn from the situation noted by these maps. Rather it seems to point the way
to more thorough local investigation.

The general locations of the major non-goods combinations (see left-hand maps, Figures 52B and 53B) were also
much the same in both years, although the combinations by
floor-space count were somewhat sparser and more scattered in 1934, and the combinations by establishment count
in 1934 were considerably more extensive.[9] In both years,
half of the floor-space combinations are low concentration,
i.e., have no first-third blocks. In the establishment combinations, however, few blocks are low concentration in
either year.

The blocks, for each sort of combination, where Retailing also occurs are shown in the right-hand maps, Figures
52B and 53B. These blocks are predominantly in the second-third by floor-space count but in the first-third by establishment count. This is to say that in blocks where Re-

---

[9] The map designations are as described above for the goods-handling combinations, Figures 52B and 53B.

tailing is combined with the services it is in a secondary
position in terms of floor space, but, when the count is by
number of establishments, then Retailing takes a strong
position in the combination. It is to be remembered, also,
that Retailing is strong throughout this entire area south
of Market Street on both sides of Broad, in blocks other
than these characterized by combinations of the services
with which we have been dealing.

The above discussion of Retailing as a secondary group
has covered a wide area. In the process some aspects of
the more generalized statements summarized in Figure 45
have been elaborated, especially as regards detailed locations. Further study of Retailing would also investigate its
role as a dominant activity. This would begin with the first-
third concentration group (Figure 73) and continue with the
combinations found in these and adjacent blocks, studying
also the establishments themselves and their linkages.

Any number of other investigations could be organized
around these data. No detailed conclusions can be drawn,
however, without looking further into the relationships
among activities at each location, the buildings in which
they are found, and their immediate surroundings, together
with the historic geography of the entire central district.
The general statements of locational relationships among
activities, made in earlier sections of this chapter, appear
to be confirmed by the more elaborate material in Figures
50 and 51. Relationships between each kind of business
and the aggregation of all kinds may also be read from these
maps. These, together with some general characteristics
applying to the various groups, are as follows:

Single blocks, since they are found within the two-thirds
concentration group for only a single kind of business, are
dominated by this business. When "heavy" enough, these
blocks command a position in the aggregate core. Single
blocks in the core, then, represent a large number of establishments per block (most likely small establishments)
or a large amount of floor space per block (with probably
only a few establishments).

Occasionally the same single block appears in both
establishment and floor-space concentrations, indicating
both a large number of establishments and much floor area
in use. Such a block is H-11 in the 1934 distribution (Figure

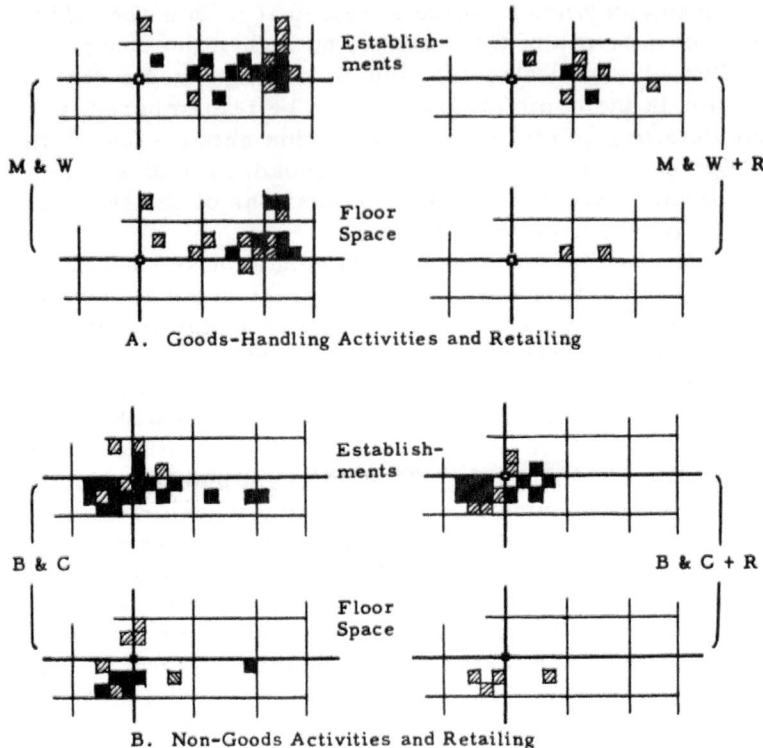

A. Goods-Handling Activities and Retailing

B. Non-Goods Activities and Retailing

Note: Blocks in major combinations (diagrams at left) are shaded where both
      activities are represented by medium concentrations and solid black
      where high concentrations occur in either or both activities.

      Blocks which also contain Retailing are shown at the right: solid for
      high concentration of Retailing and shaded for medium concentrations.

Figure 52.    COMBINATIONS WITH RETAILING, 1934

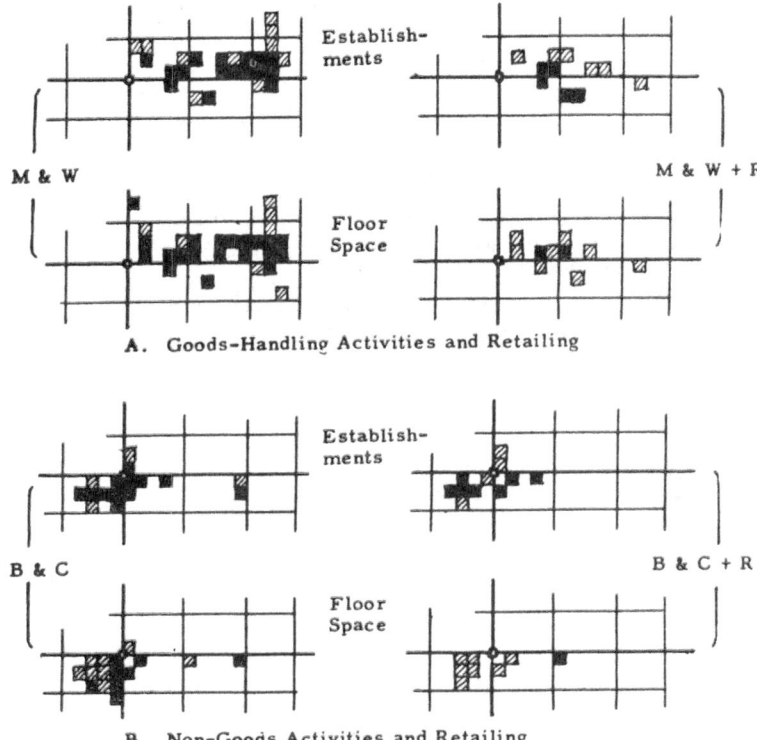

A. Goods-Handling Activities and Retailing

B. Non-Goods Activities and Retailing

Note: Blocks in major combinations (diagrams at left) are shaded where both activities are represented by medium concentrations and solid black where high concentrations occur in either or both activities.

Blocks which also contain Retailing are shown at the right: solid for high concentration of Retailing and shaded for medium concentrations.

Figure 53.    COMBINATIONS WITH RETAILING, 1949

50) in the first third for Manufacturing on both counts. The same block in 1949 (Figure 51) is still in the first third for Manufacturing and in the core, but it is "single" only by floor-space count; in terms of establishments it is now combined with Retailing. Single blocks outside of the core are also dominated by one kind of business but have not enough establishments or floor space to be included in the two-thirds concentration group for all kinds of business.

Combined blocks fall within the two-thirds concentration group for two or more kinds of business and apparently possess locational characteristics desirable for all of them. It may well be that these different kinds of business occurring in the same block have linkages with each other.

Combined blocks are more often in the core than not, but whether in or out they point to locations important to each of the constituent business groups. The degree of importance in each case and the nature of individual relationships are matters of considerable variety, however, since there are many sorts of combination.

### Factors in Locational Relationships

What do closely related groups of establishments have in common? How is it that beside the outstanding groupings that have been noted there are confusing mixtures of activities in almost every location?

Most important, of course, are linkages, which tend to pull closely related establishments into proximate locations. Sometimes a natural resource dominates whole groups of activities, as the port with its piers and warehouses and ships chandlers, and the nearby custom house with its closely linked groups of forwarders and insurance brokers and related offices. In this case the linked activities are said to be anchored to the waterfront or the custom house. A similar situation is the grouping of law offices around the courts or the banking and brokerage firms around the stock exchange. In these cases the dominant institution is relatively permanent, but when it does move, whole groups of linked establishments move with it.[10]

[10] Strictly speaking, the establishments themselves as defined in this study and in Mitchell and Rapkin, Urban Traffic (New York, 1954), do not themselves move; new ones are set up in the new locations.

Whole groups of closely linked establishments make up the overlapping centers or districts which each city dweller recognizes—the main centers of business activity, the main shopping district, the luxury shops, the various kinds of wholesale districts (foods, metals, furnishings), the garment center where both wholesaling and manufacturing are merged, and many more. All of these centers or districts are relatively free to shift, but the decision of each firm to change its location is largely conditioned by the strong network of linkages which holds "the trade" together.

In addition to linkages, the outstanding factors of location have to do with the interrelated external functioning of the individual establishments. Foremost is the need for movement, either of persons or of goods. Whole systems of movement have resulted from this need—mass transit by railroad, subway, trolley, and bus, trips by private automobile with their attendant problems of parking, systems of freight movement by rail or truck, and many subsystems within these, all related to the activities of different kinds of establishments.

The facilities for movement, especially those required by mass transit and freight handling, are themselves costly and relatively permanent, so that they tend to further fix the activities served.

In central Philadelphia, as in all large cities, the greatest concentration of buildings and of daytime population is in the area best served by mass transit, while heavy manufacturing and warehousing are concentrated along rail lines. The broadest subdivision of central activities—by goods-handling vs. persons-assembling—has been treated at considerable length. Factors which apply to both kinds of activities will help explain the many overlaps. Both kinds require frontage—show window space for retail stores and even for banks, direct access to elevator lobbies in office buildings, and either frontage or off-street trucking platforms for delivery of goods.

The structures in the central city, which reached their present form by 1900, have not yet been adjusted to the age of the automobile. Heavy goods-handling in a persons-assembling area is the cause of much congestion in street traffic; the general use of private automobiles for trips to the center is another. As both kinds of traffic are increasing,

the most stringent measures of control will soon have to be
taken in order to keep the city functioning effectively.

Low-rent space is usually second-hand space. In an
old city like Philadelphia it is provided at many locations—
some vacated by establishments which have ceased to exist,
others by firms which have removed their activities to more
up-to-date buildings or to more generous quarters or more
agreeable surroundings (or to more than one of these, as,
for example, when the offices of a firm are shifted to the
main business center and the goods-handling functions are
moved out to a more spacious location which is also more
convenient for shipping). As a rule, only establishments
which have reached a certain size and stability can afford to
put very much distance between themselves and others to
which they are linked. When the goods- and persons-as-
pects of a firm's operations are set up in separate establishments, then each can be located to advantage with, for
example, a small sales or executive office in a high-rent
central location near to linked establishments and with the
production functions (bookkeeping, files, processing of
goods, and the like) located in low-cost space which has
suitable facilities for operations, including a suitable labor
market. Older central locations, those that have seen better
days, still enjoy the advantages of good transportation and
ample public services plus reasonable rent. Since available locations are widely scattered, it is no wonder that the
land uses are extremely mixed.

## Successions of Activities

The city's physical structures are relatively permanent,
while its activities are continually shifting. In the process,
some business groups remain relatively fixed, but new
establishments are always being formed and older ones
dissolved. The character of each location and the condition
in which it is maintained will depend as much on the activities carried on there as on the original character of its
buildings. Even groups of firms that remain anchored to one
place may find that their surroundings change as some of
their neighbors go elsewhere and other activities move in.
Many a slum was once a fine residential neighborhood, and
many a commercial area that once was flourishing and high

in prestige is now blighted and decaying. At the same time
there are old neighborhoods that have been kept up and that
have enjoyed a more durable prestige than the new centers
that replaced the old. The vicinity of Independence Square,
for instance, has kept its fine character. This remains
chiefly an insurance center, and its solid stone buildings
seem in keeping with the conservative nature of their tenants.
And yet similar and contemporary buildings near City Hall
are no longer fully acceptable as symbols of their tenants'
business activities; several have recently undergone "face
liftings"—the massive masonry of the lower stories being
replaced with the flat, open look of metal and glass. Fashion
in buildings must be added to the factors of location—mainly
as an active stimulant that starts the string of moves that is
followed all along the line in other buildings and other locations. Beside providing the most up-to-date space, the
"modern" building stands as a symbol of progress. The
duration of its prestige may have no relationship to its first
evaluation.

It would be interesting to examine the durability of
successive symbols represented by the buildings of the
central district from colonial days onward. Such a time
sequence of historic fashions would, in the locations of
representative buildings, follow the growth of the town and
city as the built-up residential areas expanded westward
from the original nucleus along Dock Creek and the Delaware, followed by heavier, commercial structures. Examples from every period remain in use. With few exceptions
there has been a long succession of different uses in each
building, but in the blocks nearest the waterfront there are
whole rows of commercial structures still serving the functions for which they were built in the 1830's or 1840's. As
the entire city expanded, its base remained fixed on the
Delaware and the central functions performed by the town
of Penn's day were dispersed outward, scattering among
the residential areas, most of which converted in time to
commercial areas in the styles of successively later days
—a process that still continues.

The earlier expansion was, of course, tied to the earlier
transportation facilities. The first railroads ran on the
streets; it was only in the 1880's that the tracks were removed from Market Street. The Broad Street station was

"way up town" in 1891 when it was opened, and despite the
continued spread of central activities, with the "Old City"
given over largely to Wholesaling and Manufacturing, the
centers of gravity of Retailing or of the Services are still
east of Broad Street (Figures 69 through 73).

## SUMMARY

In this chapter a rich empirical basis for studying locational relationships among business groups has been elaborated on the groundwork of the preceding chapters by working with the block-by-block data for both establishments and
floor space in 1934 and 1949, and by also taking into account
the conceptual discussions in earlier chapters. Groupings
of activities have been examined here on a local basis, pay-
ing attention to the relatively fixed influences of the sites
themselves and their historic development in streets and
structures and especially in facilities for transportation.

Primary attention has been paid to patterns of business
groups on the map and the slowly shifting centers, consisting of different kinds and combinations of business activities,
as they have developed in the varied structures of central
Philadelphia. The rather abstract map diagrams which express the basic data have been interpreted by even more
abstract symbolic diagrams, like those developed schematically in Chapter X. These diagrams of relationship have
now been enhanced by the added dimension of relative size
of groups involved in each location.

The exploration has been carried far enough to test
the usefulness of our methods of analysis and to demonstrate the need for a more detailed functional analysis of those
operating relationships among urban activities which under-
lie the map patterns studied here. A final chapter will ex-
plore some of the possibilities that seem to be open for
making better use of the advantages inherent in urban concentrations—by expediting and, where necessary, controlling
the long processes of adjustment between needs and resources that have made the present cities what they are.

# XII
## PLANNED ARRANGEMENT
## OF URBAN LAND USES

SPACE in urban centers is used intensively by continually changing groups of activities, some quite stable, some shifting rather freely in their interrelationships and locations. The physical city, with its unique advantages of site and prior development, is slow to change, although fractional adjustments do occur all the while in response to the demands of the more vital activities. These physical changes take shape primarily in new construction, leaving a trail of consequences in the older buildings from which some of the more volatile activities have shifted. Inevitably, then, groups of linked establishments share locations with unrelated groups that require the same advantages—for example, convenient transportation or suitable space at economic rent or access to footloose crowds of pedestrians. Mixtures of related and unrelated activities become particularly complex in older centers where so many vestiges remain from earlier clusters of activities and where lowered rents in older buildings make these locations attractive for new small-scale enterprises.

The above paragraph repeats, in essence, the approach to study of urban arrangement which was stated at the beginning of Chapter I. This approach has been developed in broad outline throughout the present study, with considerable confirmation from the Philadelphia central business district, where spatial arrangements of major business groups were examined in some detail. While some degree of order is to be seen in these patterns of activities and their accommodations, the situation as a whole is very confused, with many evident inefficiencies and conflicts. Surely it must be possible to arrange things better!

But the land-use arrangement in any urban center, or in any considerable part of it, is a very complex affair. Deliberate solution of the inherent problems would have to take account of the requirements, internal and external, collaborating or conflicting, of all the activities to be accommodated. In order to minimize interference and in-

efficiency in any given area it would be necessary to choose
between activities permitted and activities excluded. It is
doubtful whether present knowledge of urban establishments
and their linkages and the systems within which they operate
is adequate for making this choice. There is so much that
we need to know about the operation of the whole fabric of
urban living—how the various groupings (of commerical and
industrial establishments and social institutions and the
population itself, by place of residence and place of employment) are now arranged in space and how they are tending
further to concentrate or to disperse.

The present study has shown what kinds of activities
do go together under "natural" conditions in one large urban center. With this as a background it is now possible
to at least specify some of the problems inherent in putting
suitable combinations together and to point out some paths
toward solution of the more general problems of urban arrangement in changing situations.

## DYNAMICS OF URBAN ARRANGEMENT

Patterns of activities as they exist in central Philadelphia, also the similar patterns found in any urban center, have been determined by reciprocal relationships between urban land uses (spatial arrangements of establishments among buildings on the map) and certain conjugates
of these land uses (things which result from and make possible their spatial differentiation) such as the following:

Transportation facilities between establishments, both
for persons and for goods: all means of transport including
the streets themselves and all factors of cost, in money and
time.

Communication facilities, mail or wire, which make
possible the separation of specialized functions (selling by
mail or from samples, for example, with delivery from
warehouse or from manufacturer.)

Preconditions or history of the city, its economic geography (physical and economic assets relative to the region
and to other cities) and culture factors (development of various centers of the professions or the arts, education or
finance, and different levels of income and social prestige.)

Other land uses which make locations desirable or undesirable for any given activity: groupings of establishments tending to comprise a common market or industry and groupings which tend not to associate. Rent, that major determinant of location, is itself largely determined by the land uses in each vicinity.

Relationships between land uses and each of the above items are subject to certain pressures and limitations. Among these are: increase or decline in production due to competition, changes in style, business cycles, or technological developments, legal or economic commitments, or trade agreements; scarcity of appropriate accommodations and even lack of understanding of the nature of changes taking place which should govern the decisions made by each firm. A prime factor, always, is timing, as it may affect the degree of development or stability reached by a firm or a productive process.

The scheme of relationships outlined here was set up for studying the internal workings of the central district as a whole, but it may be applied equally to minor centers or to the continuing adjustments that occur between central and outlying concentrations. In fact, the central business district itself functions as it does only becuse of working relationships with its satellites, both the day-to-day linkages between establishments and also the gradual reallocation of activities among the centers themselves. In the course of this latter process (wherein each activity seeks its optimum location) we begin to see the future shape of metropolitan concentrations in terms of both physical structures and institutional arrangements. As activities are regrouped, the minor centers may be strengthened or they may decay while new centers are also formed, all in response to the need for effectively located commercial or industrial space. In any case, there are efficiencies inherent in concentrations as such; weak concentrations are likely to wither away as new strong groupings are formed. The future shape of urban patterns will continue to be dominated by centers, most of all by the central business district itself.

## SELF-ARRANGING LAND USES

Current patterns of land use reflect both continuance and reorganization on the part of the underlying activities;

they reflect the adjustments to changing requirements that
are worked out separately by business, government, or social groups, each in response to its own set of interests and
limitations. In the course of this process of adjustment, the
existing patterns (both of activities and of their physical accommodations) act as moulds into which new establishments
must fit or as moulds to be broken or abandoned by expanding activities having new sets of requirements. Behind these
physical patterns the symbols attached to certain locations
or groups of establishments or buildings are also important.
They too are moulds for conformance, to be abandoned, however, when the need is strong enough. Independence Square,
for example, is a symbolic location that has kept its prestige value. The up-to-date large buildings occupied by such
solid firms as insurance companies and banks have also remained high in prestige, but the older large buildings on the
square have long been in decline. Here, as in all except
truly blighted or abandoned areas, new establishments are
always ready to move in at cheaper rents as the more pres-
tigeful groups move out, taking over whatever merit remains of the "good address." Smaller buildings on the
square, some dating from the eighteenth century and most
of them replicas of this period are themselves symbols of
prestige, occupied as headquarters by firms who value this
location. Should any considerable proportion of the large
insurance companies withdraw from this area, the rents
commanded by its buildings would drop and the quality of
the area would also drop, unless a strong nucleus of "name"
firms remained to set a standard of quality.

A strong force for continuance of present patterns is
the effort required to make any change in the organization
of a firm's activities. With a new or small enterprise this
may be critical, since a certain size is necessary before
a firm or "branch" can break up into more than one establishment. When a subsidiary establishment is set up,
it follows that it will be located apart. When a firm merely
shifts into a larger space without reorganizing its activities,
it generally finds a location nearby. Thus we find both a
shifting about of activities in the same general location and
a jumping to new locations.

Continual change is the rule, then, with a multitude of
activities milling around among available accommodations,

each establishment endeavoring to strike an economic
balance between the advantages and costs of its own location. Thus, urban activities do arrange themselves, after
a fashion, but with congestion and blight resulting all too
frequently. The big question in the study of land use is how
to arrange activities for the most effective utilization of
urban space by the entire population; how to conserve urban
resources. In line with this major goal are these tactical
questions: To what extent may the process of continuing
adjustment of activities to locations be governed? What
measures of planning control can be applied effectively to
the further changes that will inevitably take place?

It has been observed that considerable automatic
adjustments among urban land uses do take place in response to requirements of the separate activities. However,
the economic and social welfare of the entire community
is not implicit in this self-arranging scheme of things.
Planning of land uses, to be effective, must work the separate interests into a larger scheme with enough flexibility
and scope for unplanned adjustments to keep on occurring.

It is always tempting, when making plans for accom-
modating an intricate complex of activities, to presume that
their organization can be simplified and that they should be
fitted into orderly structures. The extreme mixture of different kinds and sizes of central establishments is most un-
tidy, but "cleaning up" will not necessarily lead to more efficient operations. Forcing old firms into new buildings
might, in fact, force them out of business, for the old buildings in the older parts of a city center have the combined
advantages of accessible location and cheap rent. New buildings can be provided more cheaply in outlying locations, but
the small firms that have very strong central likages find
it better to stay put.

It is also tempting to represent complex relationships
among activities by simple diagrams, often symmetrical.
These may be misleading unless the complex reality which
they are intended to represent is kept in mind continually.
For one thing, diagrams are most readily set down to represent a static situation, while the represented relationships
among land uses are almost invariably dynamic and unsym-
metrical, with both dominant and subordinate elements. Another hazard is that several different diagrams will be

needed for analyzing the activities at any one location. With
care, however, the schematic representation of land uses
and their locations and relationships can be a very useful aid
in analyzing existing situations and even planning for new
ones.

### STUDIES IN UTILIZATION OF URBAN SPACE

It is a major premise of this book that scientific management of a fairly wide range of urban resources is possible but that the factual basis has yet to be established. A
beginning has been made here in describing and measuring
and analyzing the location patterns taken by major business
groups in central Philadelphia—enough to present a scheme
of relationships among activities and some methods for
measuring patterns of land use. Much additional study will
be necessary, however, to flesh out the skeletal location
patterns with measures of the vital activities themselves.

This book, The Core of the City, has presented a general orientation and descriptive analysis of the use of space
by establishments, together with some empirical study of
location patterns among the activities found in central Philadelphia. An earlier publication of the Institute for Urban Land
Use and Housing Studies, Urban Traffic by Robert B. Mitchell and Chester Rapkin, cited frequently in the present
study, was more specifically concerned with the relationship between urban land use and transportation. A more
narrowly focused examination of the actual relationships
among establishments, i.e., a "Study of Linkages", should
also be undertaken for developing measures of the activities
engaged in by each establishment, internal and external, as
they involve the use of space in buildings and the interplay
of locations, both central and dispersed. A first step in such
a study of relationships would be the setting up of an outline for matching linkages of all kinds with the means for
effectuating these linkages. This might take the form of the
outline in Figure 5, page 44, where the needs of establishments are matched against units of space.

Both the present study and the traffic study have been
mainly concerned with the central business district; the
place of the center in relation to the life of the entire city
has been no more than touched upon. Yet a crucial element

in problems of land-use relationships is the choice between central and outlying locations. The suggested linkage study, by tracing active relationships between pairs of establishments, would also point out many threads of relationship among the various centers. A fourth study, focused on the centers themselves, will be suggested below.

Despite the internal shifts that are continually taking place, and despite the changes in balance between the main center and its satellites, the role of the central business district does not appear to have changed basically. In the continuing evolution of urban activities as they arrange themselves in space, some are properly central and some are more suitably located in the looser concentrations of activities that have developed outside. A major finding of the study of establishments made for the Philadelphia Planning Commission in 1949[1] was that goods-handling activities (at least the larger users of space) are moving out, while more and smaller establishments of all kinds continue to flourish in the center, especially those that require the presence of people: business and consumer services and retailing, especially. The close in center has been losing population for some time, of course, and retailing has increased more rapidly in the suburbs, but, despite the outward spread of population and the great increase in outlying industrial and commercial concentrations, the central business district is still a prime factor in the metropolitan scheme of things.

The importance of outlying centers has increased, of course, and comprehension of the role to be played by these newly developing concentrations will require extension of the central type of study to cover in detail the relationships between major and minor centers. This would be a "Study of Urban Nucleations." The outlying centers are themselves becoming differentiated, with the chief ones developing into a new type of urban concentration, related closely to the main center itself. The coming pattern of urbanization appears to be one dominated by a network of strong concentrations tied together by transportation lines, not the gen-

---

[1] Philadelphia Central District Study (Philadelphia, 1950). The objectives of this study are described in the opening paragraphs of our Chapter III.

eral suburban sprawl that was formerly predicted. The freedom to locate at will (brought about by motor transport) is still strongly governed by efficiencies due to nucleation of activities.

Based on the two present and two proposed empirical studies, i.e., The Core of the City and Urban Traffic, "Linkages" and "Nucleations," it would be possible to formulate for urban activities a general "Theory of Locational Arrangement." This final study would examine the relationships of establishments to activity systems and to centers: both the central district as a whole and subcenters, within or outside. Thus might be delineated a reasonably complete picture of urban space as utilized at present and as it might be utilized more effectively in the future. Once equipped with the understanding that studies such as these will give, it will be possible to plan for future changes without running counter to natural tendencies in social and economic development; it will be possible to minimize waste and to include obsolescence in the planned scheme of things. Of course, the city's further evolution will not wait until a full series of studies has provided refined tools for planning and control. Enough has been explored in this study, however, to demonstrate that the key to understanding land uses and to planning for their future development can be provided by analysis of the activities of establishments.

All of the studies discussed here are concerned primarily with material things, but they are by no means indifferent to social and economic and cultural values. Indeed, the satisfactions which people find in city life are the wellsprings that can make our studies fruitful, for only in the belief that a more livable city can be worked out is it worth while to take the broad approach, to attempt the mutual adjustment of different interests, and to reinforce the general welfare by instituting necessary public controls.

APPENDIXES

Appendix A

# DISTRIBUTIONS: ESTABLISHMENTS AND FLOOR SPACE, 1934 and 1949

This appendix is made up entirely of figures and tables which express the distributions of establishments and floor space in 1934 and 1949.

In Figures 54 through 59 are displayed the basic distributions for 1949, block by block, of establishments and floor space for the five different kinds of business and for their aggregation. Figures 60 through 65 cover the same data for 1934. The remaining figures and tables in Appendix A and all diagrammatic maps and tables in the text beginning with Chapter VII are derived from these basic distributions.

Figures 66 through 72 comprise a systematic display of concentration groups for the basic distributions listed above. Six levels are given for the aggregation of all kinds of business in Figures 66 and 67; three levels are given for the different kinds of business in Figures 68 through 72. Parts of this material (for 1949, mainly) have already been presented in the text.

Figure 73 presents simplified distribution curves for the aggregation of all kinds of business by establishments and by floor space for 1934 and 1949.

Figures 74 through 79 and Tables VII through XV present materials for 1934 which are to be compared with similar figures and tables for 1949 already presented in Chapters VIII and IX.

Figures 80 and 81 comprise a full display of the relationships between concentration groups, counted by floor space and by number of establishments, for 1934 and 1949. Three levels of concentration are examined for each kind of business and for their aggregation, after the pattern described in Chapter VIII, "Overlapping of Two Groups," beginning at page 117 and illustrated by Figures 28, 29 and 30. An additional measure of the relationship between establishment count and floor-space count introduced in Figures 80 and 81, that is, the "consistency" of each combination—the ratio between the overlapping blocks (product) and the entire combined group of blocks (sum).

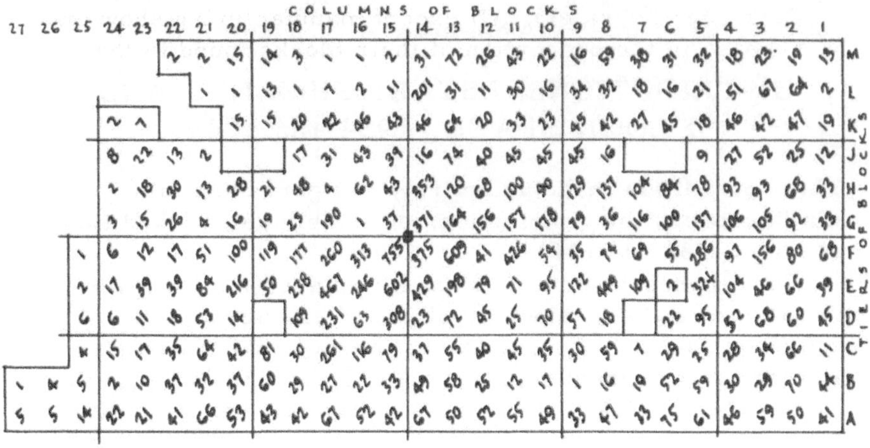

A. Establishments

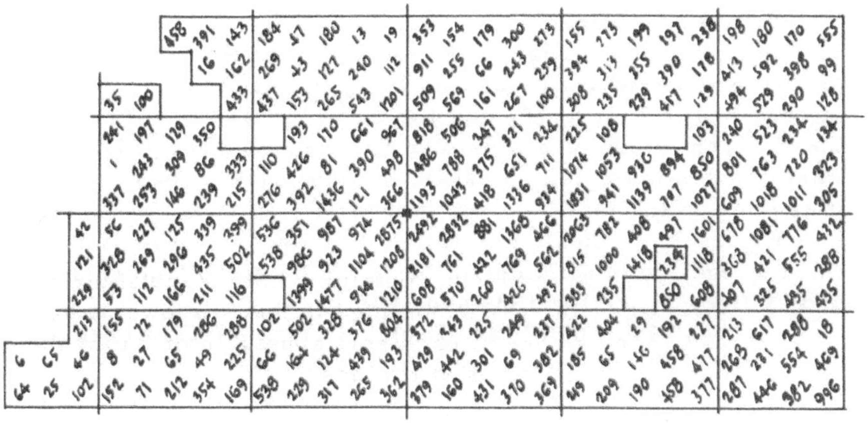

B. Floor Space

Figure 54.　DISTRIBUTION PER BLOCK, ALL KINDS OF BUSINESS BY ESTABLISHMENTS AND FLOOR SPACE, 1949

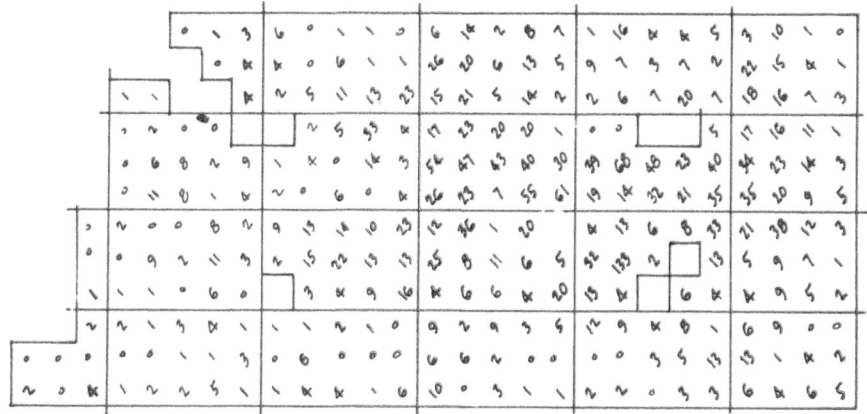

A. Establishments

Note: See Figure 54 for Key to Blocks

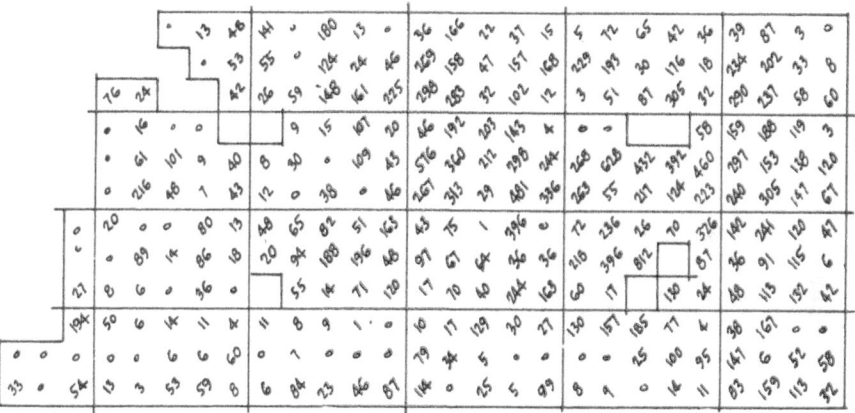

B. Floor Space

Figure 55.   DISTRIBUTION PER BLOCK, MANU-
             FACTURING BY ESTABLISHMENTS
             AND FLOOR SPACE, 1949

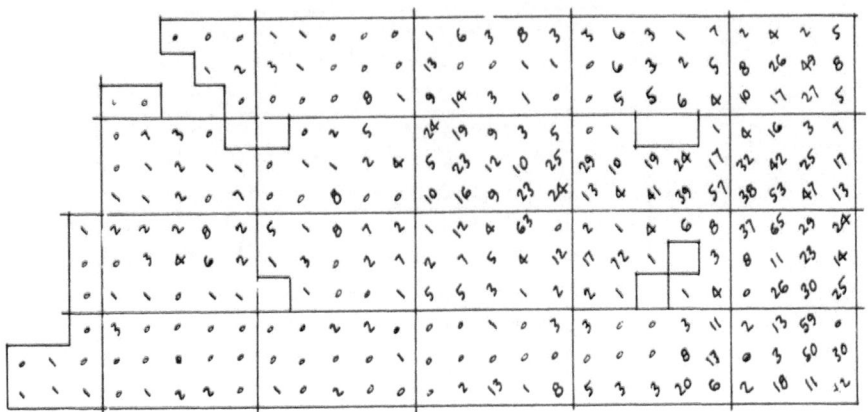

A. Establishments

Note: See Figure 54 for Key to Blocks

B. Floor Space

Figure 56.    DISTRIBUTION PER BLOCK, WHOLE-
              SALING BY ESTABLISHMENTS AND
              FLOOR SPACE, 1949

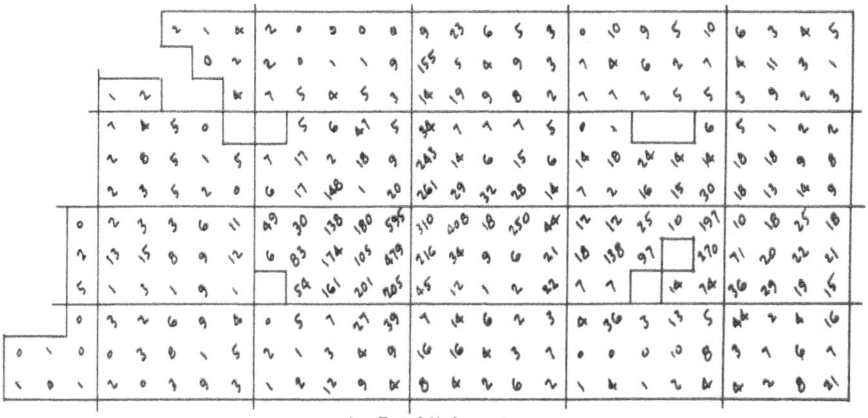

A. Establishments

Note: See Figure 54 for Key to Blocks

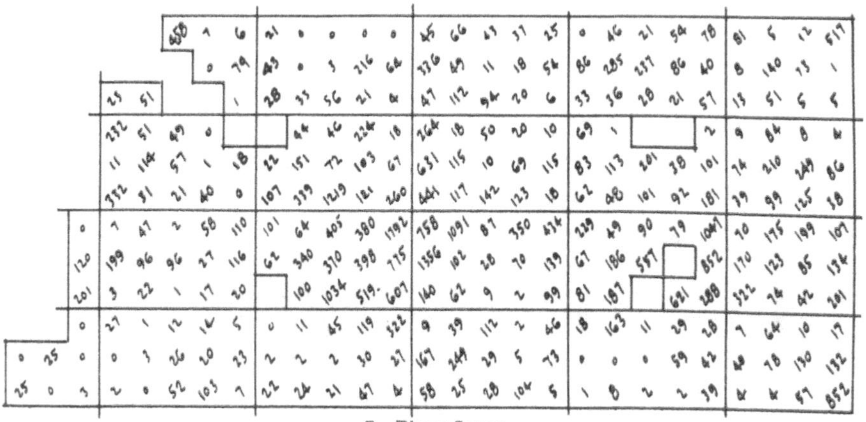

B. Floor Space

Figure 57.   DISTRIBUTION PER BLOCK, BUSI-
NESS SERVICES BY ESTABLISHMENTS
AND FLOOR SPACE, 1949

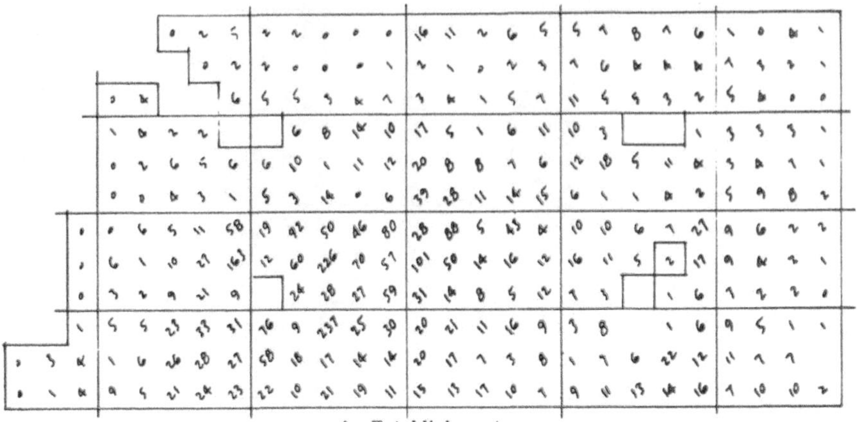

A. Establishments

Note: See Figure 54 for Key to Blocks

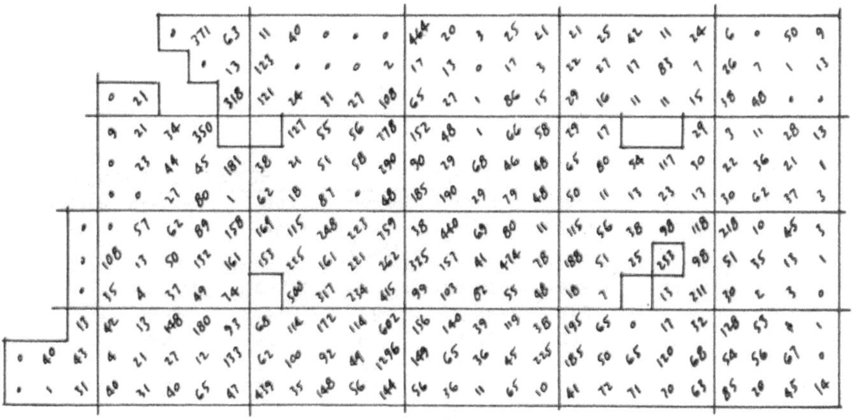

B. Floor Space

Figure 58.    DISTRIBUTION PER BLOCK, CON-
SUMER SERVICES BY ESTABLISH-
MENTS AND FLOOR SPACE, 1949

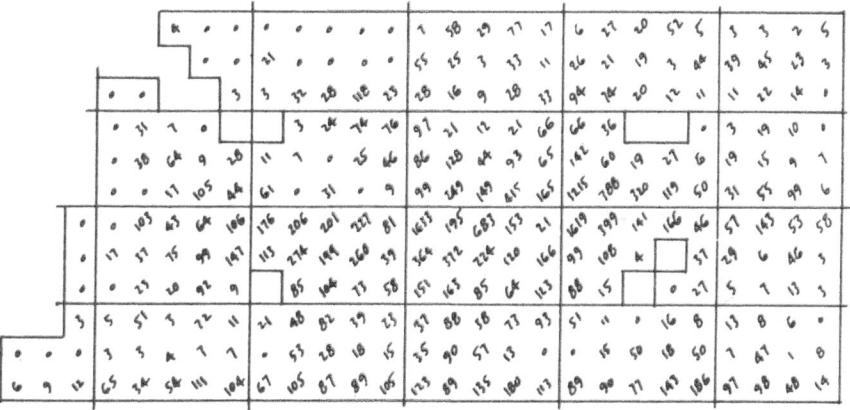

A. Establishments

Note: See Figure 54 for Key to Blocks

B. Floor Space

Figure 59.     DISTRIBUTION PER BLOCK, RETAIL-
ING BY ESTABLISHMENTS AND
FLOOR SPACE, 1949

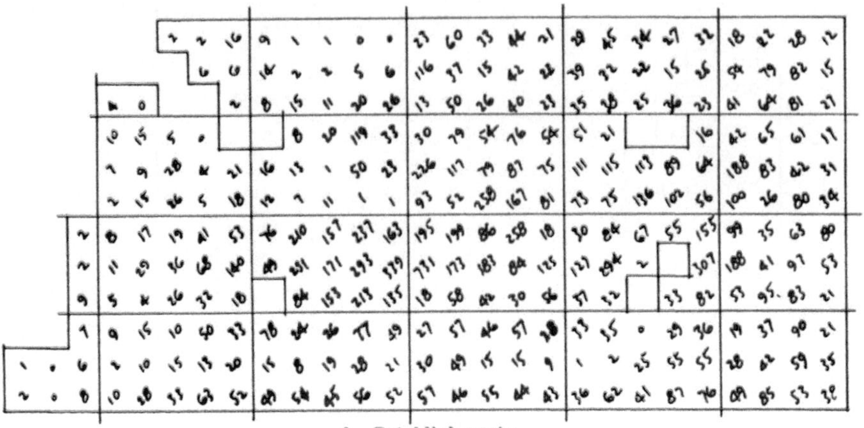

A. Establishments

Note: See Figure 54 for Key to Blocks

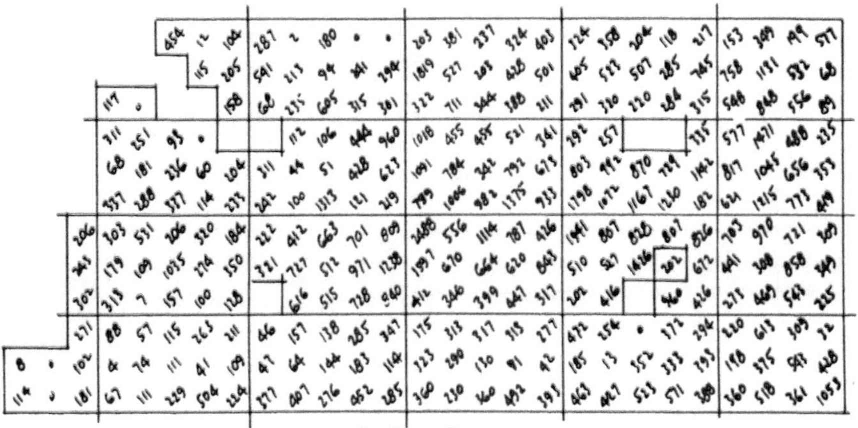

B. Floor Space

Figure 60.    DISTRIBUTION PER BLOCK, ALL
KINDS OF BUSINESS BY ESTABLISH-
MENTS AND FLOOR SPACE, 1934

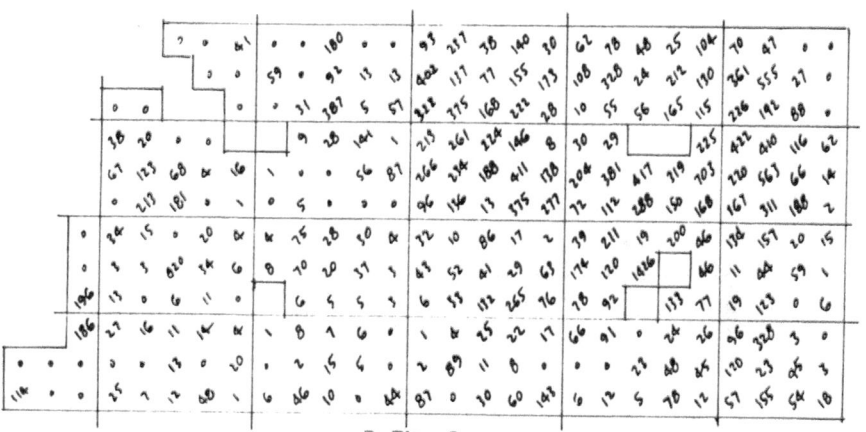

A. Establishments

Note: See Figure 54 for Key to Blocks

B. Floor Space

Figure 61.  DISTRIBUTION PER BLOCK, MANU-
FACTURING BY ESTABLISHMENTS
AND FLOOR SPACE, 1934

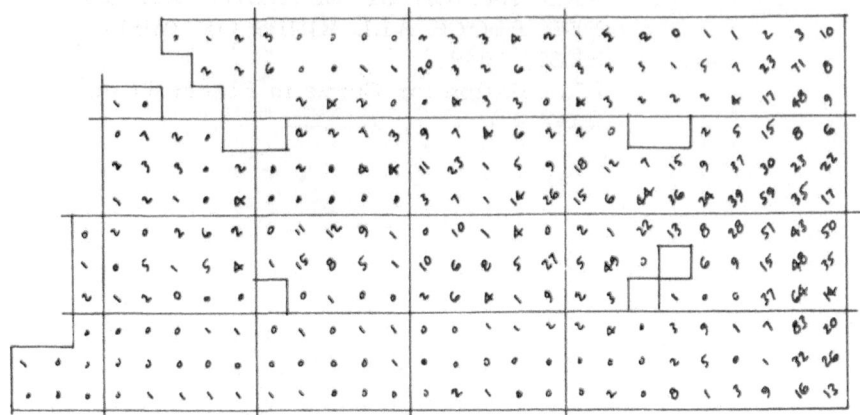

A. Establishments

Note: See Figure 54 for Key to Blocks

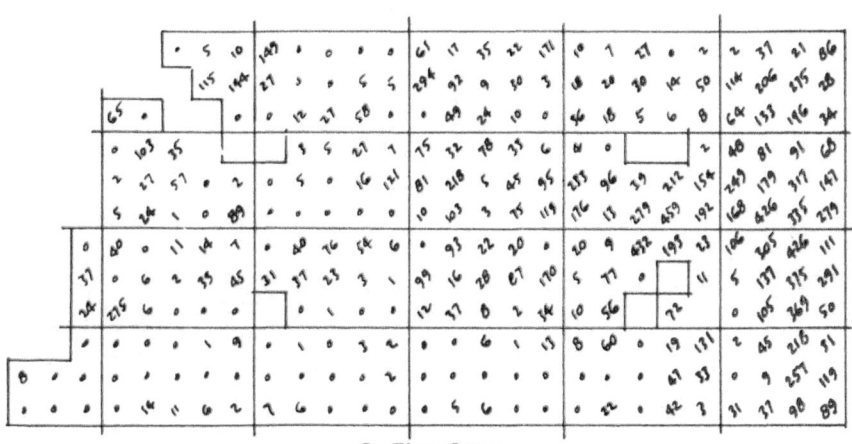

B. Floor Space

Figure 62.    DISTRIBUTION PER BLOCK, WHOLE-
SALING BY ESTABLISHMENTS AND
FLOOR SPACE, 1934

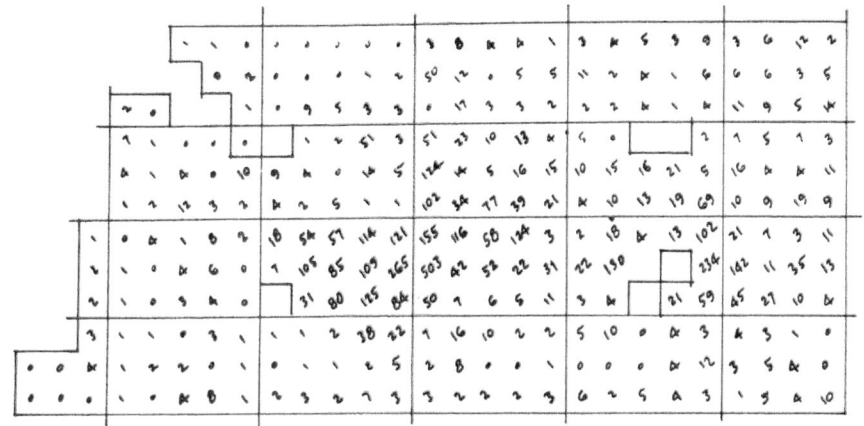

A. Establishments

Note: See Figure 54 for Key to Blocks

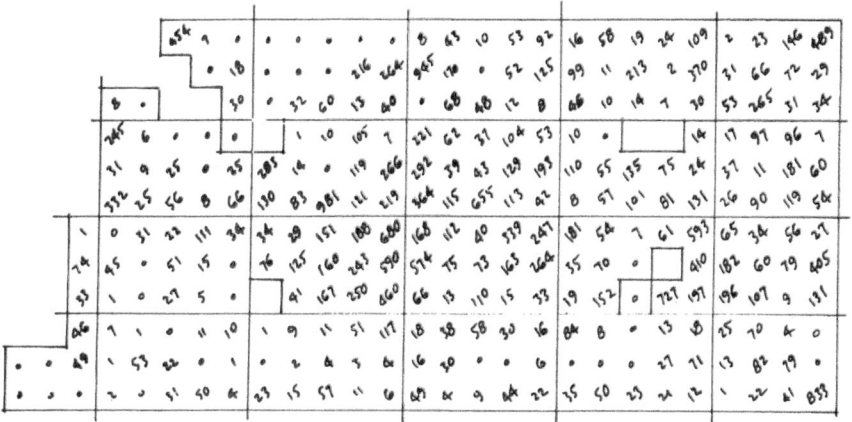

B. Floor Space

Figure 63.    DISTRIBUTION PER BLOCK, BUSI-
              NESS SERVICES BY ESTABLISHMENTS
              AND FLOOR SPACE, 1934

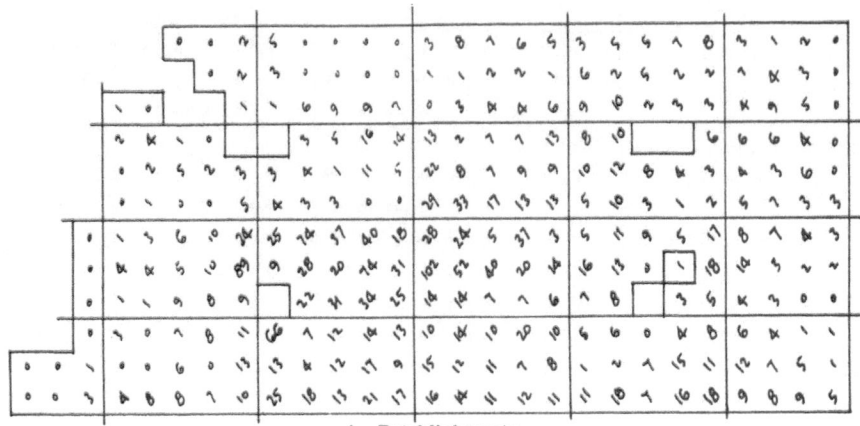

A. Establishments

Note: See Figure 54 for Key to Blocks

B. Floor Space

Figure 64.    DISTRIBUTION PER BLOCK, CON-
             SUMER SERVICES BY ESTABLISH-
             MENTS AND FLOOR SPACE, 1934

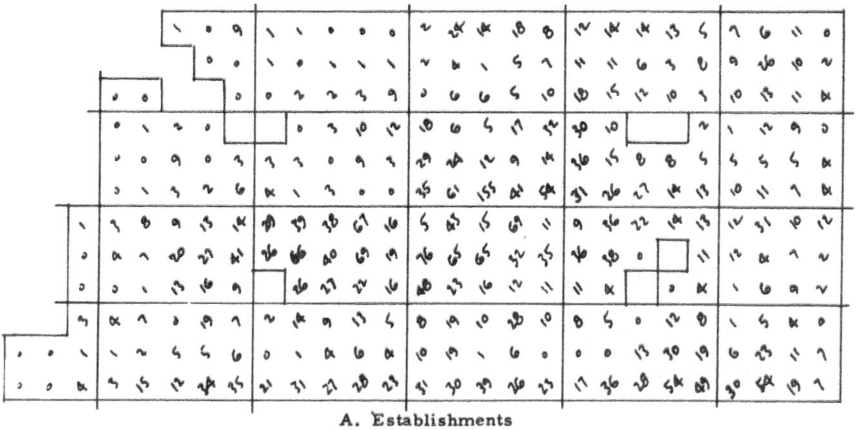

A. Establishments

Note: See Figure 54 for Key to Blocks

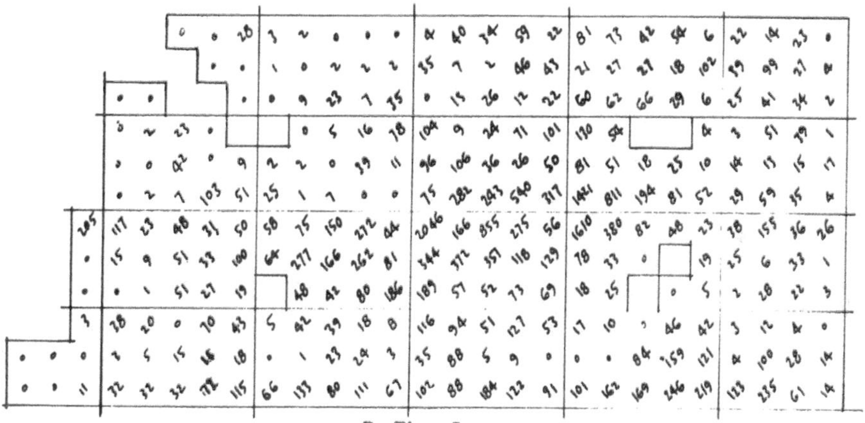

B. Floor Space

Figure 65.   DISTRIBUTION PER BLOCK, RETAIL-
ING BY ESTABLISHMENTS AND
FLOOR SPACE, 1934

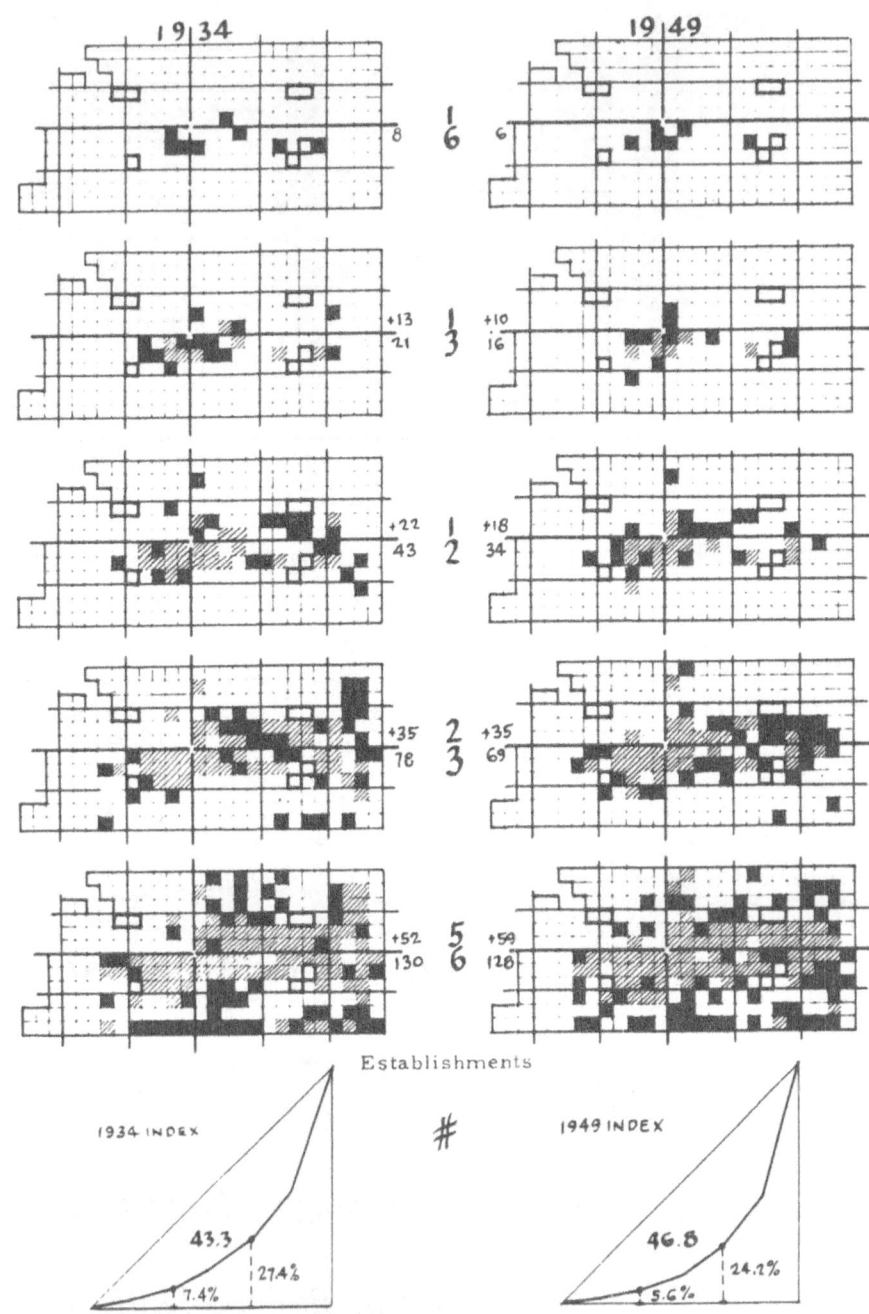

Figure 66.  CONCENTRATION BY SIXTHS, ALL
KINDS OF BUSINESS BY ESTABLISH-
MENTS, 1934 AND 1949

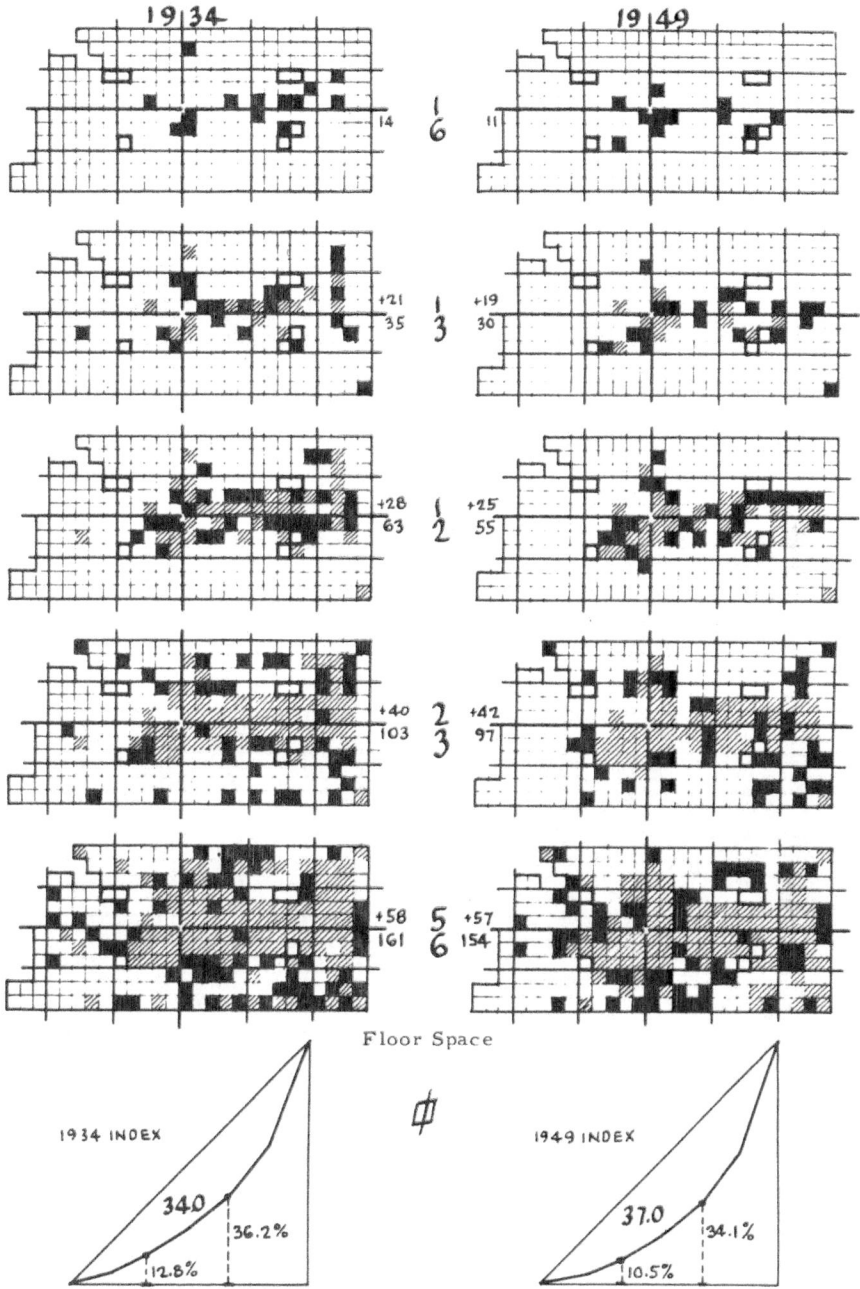

Figure 67.    CONCENTRATION BY SIXTHS, ALL
KINDS OF BUSINESS BY FLOOR
SPACE, 1934 AND 1949

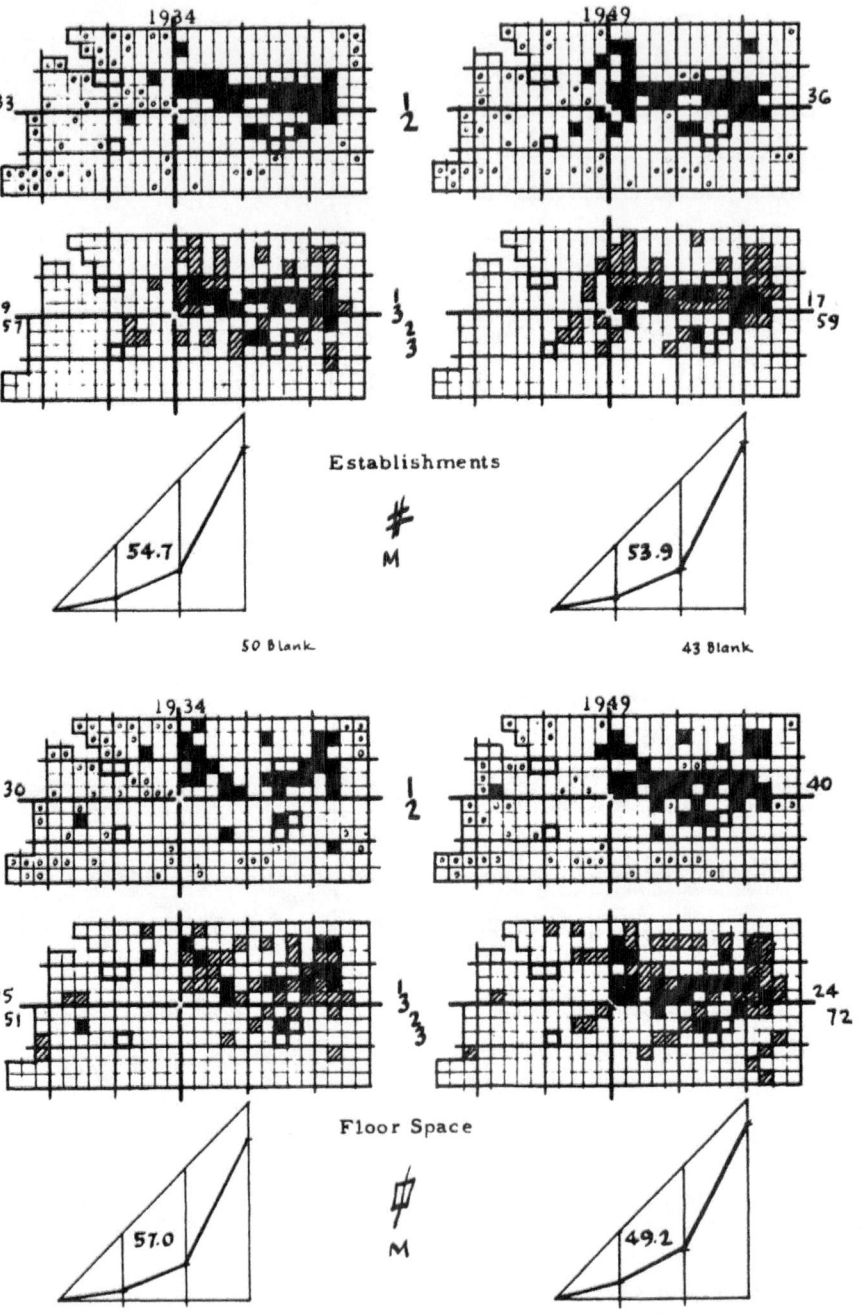

Figure 68. CONCENTRATION GROUPS, MANU-
FACTURING BY ESTABLISHMENTS
AND FLOOR SPACE, 1934 AND 1949

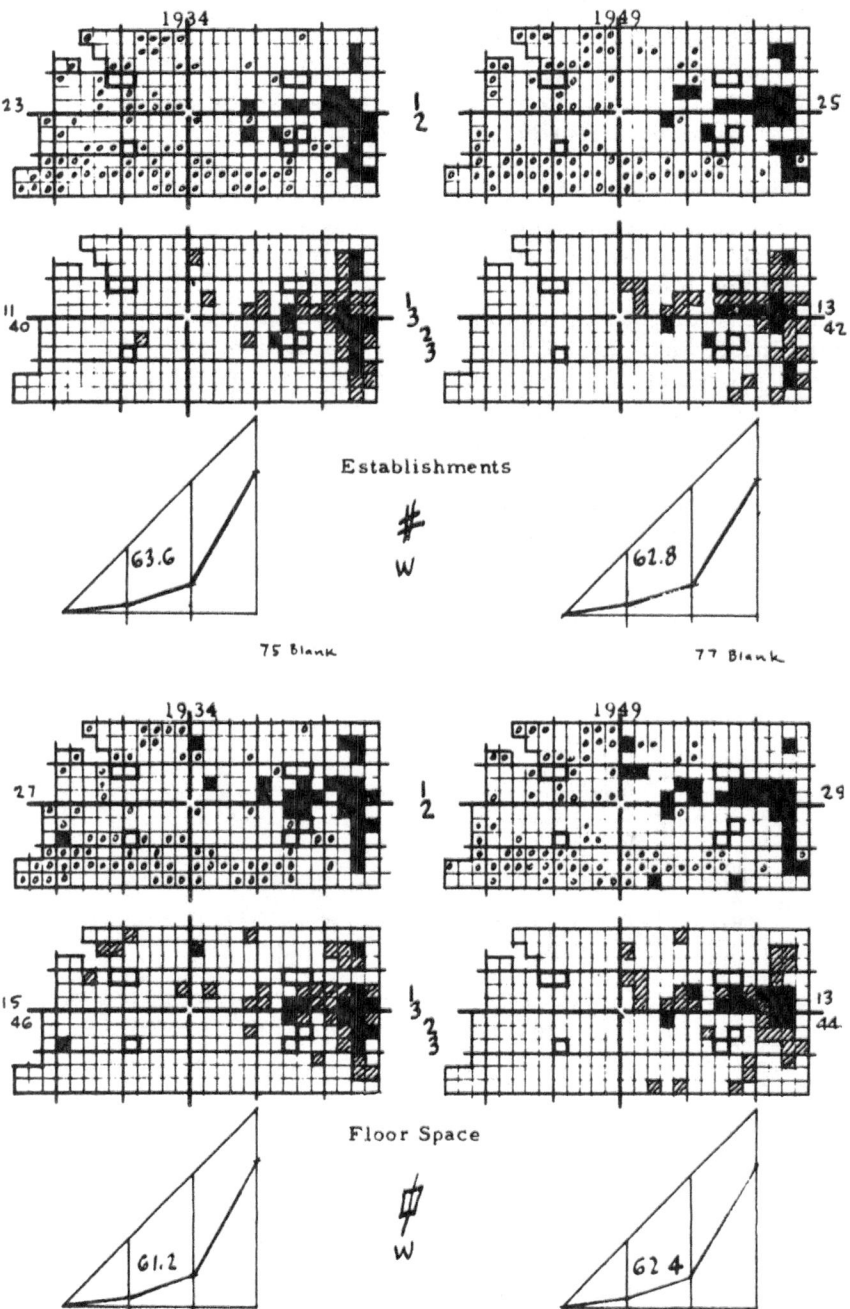

Figure 69.    CONCENTRATION GROUPS, WHOLE-
SALING BY ESTABLISHMENTS AND
FLOOR SPACE, 1934 AND 1949

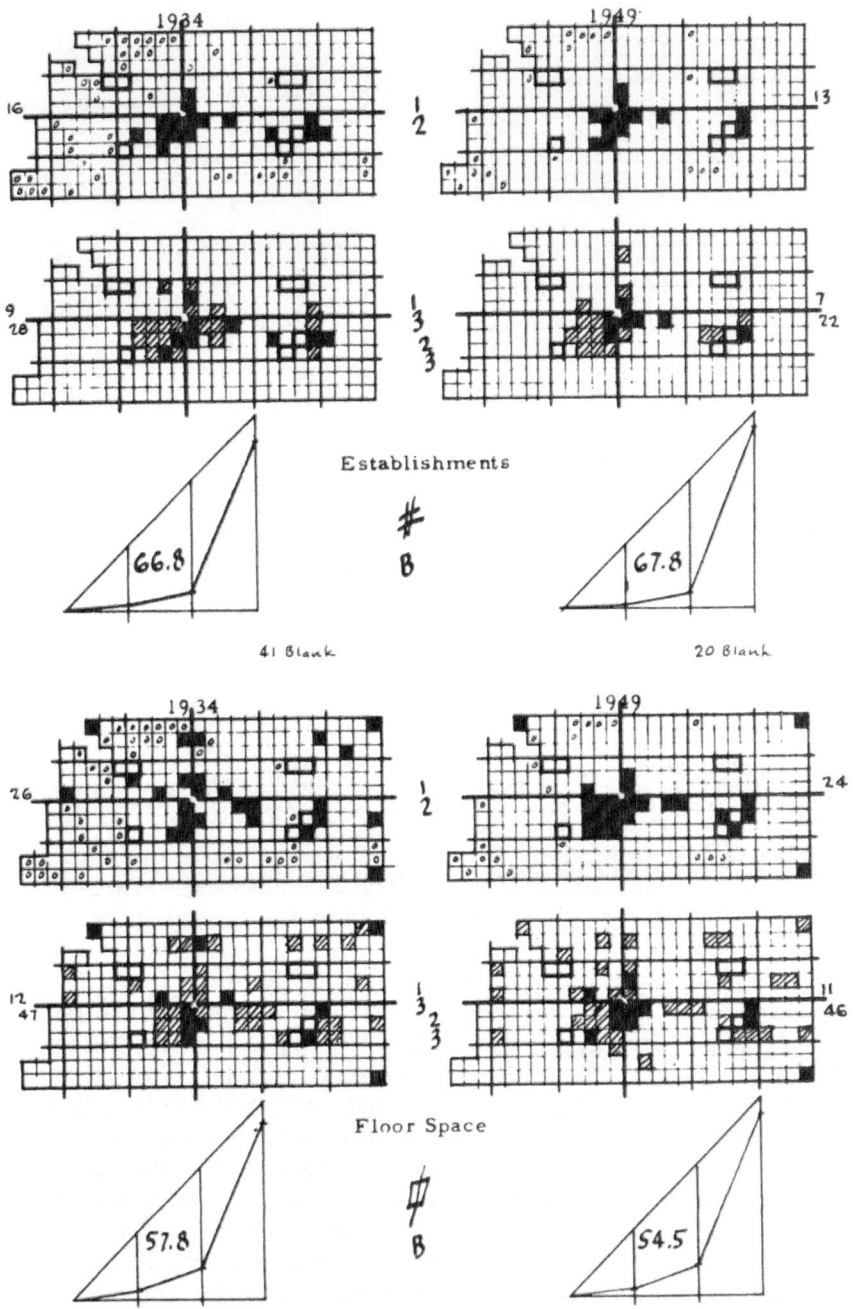

Figure 70.  CONCENTRATION GROUPS, BUSINESS
SERVICES BY ESTABLISHMENTS AND
FLOOR SPACE, 1934 AND 1949

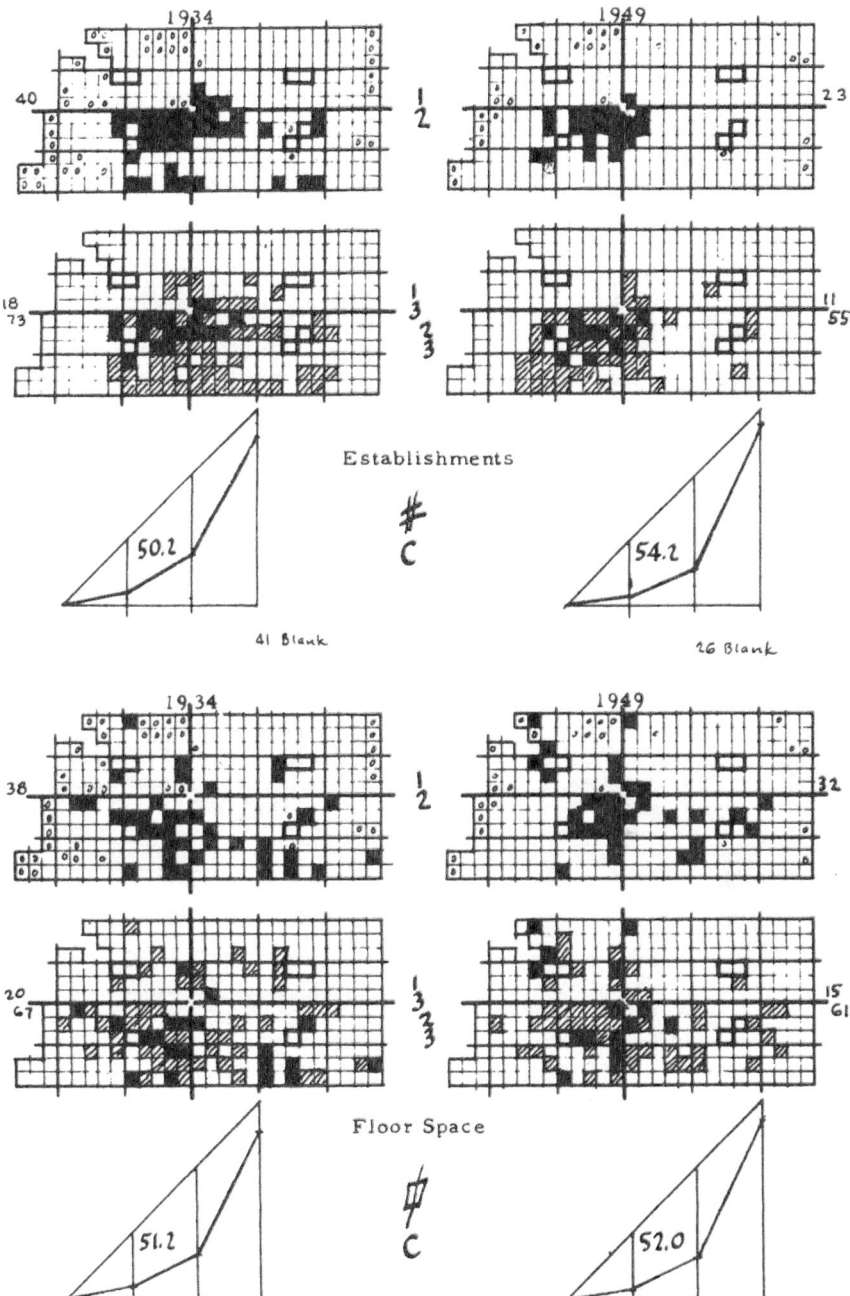

Figure 71.   CONCENTRATION GROUPS, CON-
SUMER SERVICES BY ESTABLISH-
MENTS AND FLOOR SPACE, 1934
AND 1949

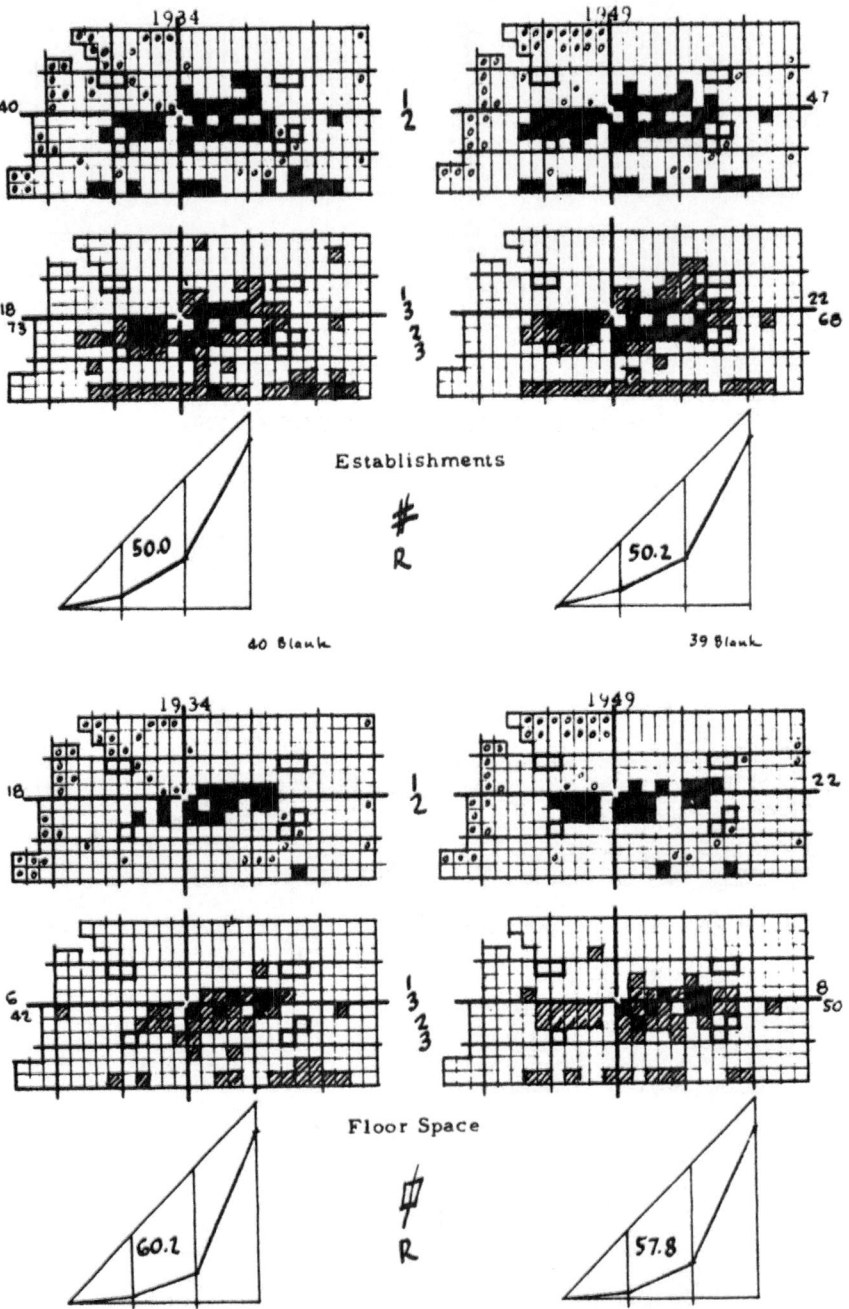

Figure 72. CONCENTRATION GROUPS, RETAIL-
ING BY ESTABLISHMENTS AND
FLOOR SPACE, 1934 AND 1949

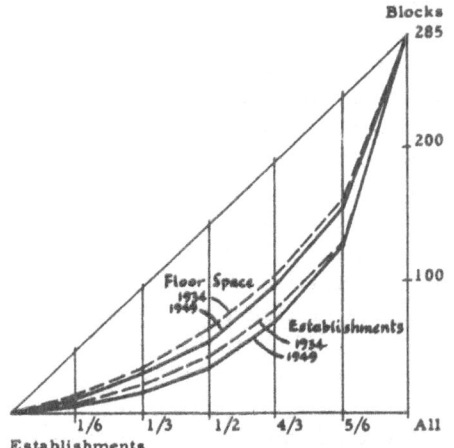

**Figure 73.   COMPARISON OF DISTRIBUTION CURVES FOR ALL KINDS OF BUSINESS**

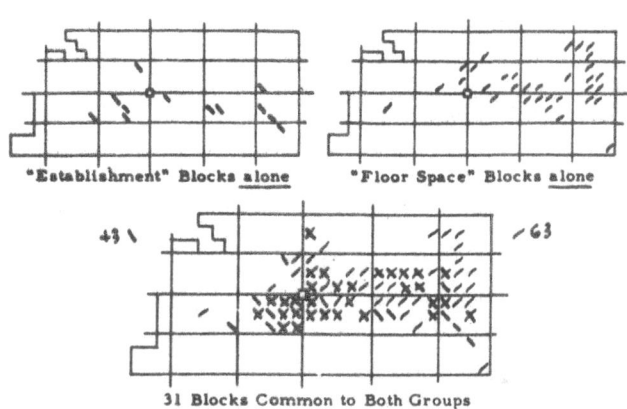

Note: See Figure 29 for 1949

**Figure 74.   OVERLAPPING GROUPS OF BLOCKS, ESTABLISHMENTS AND FLOOR SPACE, 1934**

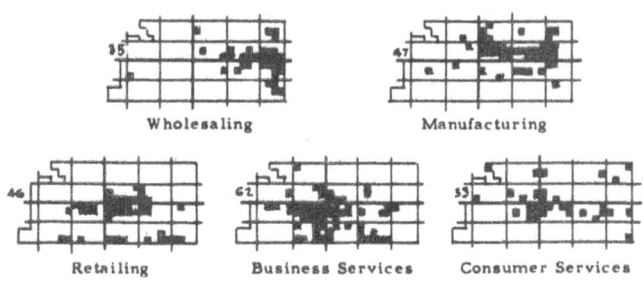

Note: See Figure 33 for 1949

**Figure 75.    FIVE MAJOR BUSINESS GROUPS, 1934 (COMBINED CORES)**

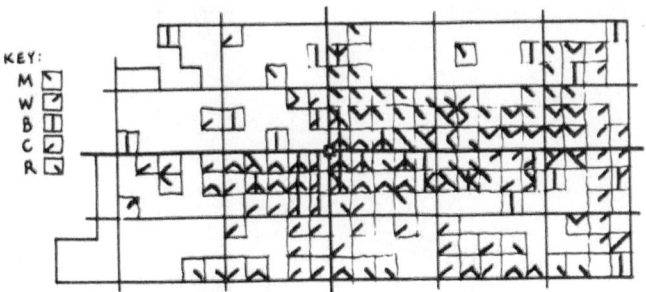

Note: See Figure 34 for 1949

Figure 76.     FIVE MAJOR BUSINESS GROUPS
               SUPERIMPOSED, 1934

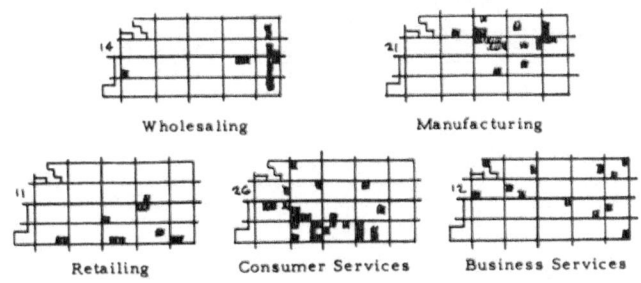

Wholesaling                    Manufacturing

Retailing        Consumer Services        Business Services

Note: See Figure 33 for 1949

Figure 77.     BLOCKS WITH A SINGLE KIND-OF-
               BUSINESS CONCENTRATION, 1934

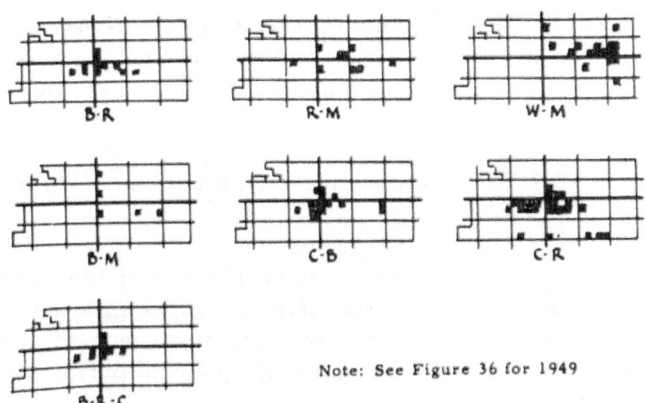

Note: See Figure 36 for 1949

Figure 78.     BLOCKS COMMON TO VARIOUS
               COMBINATIONS OF ACTIVITIES, 1934

TABLE XII   TOTAL COMBINATIONS,
            FIVE MAJOR GROUPS, 1934*

TABLE XIII
     PERCENTAGES*

| | M | W | B | C | R | "Alone" | Combined |
|---|---|---|---|---|---|---|---|
| Manufacturing | (21) | 17 | 5 | 8 | 9 | 45 | 55 |
| Wholesaling | 17 | (14) | 4 | 3 | 6 | 40 | 60 |
| Business Services | 5 | 4 | (12) | 17 | 11 | 36 | 64 |
| Consumer Services | 8 | 3 | 17 | (26) | 26 | 42 | 58 |
| Retailing | 9 | 6 | 11 | 26 | (11) | 24 | 75 |

TABLE XIV   PERCENTAGE DISTRIBUTIONS
            COMBINATIONS OF EACH KIND
            OF BUSINESS WITH EACH OTHER
            KIND*

TABLE XV
     RELATIVE PROX-
     IMITY, PAIRS OF
     BUSINESS GROUPS*

| | M | W | B | C | R | W | B | C | R |
|---|---|---|---|---|---|---|---|---|---|
| Manufacturing | — | 44 | 13 | 20 | 23 | 16 | 5 | 8+ | 8+ |
| Wholesaling | 57 | — | 13 | 10 | 20 | | 4 | 3 | 6 |
| Business Services | 13 | 11 | — | 46 | 30 | | | 16 | 10 |
| Consumer Services | 15 | 6 | 31 | — | 48 | | | | 24 |
| Retailing | 17 | 12 | 21 | 50 | — | | | | |

*Note: These Tables, for 1934, are to be compared with Tables VIII through
      XI, for 1949, in Chapter IX.

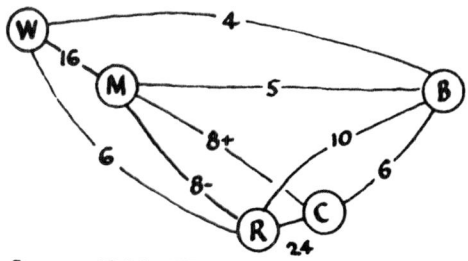

Source: Table XV

Note: See Figure 37 for 1949

Figure 79.   DIAGRAMMATIC RELATIONSHIPS, 1934

| Kind of Business | Consistencies (PROD./SUM) | | | Levels of Concentration | | |
|---|---|---|---|---|---|---|
| | 1/3 | 1/2 | 2/3 | 1/3 | 1/2 | 2/3 |
| MANUFACTURING | .21 | .34 | .46 | 19  6  15 / 13  9 / 28 | 33  16  30 / 17  14 / 47 | 57  34  51 / 23  17 / 74 |
| WHOLESALING | .37 | .47 | .69 | 11  7  15 / 4  3 / 19 | 23  16  27 / 7  11 / 34 | 40  35  46 / 5  11 / 51 |
| BUSINESS SERVICES | .11 | .31 | .36 | 9  2  12 / 7  10 / 19 | 16  10  26 / 6  16 / 32 | 28  20  47 / 8  27 / 55 |
| CONSUMER SERVICES | .19 | .24 | .40 | 18  6  20 / 12  14 / 32 | 40  15  38 / 25  23 / 63 | 73  40  67 / 33  21 / 100 |
| RETAILING | .04 | .30 | .45 | 12  1  6 / 21  5 / 27 | 42  14  18 / 28  4 / 46 | 71  35  42 / 36  7 / 78 |
| ALL KINDS | .14 | .49 | .48 | 21  7  35 / 14  28 / 49 | 43  30  63 / 13  33 / 76 | 78  59  103 / 19  44 / 122 |

Note: See Figure 28 for Key to Combinations

Figure 80. COMBINATIONS: FIVE BUSINESS GROUPS AND ALL KINDS OF BUSINESS BY ESTAB-LISHMENTS AND FLOOR SPACE, 1934

| Kind of Business | Consistencies (PROD./SUM) 1/3  1/2  2/3 | Levels of Concentration 1/3 | 1/2 | 2/3 |
|---|---|---|---|---|
| MANUFACTURING | .41   .52   .54 | 17   24 / 12 / 5   12 / 29 | 36   40 / 26 / 10   14 / 50 | 59   72 / 47 / 12   25 / 84 |
| WHOLESALING | .44   .54   .72 | 13   13 / 8 / 5   5 / 18 | 25   29 / 19 / 6   10 / 35 | 42   44 / 36 / 6   8 / 50 |
| BUSINESS SERVICES | .38   .54   .45 | 7   11 / 5 / 2   6 / 13 | 13   24 / 13 / 0   11 / 24 | 22   46 / 21 / 1   25 / 47 |
| CONSUMER SERVICES | 18   .28   .40 | 11   15 / 4 / 7   11 / 22 | 23   32 / 12 / 11   20 / 43 | 55   61 / 33 / 22   28 / 83 |
| RETAILING | .11   .35   .57 | 22   8 / 3 / 19   5 / 27 | 47   22 / 18 / 29   4 / 51 | 68   50 / 43 / 25   7 / 75 |
| ALL KINDS | .35   .51   .55 | 16   30 / 12 / 4   8 / 34 | 34   55 / 30 / 4   25 / 59 | 69   97 / 59 / 10   38 / 107 |

Note: See Figure 28 for Key to Combinations                    (Same as Figure 30)

Figure 81.   COMBINATIONS: FIVE BUSINESS GROUPS
AND ALL KINDS OF BUSINESS BY ESTAB-
LISHMENTS AND FLOOR SPACE, 1949

# Appendix B

## SYSTEMATIC COMPARISON OF
## BUSINESS GROUP LOCATIONS, 1934 and 1949

Comparative diagrams in tabular form are developed in
this appendix for demonstrating the combinations of different
kinds of business that are found together in the central
business district of Philadelphia. These diagrams are derived from the maps in Chapter XI where the five business
groups are superimposed: Figure 50 for 1934 and Figure 51
for 1949. Different levels of concentration are taken into
account by noting separately the one-third and two-thirds concentration groups for each kind of business, both by number of
establishment and amount of floor-space. Several sets of
data will be derived from these maps, organized as follows:

| | Figure |
|---|---|
| For Five Kinds of Business: | |
| Locational characteristics, both years | 83, 84 |
| Variation from average, both years | 90, 91 |
| Change in characteristics, 1934 to 1949 | 92 |
| Combinations found together, both years | 94, 95 |
| For All Kinds of Business: | |
| Average allocations, both years | 85, 86 |
| Average allocations, both years combined | 87 |
| Average of allocations for both years | 88 |
| Explanatory diagrams (no data) | 82, 89, 93 |

1 DESCRIPTION OF MAPS (Figures 50 and 51, (Chapter XI)

1.1 In Figure 50, distribution of a) establishments and b) floor
space for 1934 is shown in separate maps, with the one-
third and two-thirds concentration groups for each kind of
business indicated. In Figure 51 the same is done for 1949.
On each of these four maps the blocks in the two-thirds
group for all kinds of business taken together are shaded.
This group of blocks will be termed aggregate core and will
be used to measure the tendency of each concentration
group for each separate kind of business to be located in
or out of the concentration for all kinds of business. (This
aggregate core is closely analogous to the reference core
in Figure 31, page 123.)

1.2 These two pairs of maps will be used for deriving measures
of relationship (for each kind of business for each year)
between the five kinds of business by methods similar to
those described in Chapters VIII and IX. The elements are
more complex, however, in that the relationship of one
business group to another can now be stated in terms of
major or minor concentrations of each.

Thus, for example, block F-14 at the intersection of Broad
and Market Streets is shown in the floor-space maps for
both years, Figures 50B and 51B, as Business Service and
Retailing; in 1934 it was in the second third for Business
Service and Retailing; in 1934 it was in the second third
for Business Services and in the first third for Retailing;
in 1949 it was in the first third for both. The same block
appears in the establishment count (Figures 50A and 51A)
as Business Service and Consumer Service; in 1934 it
was in the first third for both; in 1949 it was in the first
third for Business Service and in the second for Consumer
Service. Other blocks can be made to tell different stories,
but before scrutinizing specific locations it will be best to
set down methodically the pertinent characteristics of the
five groups and of their combinations as they appear on
these maps.

2 LOCATIONAL CHARACTERISTICS

2.1 Each business group plotted on the maps, Figures 50 and 51
will be examined as to its relationship to the aggregation for
all groups and also as to its tendency to occur singly or in combination with others. These characteristics will be further
detailed by level of concentration (first third, second third).

2.2 Relationships between each business group and their entire
aggregation are set forth in Figure 83 for 1934 and Figure
84 for 1949 to show the following: number of blocks in each
group which are located in the aggregate core for all groups
or outside of this core; number of blocks in each group which
are combined with others and number in which each kind
stands alone; numbers in most-concentrated and less-con-
centrated portions of each group (first third and second
third); and the proportions, i.e., percentages, corresponding
with these numbers. The basic unit of these tables is a four-
celled cross tabulation showing, for each business group, the

number of blocks found in the aggregate core for all groups
(In - Out) and the number of blocks in which only the one
kind of business is found as against the number in which
other kinds are also found (Single - Combined). This unit
table is illustrated in Figure 82.

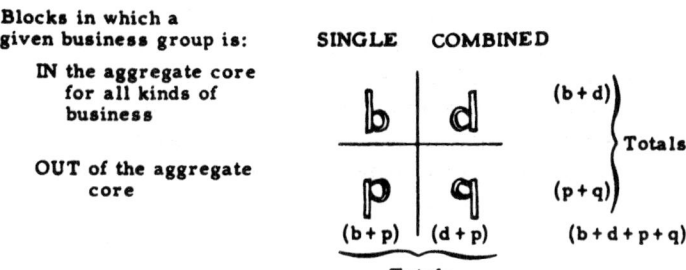

Situation of each business group relative to the aggregate core, (the two-
thirds concentration group for all kinds of business taken together) and relative to other groups.

Figure 82. KEY TO UNITS IN FIGURES 83 AND 84

2.3 There are three of these unit tables in Figures 83 and 84 for
each kind-of-business group to show the number of blocks
in: (1) the first-third concentration group, (2) the second-
third, and (3) in both, that is, the two-thirds concentration
group. Marginal totals are given for each unit table and at
the lower right of each, the total number of blocks in each
concentration group. For the first and second thirds these
totals are also expressed as percentages of their sum, that
is, the corresponding total of the two-thirds concentration
group. Finally, in order to facilitate comparison of groups,
another unit table is given for each, showing: (4) percentages
corresponding with the numbers in the third unit table.

2.4 General characteristics of the Five Business Groups can be
most readily compared by considering first the proportions
or percentages of the totals in Figures 83 and 84 (line 4 in
each) taking into account the components which make up these
totals. In general, the "heavy" cells of these unit tables are
found in the upper half and in the right half. In other words,
each business group tends to occur in the aggregate core for
all groups and to combine with others. This is most strik-
ingly the case with Business Services, by establishment

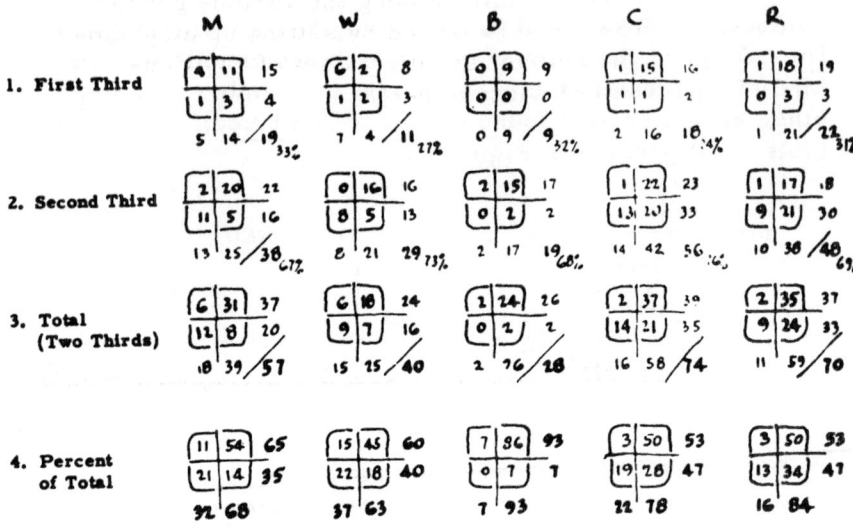

A. by Number of Establishments

Note: See Figure 82 for Key to Diagrams

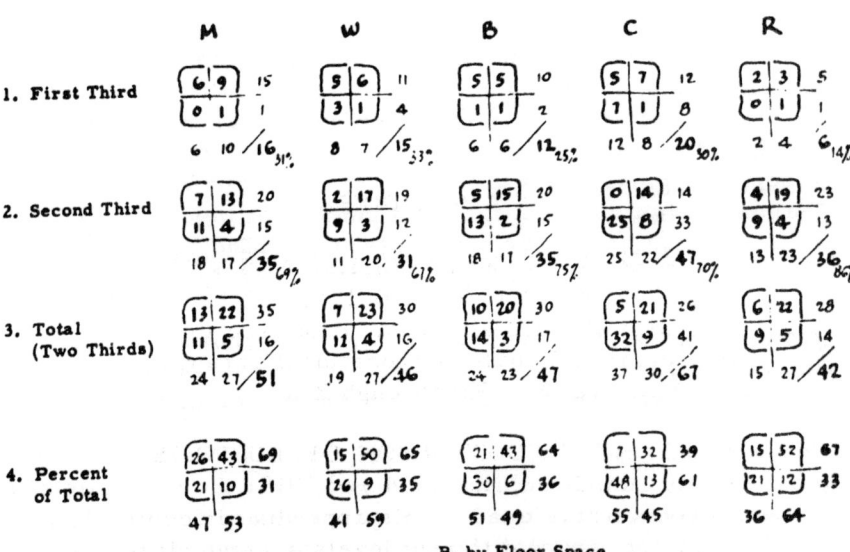

B. by Floor Space

Figure 83.   BLOCKS IN OR OUT OF CORE
BY SINGLE OR COMBINED USE,
FIVE KINDS OF BUSINESS, 1934

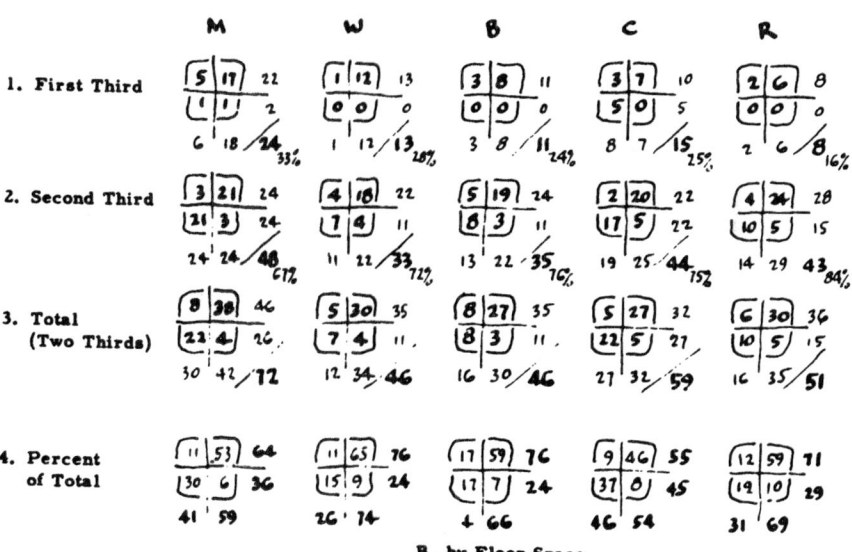

A. by Number of Establishments

Note: See Figure 82 for Key to Diagrams

B. by Floor Space

Figure 84.   BLOCKS IN OR OUT OF CORE
             BY SINGLE OR COMBINED USE,
             FIVE KINDS OF BUSINESS, 1949

count (middle of line 4 in both Figures 83A and 84A) where 86 percent of blocks are both in the core and combined, in both 1934 and 1949.

Manufacturing in 1934 by establishment count (Figure 83A, line 4) had 65 percent of its blocks in the aggregate core and 68 percent of its blocks combined. Over half (54 percent) were both combined and in the core; 21 percent were neither. The remainder were fairly evenly divided between in/single and out/combined (11 percent and 14 percent). The corresponding figures for 1949 (Figure 84A) are nearly identical with 1934 as to total percentages (64 percent in the core, 70 percent combined), but there is considerable variation in the separate cells.

It is by comparing these separate cells that uniformities and differences among the five groups can be noted and then traced to the actual functioning of each group with regard to space and location and linkages with others. The general characteristics, which apply to the single or combined blocks represented by the four cells of Figures 83 and 84, were noted in Chapter XI, pages 177 and 178.

## 3 AVERAGE ALLOCATIONS

3.1 These general characteristics may be summarized for the aggregation of all business groups by computing the average allocations for each year, by number of establishments and by floor space. In this summary statement the distinction between levels of concentration (first third, second third) will be disregarded and only the totals will be taken into account, that is, only lines 3 and 4 in Figures 83 and 84.

3.2 The average allocations for all kinds of business are set forth in Figures 85 and 86. These are computed from the totals in the third lines of Figures 83 and 84, thus taking into account each occurrence of a business group, as designated on the maps in Figures 50 and 51.

3.3 Changes in average allocations for all kinds of business are revealed by comparing the average percentages for 1934 and 1949 as follows: Proportion in the aggregate core increases (totals at right of each unit table on Figures 85 and 86) whether measured by number of establishments (+1 percent; 61 to 62) or by floor space (+8 percent; 59 to 67). The proportion of combined blocks, on the other hand (totals at

|       | Single | Combined |     |
|-------|--------|----------|-----|
| In    | 7      | 54 \|    | 61  |
| Out   | 16     | 23 \|    | 39  |
|       | 23     | 77       | 100 |

a. by Establishment Count

|       | Single | Combined |     |
|-------|--------|----------|-----|
| In    | 7      | 55 \|    | 62  |
| Out   | 25     | 13 \|    | 38  |
|       | 37     | 68       | 100 |

a. by Establishment Count

|       |    |      |     |
|-------|----|------|-----|
| In    | 16 | 43 \| | 59  |
| Out   | 31 | 10 \| | 41  |
|       | 47 | 53   | 100 |

b. by Floor-Space Count

|       |    |      |     |
|-------|----|------|-----|
| In    | 12 | 55 \| | 67  |
| Out   | 25 | 8 \|  | 33  |
|       | 37 | 63   | 100 |

b. by Floor-Space Count

Figure 85. PERCENTAGE OF BLOCKS IN OR OUT OF CORE BY SINGLE OR COMBINED USE, ALL KINDS OF BUSINESS, 1934

Figure 86. PERCENTAGE OF BLOCKS IN OR OUT OF CORE BY SINGLE OR COMBINED USE, ALL KINDS OF BUSINESS, 1949

Note: The percentages in Figures 85 and 86 are computed by adding the numbers in each corresponding cell of the unit tables (line 3 of Figures 83 and 84) and expressing these sums as percentages of the totals for all cells.

bottom of each unit table), is seen to decrease when counted by establishments (-9 percent; 77 to 68) but to increase when counted in terms of floor space (+10 percent; 53 to 63). The components of these changes in percentage from 1934 to 1949 are repeated in Figure 87.

3.4 The greater total percentages in the aggregate core in 1949, on both counts (+1 and +8), indicate an increasing tendency to locate centrally, that is, where others locate or where "the most" locate. It is accompanied by an increasing tendency to combine. By establishment count, the total increase in the core is accounted for entirely by the combined blocks (no change in percentage of single blocks) but by floor-space count the combined blocks have an even greater increase (+12) than the total since there was a 4 percent decrease in single blocks.

|     | Single | Combined |     |     | Single | Combined |     |
|-----|--------|----------|-----|-----|--------|----------|-----|
| In  | 0      | + 1      | + 1 | In  | - 4    | + 12     | + 8 |
| Out | + 9    | - 10     | - 1 | Out | - 6    | - 2      | - 8 |
|     | + 9    | - 9      |     |     | - 10   | + 10     |     |

a. by Establishment Count          b. by Floor-Space Count

Source: Figures 85 and 86

Figure 87.    CHANGES IN AVERAGE PERCENT-
              AGE FROM 1934 TO 1949, BLOCKS IN
              OR OUT OF CORE BY SINGLE OR
              COMBINED USE, ALL KINDS OF BUSI-
              NESS

3.5 The total combined blocks show opposite tendencies on the
    two counts (-9 and + 10) due to a different balance in their
    components. In both cases the percentage change is posi-
    tive in the core and negative out of the core. By floor-space
    count the positive predominates (+12, -2); by establishment
    count the net balance is negative (+1, -10). The important
    item here, as in the preceding paragraph, appears to be the
    increasing tendency of business groups to concentrate in the
    core and to combine with others, and this is especially
    noticeable in the case of floor space.

3.6 One cell in each table remains to be noted: single blocks
    out of the aggregate core. These blocks, representing more
    or less isolated business groups, increased 9 percent by
    establishment count and decreased 6 percent when counted
    by floor space.

3.7 However, all of these differences between the years 1934 and
    1949 are not so great as to change the general picture. Re-
    turning to Figures 85 and 86, the most noticeable differences
    are those between the allocations by establishments and by
    floor space; the changes over time within each type of count
    are comparatively minor. Recasting the tables in the form
    of averages for the two years gives us Figure 88 as a basis
    for generalizing on the allocation of blocks as they are shown
    by the two kinds of count.

|        | Single | Combined |    |
|--------|--------|----------|----|
| In     | 7      | 55       | 62 |
| Out    | 20     | 18       | 38 |
|        | 27     | 73       |    |

|        | Single | Combined |    |
|--------|--------|----------|----|
| In     | 14     | 49       | 63 |
| Out    | 28     | 9        | 37 |
|        | 42     | 58       |    |

a. by Establishment Count          b. by Floor-Space Count

Source: Figures 85 and 86

Figure 88.    AVERAGE OF PERCENTAGES FOR
1934 AND 1949, BLOCKS IN OR OUT
OF CORE BY SINGLE OR COMBINED
USE, ALL KINDS OF BUSINESS

3.8 On both counts, the percentages in Figure 88 are roughly
consistent up the right-hand diagonal ($20\text{-}^{55}$ and $28\text{-}^{49}$) but
not on the left where the balance in diagonal cells is reversed
($^{7}\text{-}18$ and $^{14}\text{-}9$). This is to say that:

Within the two-thirds concentration groups, whether taken
by number of establishments or by amount of floor space,
about half of the blocks for any kind of business are found
combined with others inside the aggregate core (the two-
thirds group, for all kinds of business). Likewise, about
one-fourth of the blocks for any kind of business are found
outside of the core and not combined. These "single"
blocks, it will be recalled, are dominated by one kind of
business, either in terms of number of establishments or
amount of space. (The range of variations in these percentages for the years 1934 and 1949 is 43 to 55 for combined, inside; 16 to 31 for single, outside, as seen in the
corresponding cells of Figures 85 and 86.)

In the remaining blocks (roughly one-fourth of the total)
the counts by establishments and by floor space show opposite tendencies; that is, there are roughly twice as many
single blocks within the core dominated by floor space as
by number of establishments, while in the case of combined
blocks out of the core there are about twice as many when
counted by number of establishments as by floor space.

3.9 So much for the general tendencies, the similarities and
differences in the aggregate distribution of business estab-

lishments among the blocks of the central district as counted
in two different ways—by number of establishments and by
floor area. The variation in these tendencies from 1934 to
1949 have been noted in Figure 87, corresponding with the
data for each year, Figures 85 and 86. These tables, in,
turn, summarize the characteristics detailed in Figures
83 and 84 where the allocation of blocks for each kind of
business is shown separately by both sorts of count and for
both years. All of these tables will now be used for comparing the general or average tendencies which have just been
described with the separate tendencies shown by individual
kinds of business.

## 4  VARIATIONS AMONG BUSINESS GROUPS

4.1  The locational characteristics of each business group, as
displayed in Figures 83 and 84 can be studied in great detail
by examining the individual units of these tables as suggested
above at 2.4: "General characteristics, etc." Detailed comparisons between groups can be made readily enough by taking appropriate unit tables in pairs and changes over time
can be traced in like manner. These tables and the maps
from which they are derived (Figures 50 and 51) provide
an elaborate basis for analysis of differences among groups.
In general it will suffice to point up these differences by
comparing each kind-of-business group with the aggregation of all of them.

4.2  Variation from average for each business group is stated as
a comparison with the aggregate allocation of blocks represented by Figures 85 for 1934 and 86 for 1949. This is
done for 1934 in Figure 90 by setting down the differences
between each cell in each unit table in Figure 85 and the
corresponding cells for each kind-of-business in line 4 of
Figure 83. Repeating the process and using Figures 86 and
84 gives the differences for 1949 as presented in Figure 91.
The degree of variation from average for each kind of business (the circled number below each unit table) is the total
of the differences for each unit table; the amount and sign
of the differences in each cell are indications of different
characteristics of the separate business groups. A typical

For Manufacturing by Establishment Count in 1934. See Figure 82 for key
to tabular units.

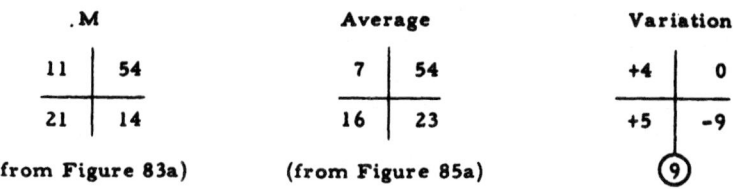

| .M | | | Average | | | Variation | |
|---|---|---|---|---|---|---|---|
| 11 | 54 | | 7 | 54 | | +4 | 0 |
| 21 | 14 | | 16 | 23 | | +5 | -9 |
| (from Figure 83a) | | | (from Figure 85a) | | | ⑨ | |

Figure 89.  SAMPLE CALCULATION FOR COM-
            PARISON OF PERCENTAGES IN FIG-
            URES 90 AND 91.

computation (Manufacturing by Establishment Count in 1934)
is illustrated in Figure 89.

Figure 89 shows a degree of variation of 9 in the allocation of Manufacturing blocks. This is fairly typical, as
will be seen in the tabulations for all groups in Figures
90 and 91. The greatest discrepancy between Manufacturing and the average is found in the combined blocks outside of the core, 9 percent less than average; this is
balanced by increases of 4 percent for single blocks in
the core and 5 percent for single blocks outside. Combined blocks in the core show zero variation.

4.3 Changes from 1934 to 1949 for each business group can be
    found by comparing the appropriate unit tables in Figures
    83 and 84. For the present only percentages will be used
    for illustration (line 4 of each figure).

    Inspection of the percentage in the aggregate core by
    establishments reveals virtually no change between 1934
    and 1949 (see Figures 83A and 84A). The greatest change
    in this item occurs in Retailing (from 53 percent to 58
    percent) while the others change by 2 percent or less.

    A similar inspection by floor space, however, shows con-
    siderable fluctuation (see Figures 83B and 84B). In this
    case, Retailing has the least change, from 67 percent to
    71 percent, while others differ by as much as 16 percent
    (Consumer Services). All except manufacturing show an
    increase in the proportion of their blocks found in the
    aggregate core.

| | M | | W | | B | | C | | R | |
|---|---|---|---|---|---|---|---|---|---|---|
| **A** **Establishments** | +4 | 0 | +8 | -9 | 0 | +32 | -4 | -4 | -4 | +9 |
| | +5 | -9 | +6 | -5 | -16 | -16 | +3 | +5 | -3 | +11 |
| | 9 | | 14 | | 32 | | 8 | | 11 | |
| **B** **Floor Space** | +10 | 0 | -1 | +7 | +5 | 0 | -9 | -11 | -1 | +9 |
| | -10 | 0 | -5 | -1 | -1 | -4 | +17 | +3 | -10 | +2 |
| | 10 | | 7 | | 5 | | 20 | | 11 | |

(Computed from Figures 83 and 85 as outlined in Figure 89.)

Figure 90.    COMPARISON OF PERCENTAGES,
EACH KIND OF BUSINESS WITH ALL
KINDS, 1934

Inspection of the percentages of combined blocks reveals changes somewhat less consistent than those just
described. By establishment count (Figures 83A and
84A again) there is little change (2 percent to 4 percent)
in Manufacturing, Wholesaling, and Business Services,
but heavy decreases in Consumer Services and Retailing
(13 percent and 22 percent). Comparison of percentage
of combined blocks in terms of floor space (Figures
83B and 84B) reveals a general increase, ranging

| | M | | W | | B | | C | | R | |
|---|---|---|---|---|---|---|---|---|---|---|
| **A** **Establishments** | -4 | +6 | 0 | -2 | -2 | +31 | +1 | -8 | +2 | -6 |
| | +2 | -4 | +1 | +1 | -25 | -8 | +2 | +5 | +4 | 0 |
| | 8 | | 2 | | 33 | | 8 | | 6 | |
| **B** **Floor Space** | -1 | -2 | -1 | +10 | +5 | +4 | -3 | -9 | 0 | +4 |
| | +5 | -2 | -10 | -1 | -8 | -1 | +12 | 0 | -6 | +2 |
| | 5 | | 11 | | 9 | | 12 | | 6 | |

(Computed from Figures 83 and 85 as outlined in Figure 89.)

Figure 91.    COMPARISON OF PERCENTAGES,
EACH KIND OF BUSINESS WITH ALL
KINDS, 1949

from 5 percent for Retailing to 17 percent for Business Services.

4.4 Certain consistencies in the changes from 1934 to 1949 are noted in the two preceding paragraphs: the proportion of blocks found in the aggregate core changes but little when measured by number of establishments but increases considerably when measured in terms of floor space; in general the proportion of combined blocks, by establishment count, decreases or remains virtually unchanged, but in terms of floor space all kinds of business show an increasing tendency to combine, that is, to be found in the same location with others. These average tendencies have already been summarized in Figure 87. The changes for each business group are given in Figure 92 and the average change for all of them (repeated from Figure 88) is also given for comparison of the individual changes with the general tendency.

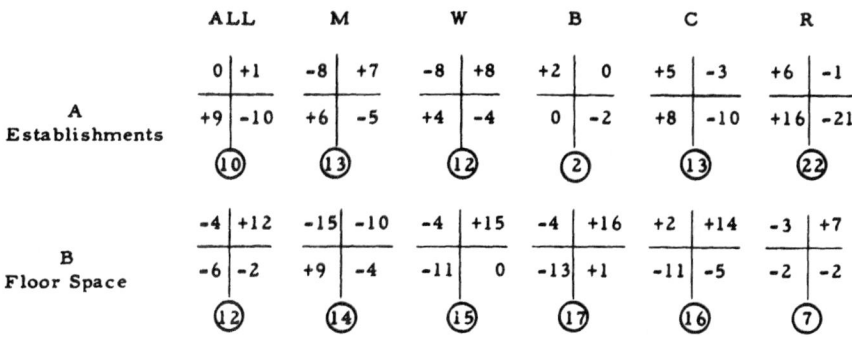

Derived from Figures 83 and 84 by subtracting percentages (line 4 of each). Circled figures indicate degree of change (the total of the differences in each table, see 4.2.1). The left-hand units (ALL) are repeated from Figure 87 for ready comparison with each kind of business.

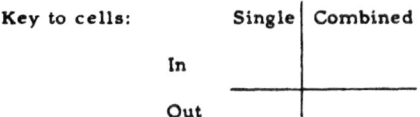

Figure 92.    PERCENT CHANGE, 1934 TO 1949,
              FIVE KINDS OF BUSINESS

4.5 The variations among business groups which have been discussed in this section are of two kinds: (1) variations from
average, summarized in Figure 90 for 1934 and Figure 91 for
1949: and (2) changes from 1934 to 1949, summarized in Figure 92. These figures focus on the differences in allocation
which are characteristic of the various groups. Thus, for
example, Business Services by establishments (middle of
top row in each figure) is by far the most concentrated of
all in the aggregate core and in combination with other groups
in both years (Figures 90 and 91). Another example is seen
in Retailing, still on the establishment side. It has the
greatest variation over time.

## 5 COMBINATIONS OF BUSINESS GROUPS

5.1 In the foregoing discussion, blocks have been noted as
"single" (occurring in only one kind-of-business group) or
"combined" (with two or more kinds represented in the same
block). The combined blocks, however, may consist of any
one of 10 pairs of the 5 groups, or, taking two levels of concentration into account, any one of 40 combinations. Further
subdivision by the occurrence of each combination within or
outside of the combined core for all groups makes 80 more
possible paired combinations. Combinations of more than two
per block will not be considered at present.

5.2 Combinations of each group with the others are all stated in
Figure 94 for 1934 and Figure 95 for 1949 in four-cell units
arranged diagonally so that they can be read from either
side. These include all the combinations, taken two at a time,
in each block as shown in the maps, Figures 50 and 51. The
arrangement of units is illustrated by Figure 93 where the
first combination in Figure 94 (for Manufacturing and Wholesaling by establishment count) is repeated so that the designations may serve as a key for all the other combinations.

5.3 The upper unit in Figure 93 shows the total combined blocks
shared by the two groups (22) circled in the center. These
are broken down four ways as follows: those in the first
third concentration group for both kinds of business (4),
those in the second third for both (11), and those in which
one is first and the other second and vice versa (7 and 0).

This total tabulation of blocks containing both Manufacturing and Wholesaling is further subdivided in the two lower units to show how many blocks of each sort appear in or out of the aggregate core for all kinds of business.

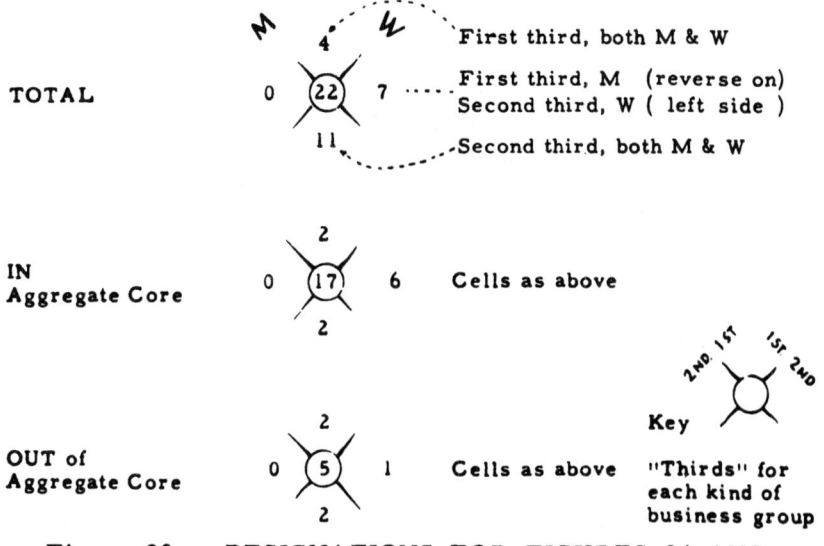

**TOTAL**

First third, both M & W

First third, M  (reverse on)
Second third, W ( left side )

Second third, both M & W

**IN**
**Aggregate Core**

Cells as above

**OUT of**
**Aggregate Core**

Cells as above

Key

"Thirds" for
each kind of
business group

Figure 93.    DESIGNATIONS FOR FIGURES 94 AND 95: COMBINATIONS OF BUSINESS GROUPS SHOWING BREAKDOWN OF EACH COMBINATION BY "CONCENTRATION GROUP" FOR EACH KIND OF BUSINESS, THAT IS, BY THIRDS

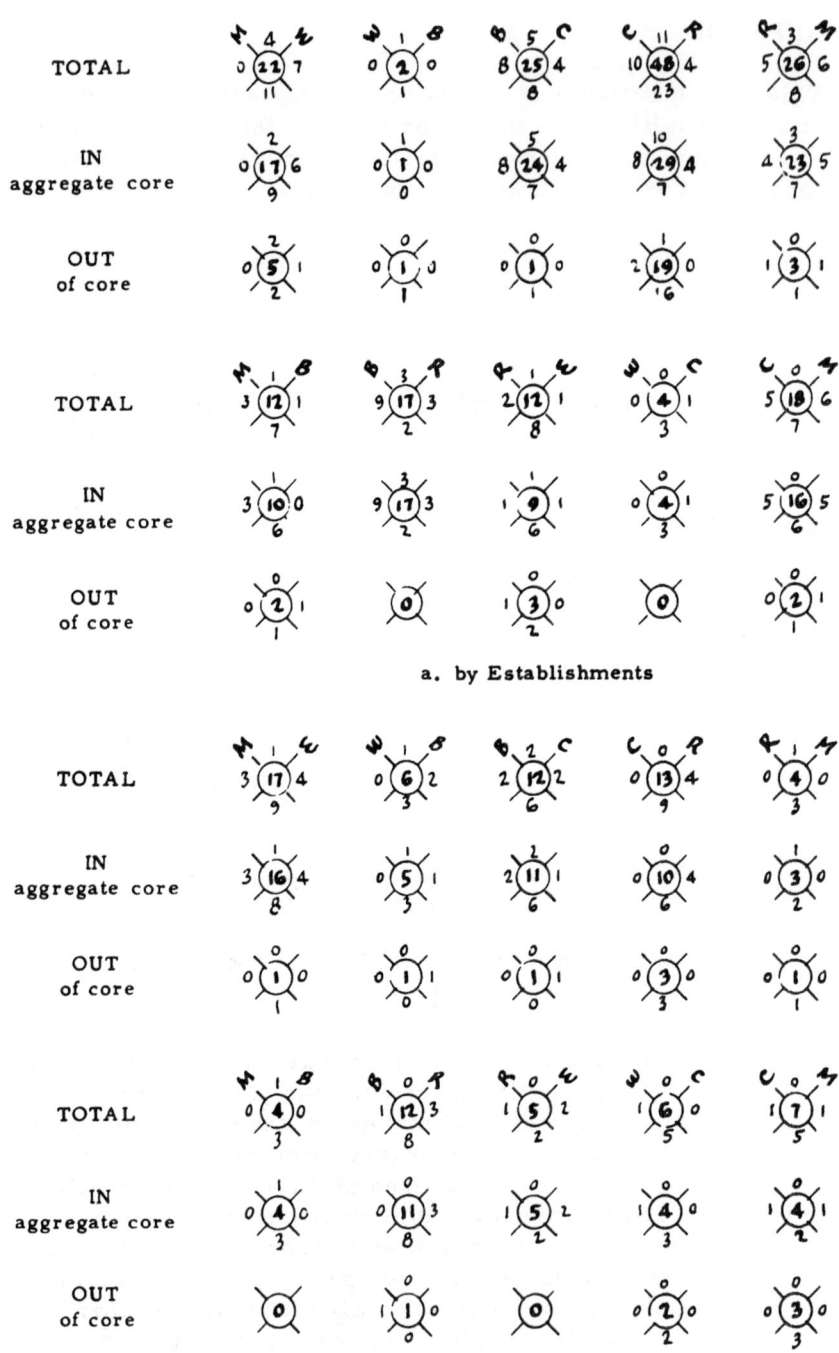

a. by Establishments

b. by Floor Space

Figure 94.  COMBINATIONS OF FIVE KINDS OF BUSINESS
BY ESTABLISHMENTS AND FLOOR SPACE, 1934

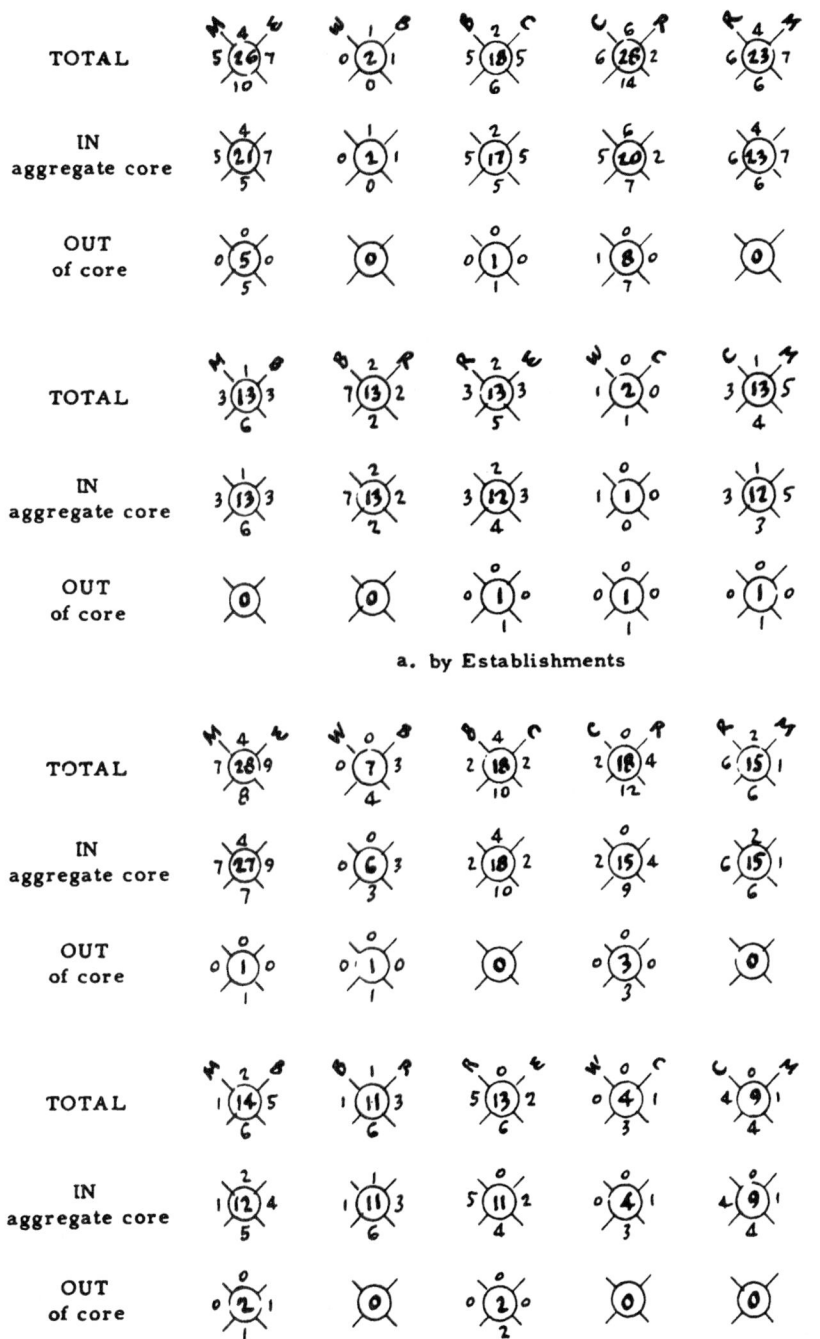

a. by Establishments

b. by Floor Space

Figure 95.   COMBINATIONS OF FIVE KINDS OF BUSINESS
BY ESTABLISHMENTS AND FLOOR SPACE, 1949

# Appendix C

## CALCULATION OF DISTRIBUTION CURVES

The full Lorenz Curve illustrated in Figure 11 is derived from the tabulation on the opposite page, as itemized below for each successive column:

1. Number per block of establishments, from Figure 9, arranged in sequence, i.e., lowest number first, and so on.
2. Number of times that each number in column 1 occurs on the map, Figure 9.
3. Summation of blocks, counting largest first, i.e., working up from the bottom.
4. Percent of total blocks, ordinate of each point on curve in Figure 11.
5. Groups of establishments, either single blocks or blocks with equal numbers.
6. Summation of establishments, working up from bottom as in column 3.
7. Percent of total establishments, abscissa of each point on curve in Figure 11.
8. Fractions (sixths of total) for comparison with actual numbers in column 6.

Six-segment approximations of the full curve are computed from the maps, Figures 54 through 65, as follows:

A. Determine total number of establishments and set up six equal divisions, as in column 8.
B. Add numbers per block, starting with largest, until total is nearest to the first sixth; check off blocks comprising this first sixth on the map.
C. Continue thus for each sixth in turn, checking off corresponding blocks.
D. Blocks in each sixth will be indicated on the map (concentration groups) and their successive percentages will provide ordinates for the distribution curve. Maps and curves, Figures 66, 67 and 73, were derived in this manner; Figures 68 through 72 were derived similarly.

| Estab's per block (1) | Times (2) | BLOCKS Total (3) | Percent (4) | Number (5) (1x2) | ESTABLISHMENTS Total (6) | Percent (7) | Sixths* (8) |
|---|---|---|---|---|---|---|---|
| 1 | 4 | 285 | 100.00 | 4 | 19425 | 100.00 | |
| 2 | 11 | 276 | 96.2 | 22 | 19413 | 99.95 | |
| 3 | 2 | 265 | 93.1 | 6 | 19391 | 99.84 | |
| 4 | 3 | 263 | 92.5 | 12 | 19385 | 99.81 | |
| 5 | 3 | 260 | 91.4 | 15 | 19373 | 99.74 | |

the middle portion is omitted

| Estab's per block (1) | Times (2) | BLOCKS Total (3) | Percent (4) | Number (5) (1x2) | ESTABLISHMENTS Total (6) | Percent (7) | Sixths* (8) |
|---|---|---|---|---|---|---|---|
| 116 | 2 | 37 | 13.0 | 232 | 10092 | 52.0 | |
| 119 | 1 | 35 | 12.3 | 119 | 9860 | 50.8 | |
| 120 | 1 | 34 | 11.9 | 120 | 9741 | 50.2 | |
| 122 | 1 | 33 | 11.6 | 122 | 9621 | 49.5 | 9713 (1/2) |
| 129 | 1 | 32 | 11.2 | 129 | 9499 | 48.9 | |
| 137 | 2 | 31 | 10.9 | 274 | 9370 | 48.2 | |
| 156 | 2 | 29 | 10.4 | 312 | 9096 | 46.8 | |
| 157 | 1 | 27 | 9.5 | 157 | 8784 | 45.2 | |
| 164 | 1 | 26 | 9.1 | 164 | 8627 | 44.4 | |
| 177 | 1 | 25 | 8.8 | 177 | 8463 | 43.6 | |
| 178 | 1 | 24 | 8.4 | | 8286 | 42.7 | |
| 190 | 1 | 23 | 8.1 | · | 8108 | 41.8 | |
| 198 | 1 | 22 | 7.7 | · | 7918 | 40.8 | |
| 201 | 1 | 21 | 7.4 | · | 7720 | 39.6 | |
| 216 | 1 | 20 | 7.0 | · | 7519 | 38.7 | |
| 231 | 1 | 19 | 6.7 | · | 7303 | 37.6 | |
| 238 | 1 | 18 | 6.3 | · | 7072 | 36.4 | |
| 246 | 1 | 17 | 6.0 | | 6834 | 35.2 | |
| 260 | 1 | 16 | 5.6 | | 6588 | 33.9 | 6475 (1/3) |
| 261 | 1 | 15 | 5.3 | | 6328 | 32.6 | |
| 286 | 1 | 14 | 4.9 | Same as Column 2 | 6067 | 31.2 | |
| 308 | 1 | 13 | 4.6 | | 5781 | 29.8 | |
| 313 | 1 | 12 | 4.2 | | 5473 | 28.2 | |
| 324 | 1 | 11 | 3.9 | | 5160 | 26.6 | |
| 353 | 1 | 10 | 3.5 | | 4836 | 24.9 | |
| 371 | 1 | 9 | 3.1 | · | 4483 | 23.1 | |
| 375 | 1 | 8 | 2.8 | · | 4712 | 21.2 | |
| 426 | 1 | 7 | 2.5 | · | 3737 | 19.2 | |
| 429 | 1 | 6 | 2.1 | · | 3311 | 17.1 | 3238 (1/6) |
| 449 | 1 | 5 | 1.7 | · | 2882 | 14.8 | |
| 467 | 1 | 4 | 1.4 | · | 2433 | 12.5 | |
| 602 | 1 | 3 | 1.0 | · | 1966 | 10.1 | |
| 609 | 1 | 2 | 0.7 | · | 1364 | 7.1 | |
| 755 | 1 | 1 | 0.35 | 755 | 755 | 3.9 | |

* $\frac{19425}{6}$ = 3237.5; 1/3 = 6475; 1/2 = 9713; 2/3 = 12940; 5/6 = 16188

Table XVI.   TABULATION OF ESTABLISHMENTS PER BLOCK ALL KINDS OF BUSINESS, 1949
(Calculation for Curve in Figure 11 on Page 93)